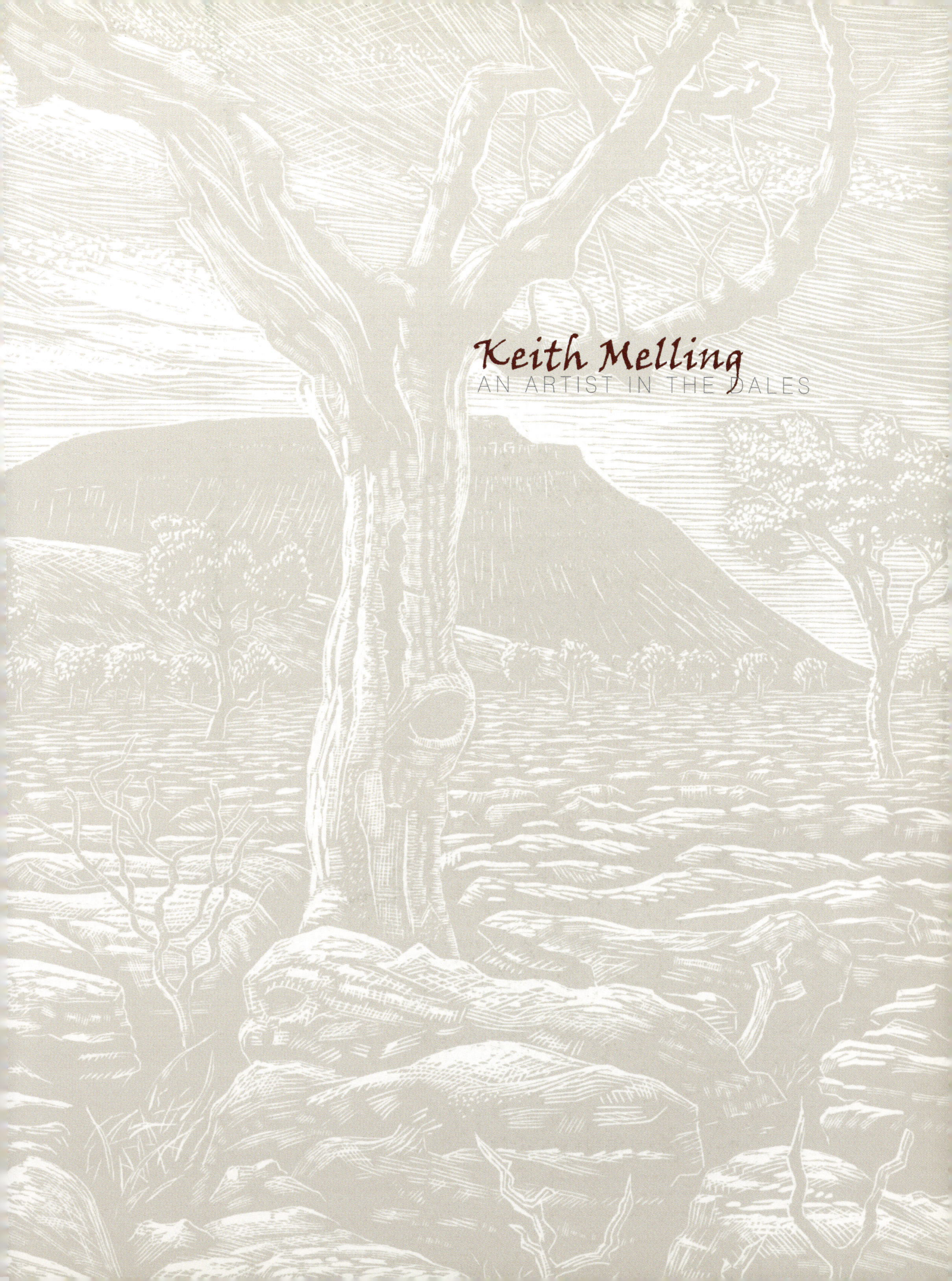

Keith Melling

AN ARTIST IN THE DALES

Keith Melling
AN ARTIST IN THE DALES

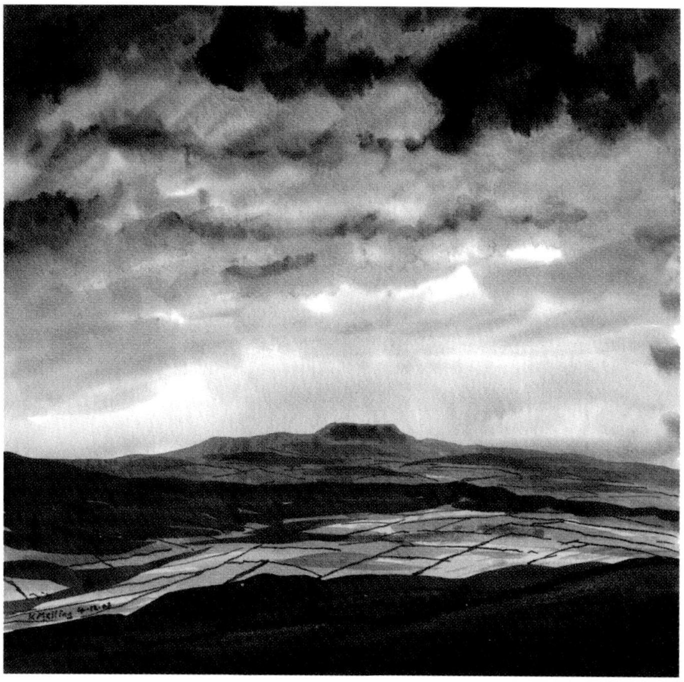

'I like a painting which makes me want to stroll in it.'
(Pierre-Auguste Renoir, 19th century)

'...almost everything, if one keeps one's eyes open,
is potential for painting.'
(Graham Sutherland, 20th century)

First published in 2008 by Plover Publications

www.ploverbooks.com

www.kmelling.com

British Library Cataloguing-in-Publication data
A catalogue record for this book is available from the British Library

ISBN: 978-0-9560938-0-6

Typeset by Carnegie Book Production, Lancaster
Printed and bound in the UK by Cromwell Press

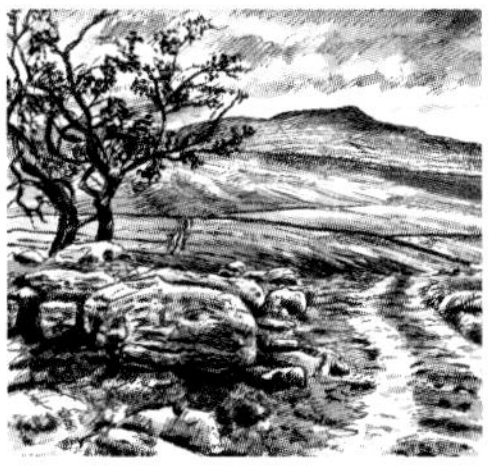

Contents

To my family

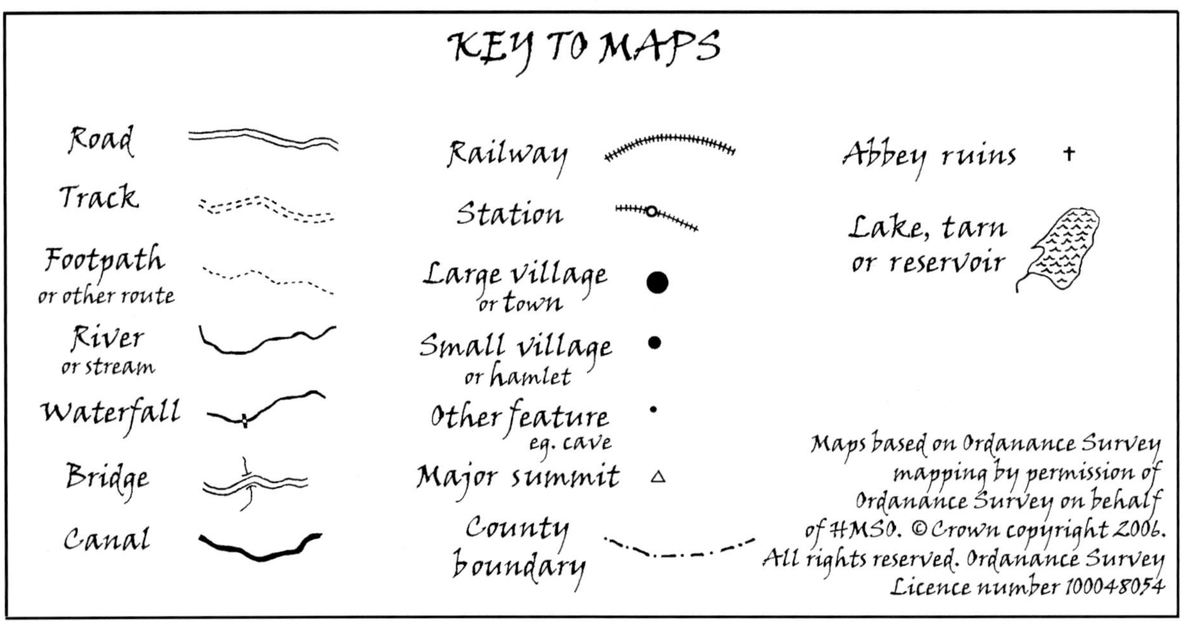
KEY TO MAPS
Road
Track
Footpath or other route
River or stream
Waterfall
Bridge
Canal
Railway
Station
Large village or town
Small village or hamlet
Other feature eg. cave
Major summit
County boundary
Abbey ruins
Lake, tarn or reservoir
Maps based on Ordanance Survey mapping by permission of Ordanance Survey on behalf of HMSO. © Crown copyright 2006. All rights reserved. Ordanance Survey Licence number 100048054

Preface

The idea for this book grew from attempts to write picture commentaries for my website. It was a vague half-baked idea at first: shapeless as a tadpole beginning to change into a frog, hazy as the distant hills under a veil of damp fog. Should all areas where I have mostly painted be included — Lake District, Yorkshire Dales and my home patch around Pendle? Or would three separate studies be better? If the latter, which first?

As time passed, the fog lifted and the tadpole began to look more like a frog. I would start with the Yorkshire Dales, simply because I had a greater body of work for that region and because it has been the regular object of my weekly forays for several years. I figured this would give me a head start. Not that there was any rush — this was basically a labour of love with no deadline to meet. However, it did take much longer than I envisaged. There were maps to draw, places to research and, even though I had many Yorkshire images, they were mainly of the southern and western Dales. Then there was the writing, which I thought should be kept to a minimum, after all this was mainly going to be a picture book and I considered myself to be a painter not writer.

I set about my task with enthusiasm and, all in all, the project proved to be very enriching. I learned a lot, my appreciation deepened and although I'm no expert on any aspect of the Dales, I feel now to know the region more intimately.

After perusing my final illustrations, I realise there is still an imbalance. For example, I've scant material for Coverdale, plenty for Ribblesdale and nothing for Garsdale. This is not because of preference but of convenience. No excuse I know. I just happen to live nearer the southern and western Dales and visit them more often. So, in no way have I managed perfection, the tadpole has turned into a frog of sorts, but falls a long way short of becoming a prince.

On nearing the end I was struck by a faint feeling of trepidation. What to do with it next, and, if I manage to launch it into the world, what would my fellow Lancastrians think? Would they consider me a traitor for producing a book on Yorkshire? Conversely, what would be the view from over the border? Would Yorkists see the endeavours of a foreigner painting and writing about their beloved territory as audacious?

Well, there's only one way to find out, so here goes.

Keith Melling
Fence 2008

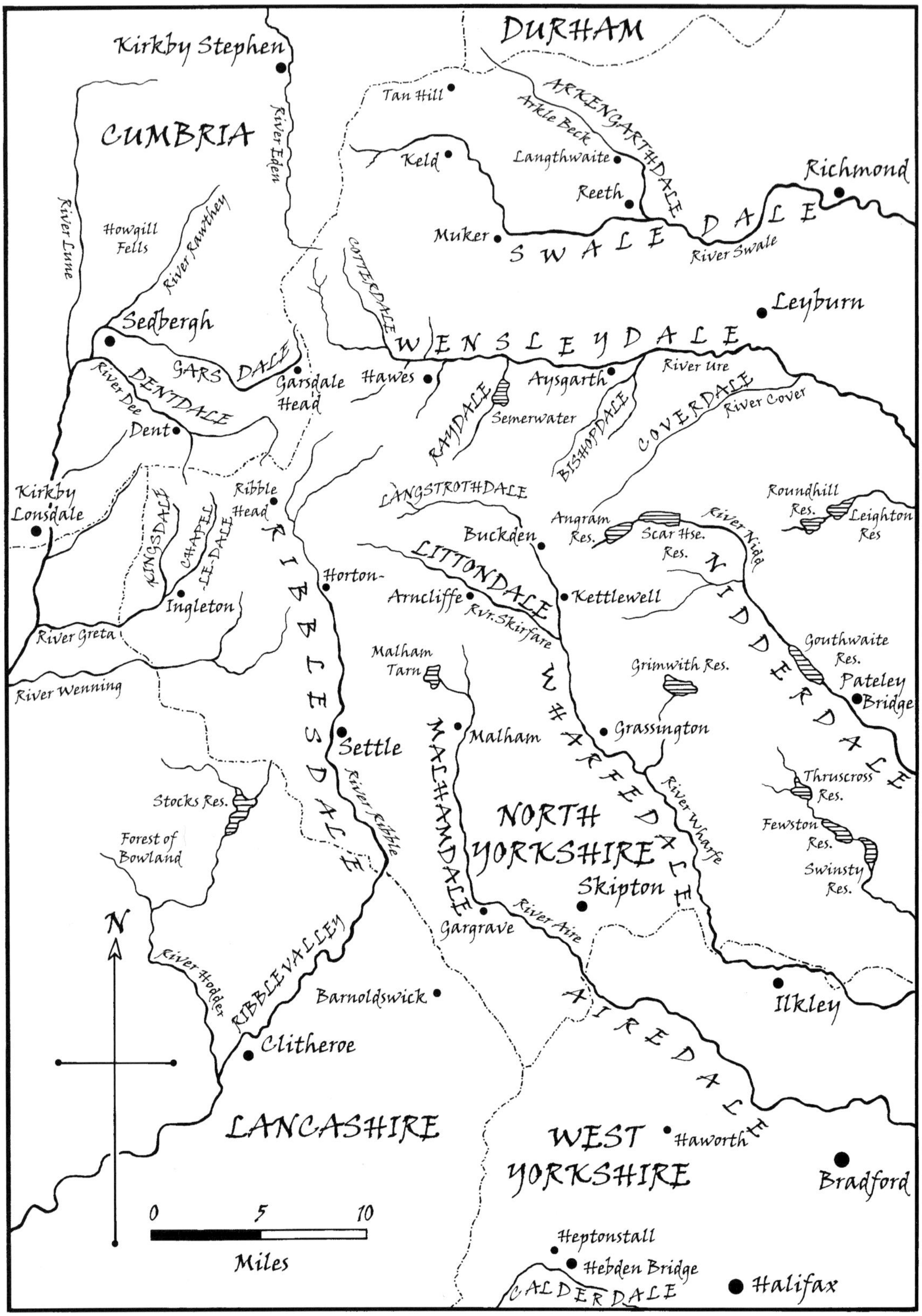

The Yorkshire Dales an overview showing principal rivers and dales

Introduction

The diverse scenery of the Yorkshire Dales is stunningly beautiful. It means many things to many people, but to the landscape painter, it offers an inexhaustible variety and wealth of superb subject matter.

Geographically the area is quite well defined and very extensive, covering some 683 square miles in the National Park alone. Each dale has its own individual character, formed mainly by the forces of nature; geological upheavals, glaciation and the action of the elements, all very evident, especially when pointed out to us. However, the country has been given its topmost layer (most noticeably in the valley bottoms), by the people who from the earliest times have settled and worked there, transforming rough wilderness into a more ordered and managed environment. Of course this has not been a one-way process, the environment has also had its effect on the people, contributing to the psyche of Dalesfolk.

Sweeping whalebacked fells adorned with purple heather or awash with wind-scorched grass rise majestically to apparently great heights, though most are less than 2000 ft. A few even higher flat-topped peaks with rugged outcrops of rock appear sometimes to have their own weather systems. Some lesser green hills are crowned with tall trees. All look down into lush valleys patterned with patchwork fields, limestone walls gleaming white where (and when) they catch the sun. Sparkling becks, which gurgle to life in the high hills, cascade through wooded gills, rush between rocky ravines then move more sedately on the level valley floors. Lakes and tarns are few but are delectable when found; water always invites meditation and is a great source of inspiration. Farms abound, mainly with their mix of cattle and sheep. Field-barns there are aplenty. Picturesque villages and small hamlets are strung out here and there; some close together, others more isolated. Romantic ruined abbeys feed the imagination and the remains and relics of long gone industries stir curiosity. The weird world of limestone is never far away, its unexpected moonscape pavements and scars invoke a sense of wonder, and its caves and crags inspire awe.

The wildlife, flora and fauna are as rich and varied as anywhere in England and add greatly to the atmosphere of the Dales. The melancholy call of the curlew as it wheels over the lower slopes is so evocative. The sight of a fox running below the steep escarpments can be mesmerising and unforgettable if you are lucky enough to see it.

There is surely more than sufficient subject matter in the Dales for an artist, yet there is also something else to consider. That is — the question of the transient elements of the landscape. The changeable Pennine weather and variable northern light with subtle or dramatic influence can change a scene almost beyond recognition. A view seen often and considered quite ordinary, may suddenly be transformed by a certain trick of the light and appear exceptional. Then we have the cycle of the seasons bringing their more predictable but sometimes still surprising changes.

The transitory effects of weather, light and seasons might alter the landscape's appearance dramatically but the underlying physical features remain intact like a bone structure. This combination of the ephemeral and the everlasting has always fascinated landscape artists and no more so than here in the Dales.

This book then, which is primarily a picture book, is really a 'work in progress', for a complete survey of the Yorkshire Dales from an artist's point of view could never be completed.

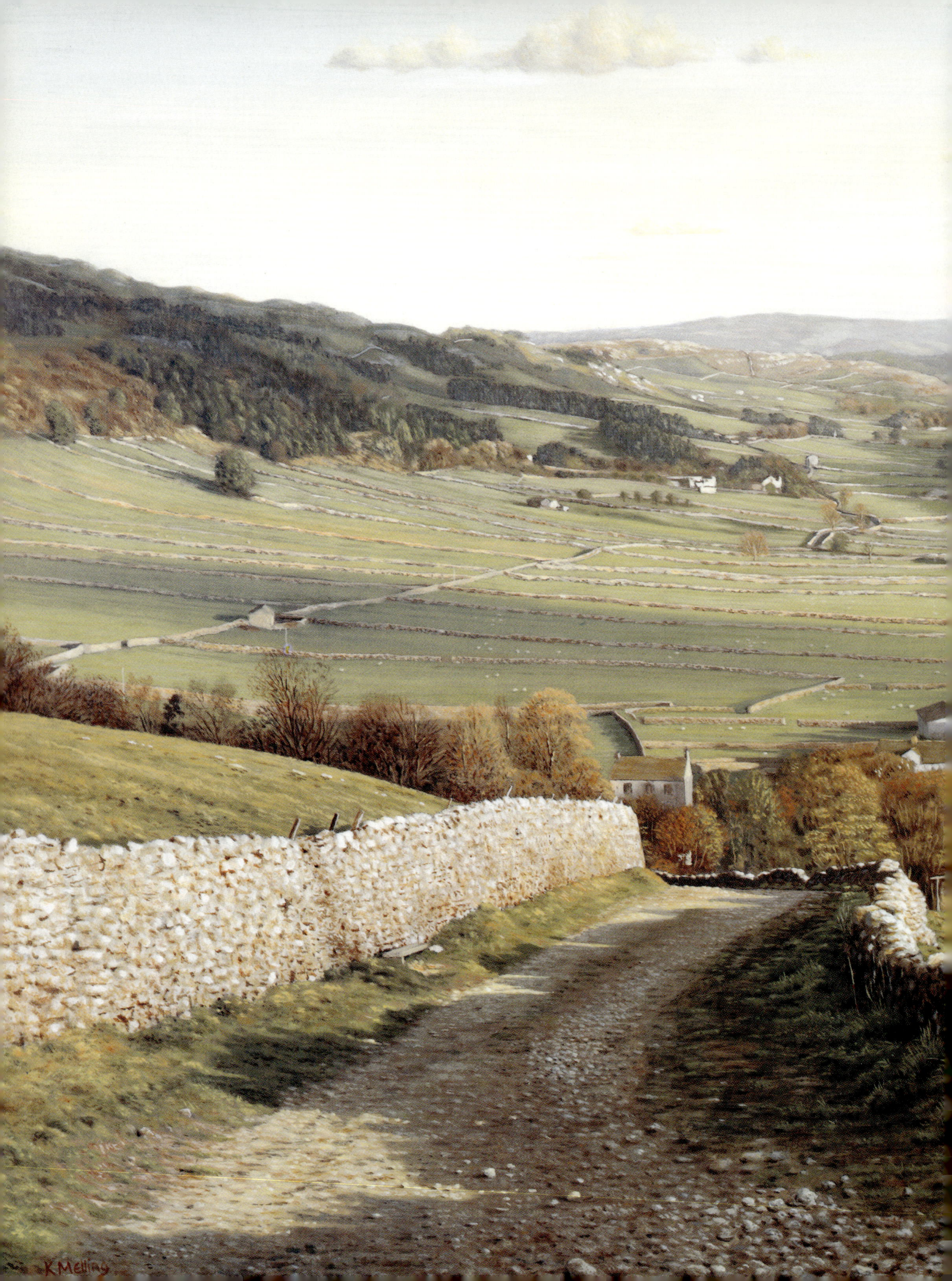
K Melling

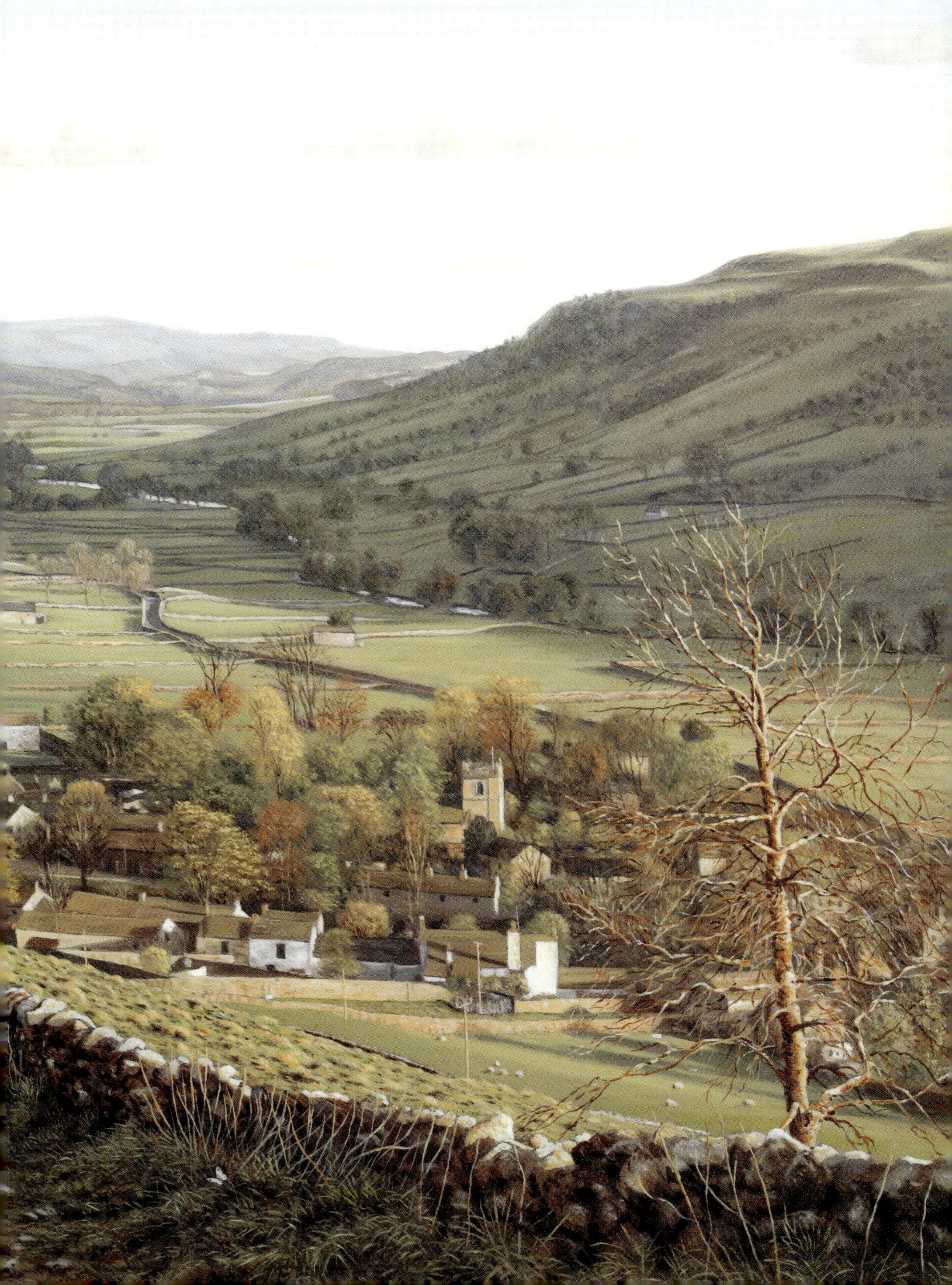

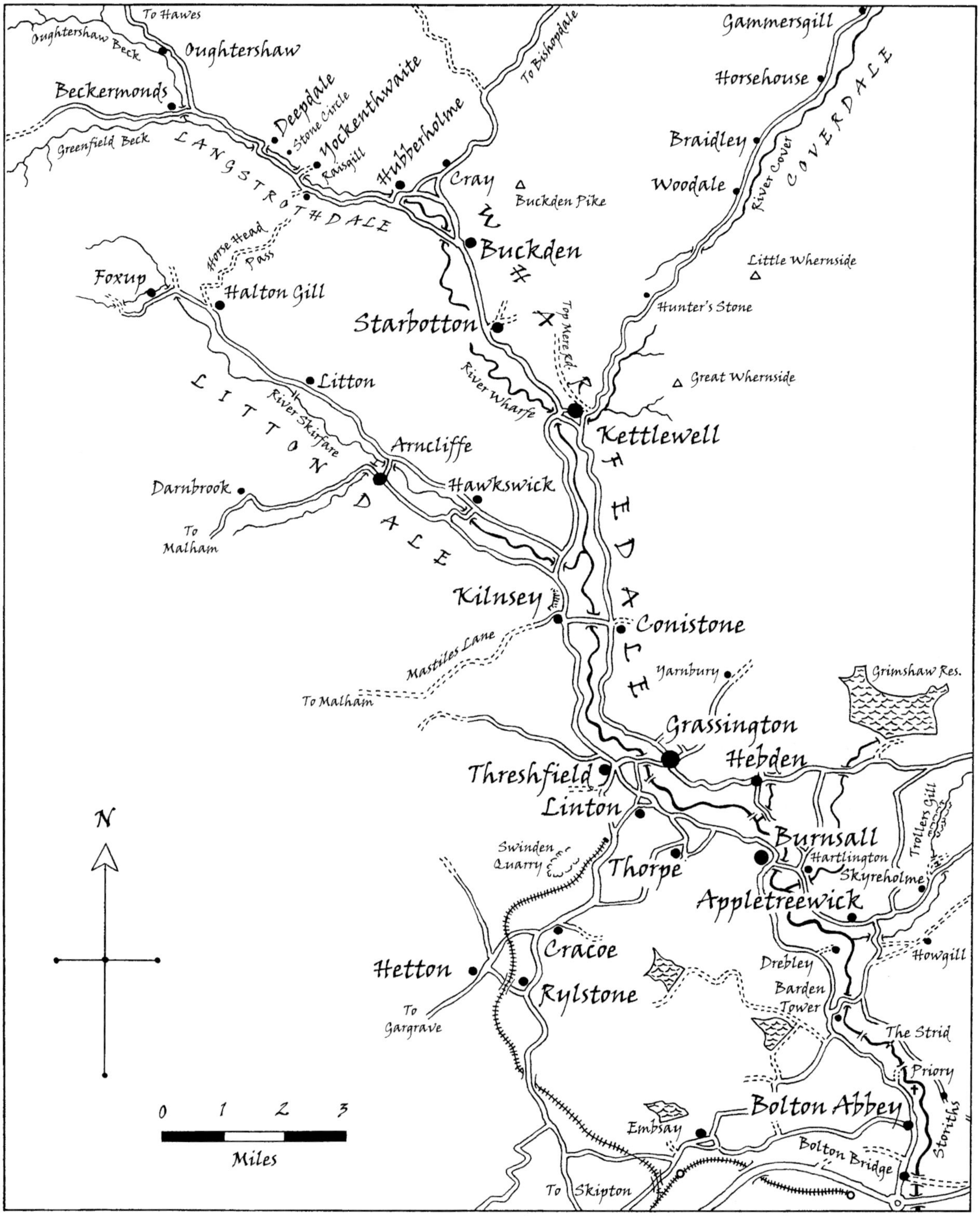

Wharfedale showing Littondale and part of Coverdale

Wharfedale

If any dale typifies the district it must be Wharfedale. Beautifully proportioned it has variety in abundance. Its attributes compete favourably with any other dale in every department — a fine river, ample woodlands, many limestone features, attractive villages, high fells and expansive moorland. Wensleydale may be grander and Swaledale more dramatic but in my opinion this is the quintessential dale.

Geologically Wharfedale is split into two by the Craven Fault. Near Burnsall the prominent dark gritstone much in evidence in the south of the valley, gives way to lighter limestone, which renders the scenery softer and brighter. Even the grass grows a more vibrant green on the lime rich soil — not always appreciated by artists as green is often viewed as a problematic colour. Some painters may emphasize red, blue or other colours if they see it in the landscape but rarely green.

The dale, which approximately lies on a north south axis, has its humble beginnings high up in the fells near Cam, where a spring rises in rough marshy ground to form the infant Wharfe. The stream hurries down to meet Greenfield Beck at Beckermonds (meeting of becks) then twists and tumbles through the wild scenery of Langstrothdale. The small hamlets in this upper dale have names of Norse origin, Oughtershaw, Beckermonds, Yockenthwaite and Hubberholme. A Bronze Age stone circle, still reasonably intact, is easily accessible near Yockenthwaite. Nobody really knows the purpose of these stone circles, but they are good places to contemplate and ponder ancient history. I think of them as works of art as they have such a profound effect on the senses.

After serving its apprenticeship in Langstrothdale, the Wharfe passes under the handsome stone bridge at Hubberholme as a fully-fledged river, and enters Wharfedale proper.

The first village encountered is Buckden (valley of the bucks), situated on the meeting of three ways — to Bishopdale, Langststrothdale and south through Wharfedale. Tucked under the bulk of Buckden Pike it seems that this place has always been geographically important. The area, rich in archeological history has ancient settlement sites from Bronze Age, Iron Age and Romano British times. A scattering of woodlands on the hillsides here makes it especially pleasing — a good place to draw or paint.

During the ice age the action of the glaciers scooped and ground out the valley into a flat-floored U shape, which, from Buckden through Starbotton to Kettlewell is strikingly obvious once we are told. The winding road through Wharfedale keeps an eye on the river, clinging tightly on some sections and wandering further away on others. Almost every village boasts a fine stone bridge; the best at Burnsall, but perhaps Conistone or Barden would challenge that opinion. Bridges are

"A scattering of woodlands on the hillsides here makes it especially pleasing — a good place to draw or paint"

usually very photogenic subjects and act as magnets to artists and photographers (and motorcyclists in the case of Devil's Bridge at Kirkby Lonsdale). Maybe though, the attraction is a little subtler. Subconsciously, bridges are symbols of life or time, 'a lot of water has flowed under the bridge since then'. Also they are symbolic of overcoming obstacles and making the transition from one side to the other.... That's enough amateur psychology — bridges are simply aesthetically pleasing structures.

Kettlewell, a very appealing village, could be said to be the centre of the upper dale. Strategically placed on the confluence of the Wharfe and Cam Gill Beck, a steep road from here winds its way over to Coverdale under the watchful Great Whernside, the highest fell in Wharfedale at 2310 ft. (not to be confused with Whernside of the Three Peaks).

The Wharfe now joined and bolstered by the Skirfare of Littondale, flows lazily past the impressively undercut Kilnsey Crag. A little downstream, the bridge at Conistone appears to tether the villages of Kilnsey and Conistone together. Turner made some interesting drawings here, exaggerating the famous crag and trying to include both villages in the same composition.

Grassington is the honey-pot of the dale and is often buzzing. More a small town than village, its assortment of shops, pubs, and cafes set around a quaint cobbled square and unspoiled narrow streets lend it much character. The atmosphere and movement would challenge any painter, and would be an interesting diversion from other Dales subjects.

In stark contrast to the hustle and gentle bustle of Grassington, the surrounding hills offer solitude and quietude, where the only sounds are those of nature; the calls of moorland birds and the whispering of the wind through rough grass and heather. This area is particularly profuse in ancient settlement sites, though more noticeable is the scarring left by 17th, 18th and 19th century lead mining activities. Rusty relics and ruined buildings combine to infuse into the lonely expansiveness, a haunted ghostly feel. With a little imagination it is possible to conjure up in the minds eye the sights and sounds of men working and the clatter and groan of machinery. Watch out for unfenced mine shafts!

A popular walk from Grassington by a lovely stretch of the river to Burnsall — passes the dynamic Linton Falls and the limestone gorge of Loup Scar. A line of horse chestnut trees at the waters edge below Hebden makes a colourful sight in autumn. I have dawdled and doodled some time away here, observing and sketching the sunlight filtering through the yellow leaves.

At Burnsall life seems leisurely. A captivating village by a wide bend in the river, with many large trees, well-kept green, splendid five arched bridge and a backdrop of fells second to none, making this a very picturesque spot. Burnsall has been for decades the destination of day-trippers. And why not, it's beautiful here.

Near Burnsall and the secret hamlet of Thorpe, exist some interesting conical hills. These (geologists tell us) are reef knolls, which were formed millions of years ago when the remains of sea creatures were deposited near the shore of a shallow tropical sea. The limestone is quite pure and contains many fossils. The views from these moderate hills are surprisingly extensive.

A little side valley near Appletreewick and Skyreholme narrows to the bottleneck of Trollers Gill. This steep sided rocky chasm is a spooky place at dusk. Sat alone drawing here one balmy evening,

> *"Sat alone drawing here one balmy evening, I felt the hairs on the back of my neck stand up as I sensed something behind me"*

I felt the hairs on the back of my neck stand up as I sensed something behind me. Of course there was nothing, it was just imagination, but apparently, there are many folk tales of a spectral hound or 'Mauthe Dog' with huge staring eyes which has a lair in the rocks here.

Some of the boulders dotted on the hillside above Skyreholme have Neolithic cup marks. There has been much speculation into the meaning of these marks, usually based on ritual and belief. I am no expert on these matters, but if I can put my two penn'oth in, I think they may have had a more practical use. The forest Indians in California made similar holes in rock for pounding acorns into mush (their staple diet). These rocks were important for survival, so were respected and revered. The Yorkshire cup marks are always carved into the horizontal part of the rock at a convenient working height, so perhaps they had a similar use.

The sprawling high fells towering over this lower dale have a sombre austere appearance. This is due to the underlying hard sandstone known as millstone grit, which doesn't allow the land to drain easily, and therefore encourages the formation of acid soils and peat. Heather grows well on this terrain and is a wonderful sight in August and September when in bloom. From the rocky outcrop of Simons Seat, the waves of a purple ocean stretch eastwards into the hazy distance. This subtle colour is elusive and can be very difficult to paint. The artist could easily overstate it, for what we think we see, does not always correspond to what is actually there.

The exposed airiness of the moors with its all-encompassing sky is the complete antithesis to the valley directly below, where, the Wharfe flows under the graceful Barden Bridge, and — if likened to a symphony, enters its most richly orchestrated and tempestuous movement. Through the mature woodland of Bolton Woods the water gathers momentum before being squeezed through the narrow rock channel of the awesome Strid as a thundering raging torrent. A good way to sketch or paint rushing water is to emulate its movement by working rapidly and spontaneously.

Two miles downstream, peace is restored as the river slows to respect the quiet compelling beauty of Bolton Priory. At Bolton Bridge the River Wharfe leaves the national park and continues its journey through Ilkley to meet the Ouse nine miles south of York.

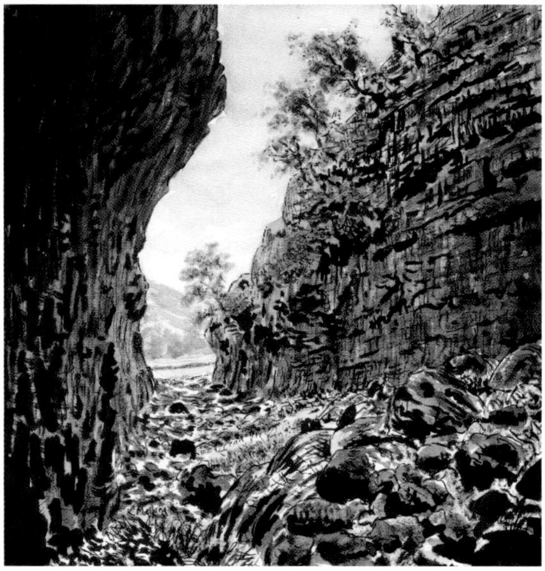

Trollers Gill

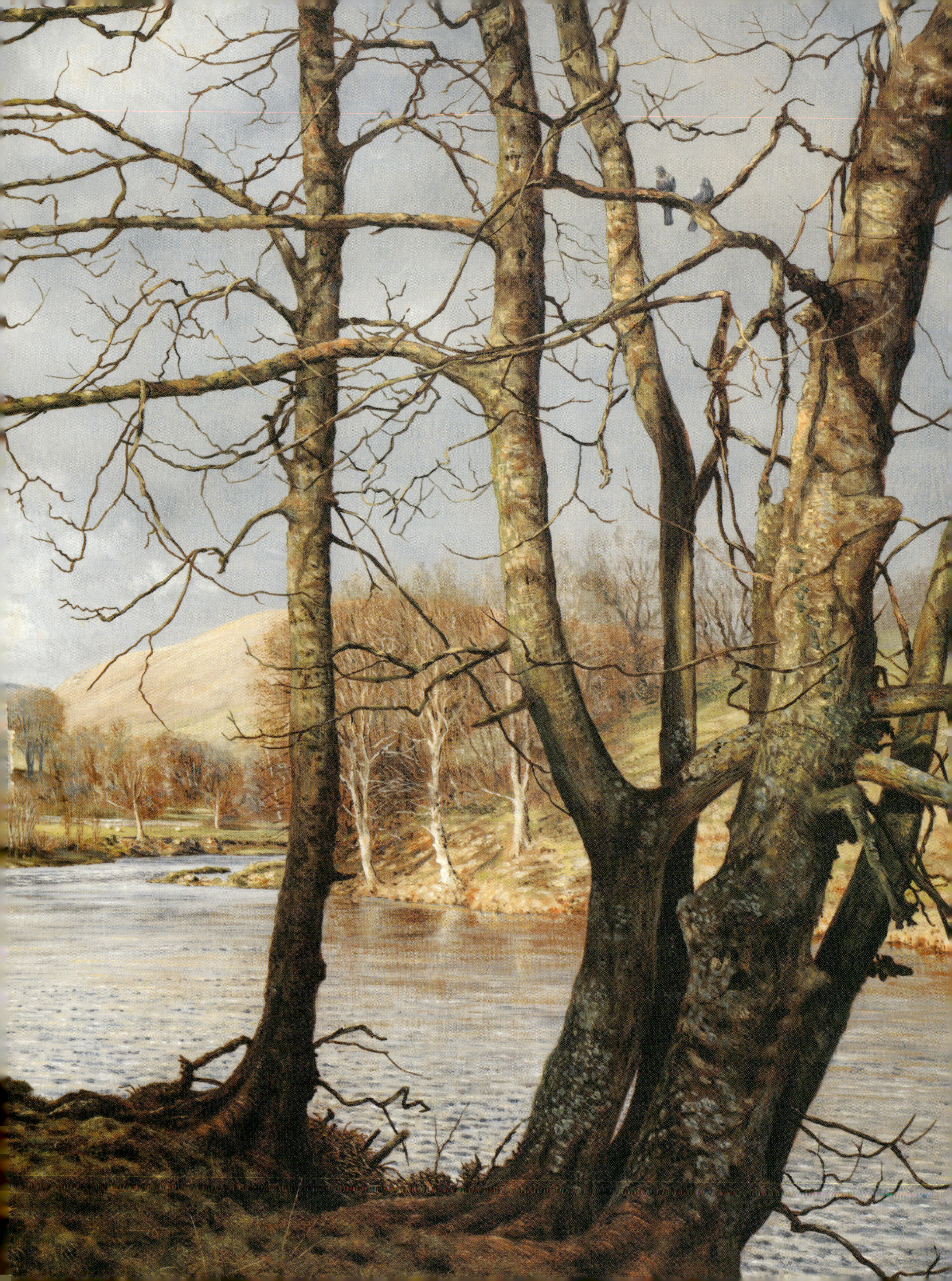

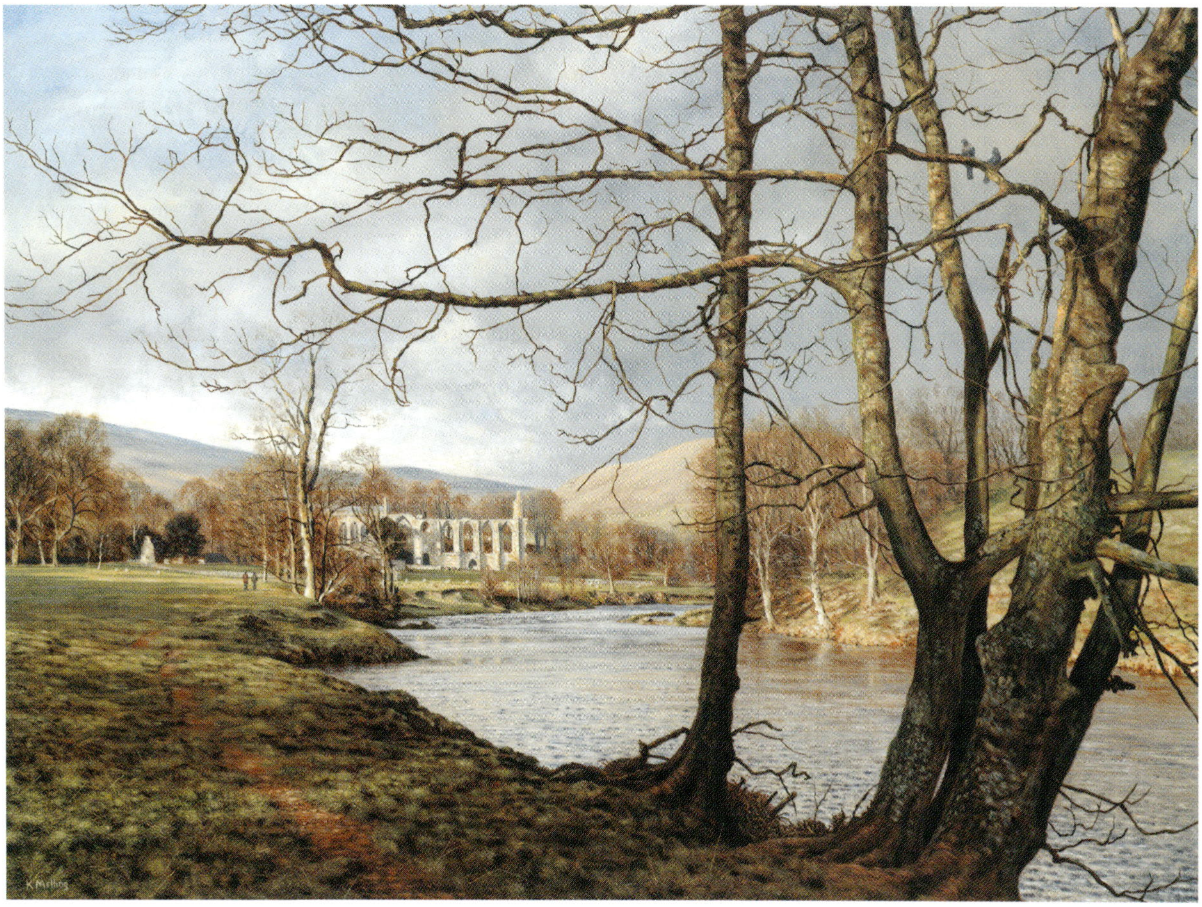

The River Wharfe at Bolton Abbey
1989 Oil 14.25 x 19.5in

Deciding on a title for this painting was a little problematic. Although the ruin is often referred to as an abbey, it was really a 'priory'. The village that grew nearby is actually called 'Bolton Abbey' through common usage I suppose. I needed a title that would suit both the sticklers for correctness and the majority of folk whom like me had always used the name 'Bolton Abbey'. So I devised the title 'The River Wharfe at Bolton Abbey' which, I hope, nobody can say is wrong.

Many notable artists over the centuries have painted this subject and it is interesting to see their chosen viewpoints and how the trees have grown or in some cases disappeared. For my composition I tried to strike a balance between the ruin and its surroundings so that the building didn't dominate but still retained a presence as the focal point. The trees in the foreground were in reality much denser, so I thinned them out quite a lot (not literally) so as to see the rather moody sky through them — which made me wonder about the trees in those older pictures.

To animate a painting further I like to add a bit of life, hence the two doves in the branches, which perhaps connect in some way to the couple walking on the riverbank.

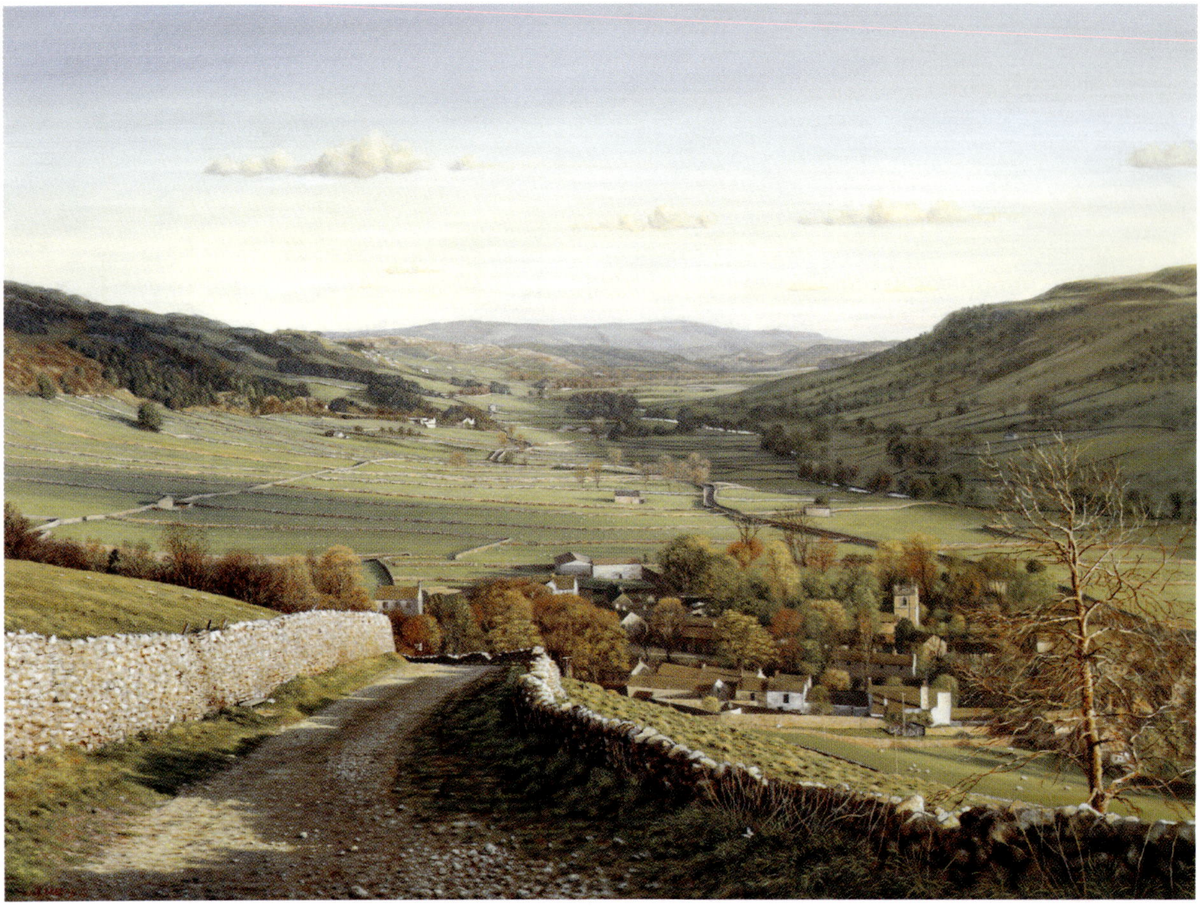

Above Kettlewell, Wharfedale

1989 Oil 14.25 x 19.5in

This was my first Dales picture and possibly my favourite. I cannot think of Kettlewell without thinking back to cycling there from Colne in Lancashire with two of my old teenage pals 'Buck' and 'Peck' in the early 1960's. We camped by the river and spent many happy hours catching fish by the 'tickling' method. We didn't have much money but we ate like kings — eating trout for breakfast, dinner and tea, deliciously cooked in butter on a roaring Primus stove. A farmer sprang up on us one day and gave us a good telling off. He seemed most concerned afterwards that we were Lancashire lads poaching fish in a Yorkshire river.

The view in this painting is looking south from Top Mere Road with the village in a huddle on the glaciated valley floor. Grass Wood is in the distance and you can catch a glimpse of Kilnsey Crag peering over the flank of the fell on the right. The early evening sun is casting elongated cloud shadows, which move slowly over the lush fields and rough fellsides. The mellow sun also picks out the limestone walls making them glow. When I was sketching on the lane, it was very still and quiet. A hot air balloon was ascending from a field nearby and it was possible to hear the conversation of the occupants of the basket and the intermittent roar of the burner for a long time afterwards as it gracefully gained height. I remained working on the spot for quite some time until a man festooned with many rabbits and a gun walked passed and gruffly said - 'can ta see lad.... leeat's lowin'.

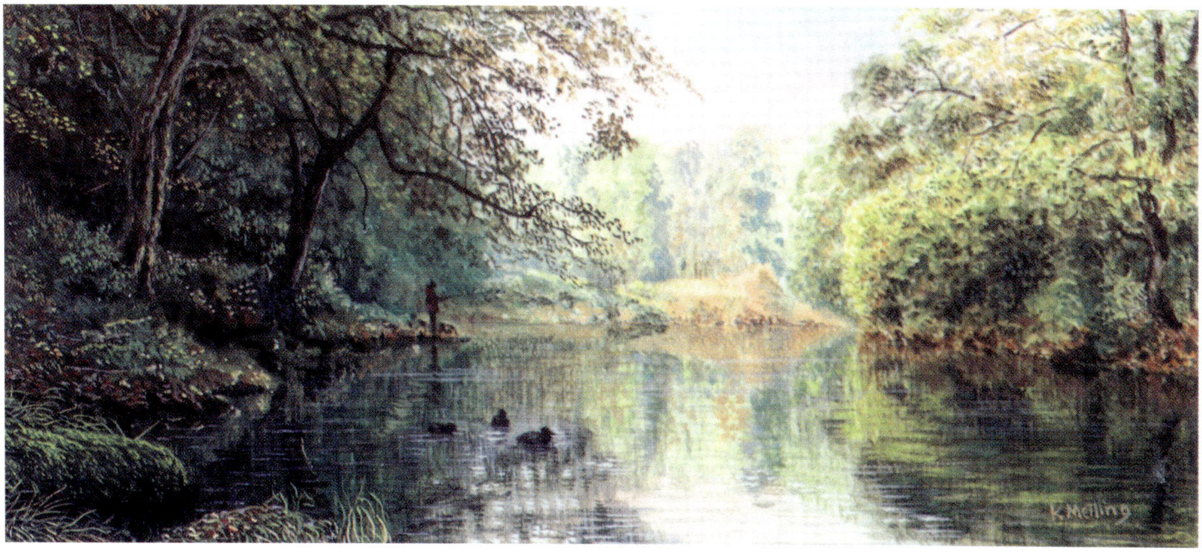

Morning Light on the River Wharfe
1991 Gouache and watercolour 3 x 6.5in

The moody Wharfe has many guises — this tranquil stretch just downriver from the boisterous Strid is not the river's full width, but is between the west bank and a small island. The well-managed woodlands close to the water provide a rich wildlife habitat, attracting a great variety of birds. Nuthatch and treecreeper perform impossible antics on the tree trunks and further away the drumming of the elusive woodpecker might be heard. Over the water the dash of the dipper and the flash of the colourful kingfisher may be glimpsed.

For this little picture, I used a mixture of gouache and watercolour. Watercolour seemed an obvious choice for painting a watery subject.

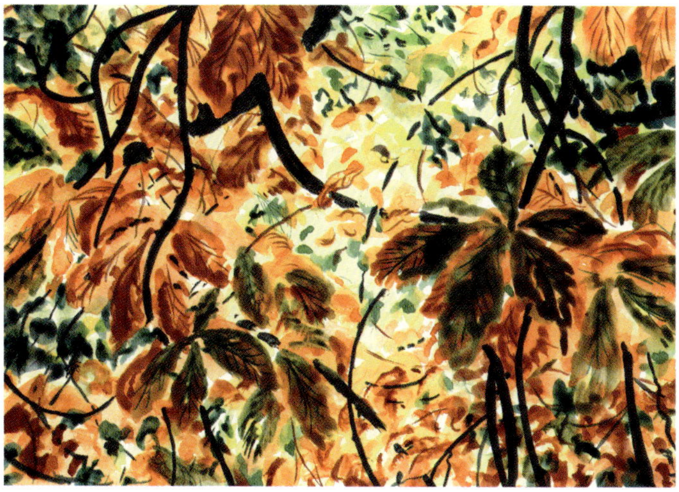

Autumn Leaves, Grassington
1996 Watercolour 7 x 10.25in

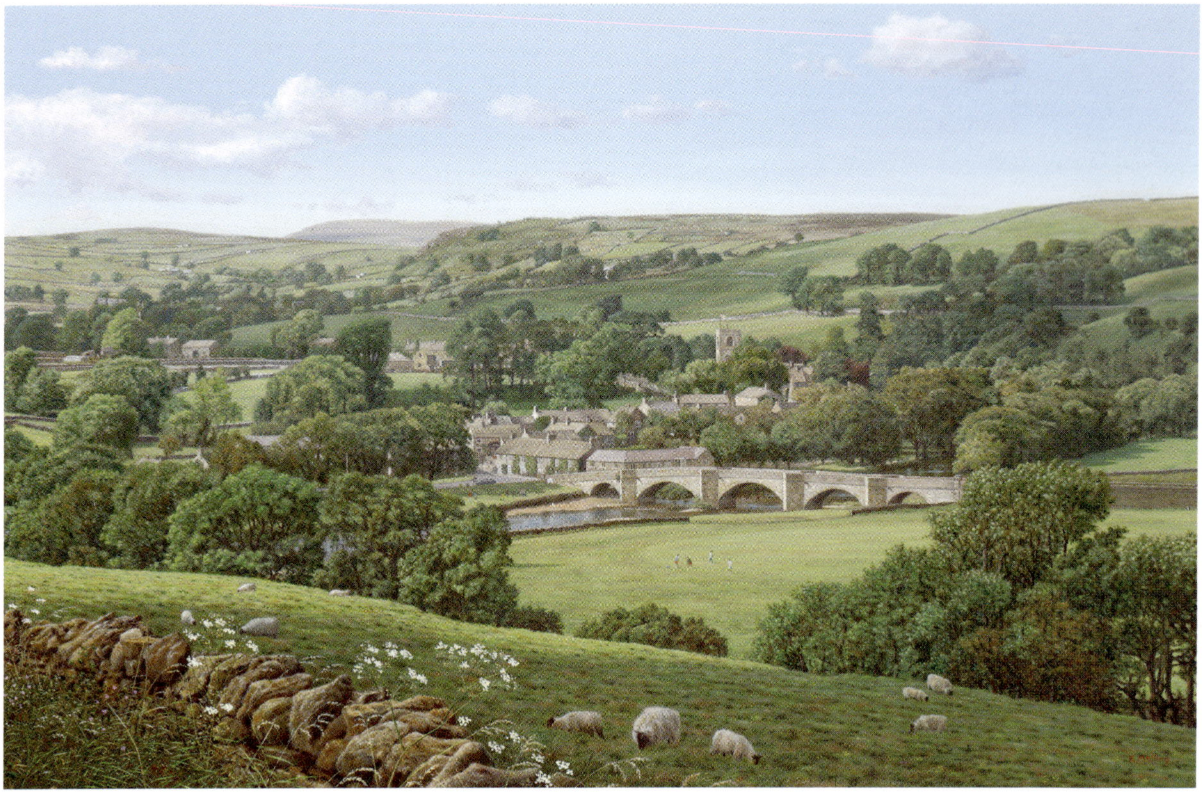

Summer in the Dales, Burnsall

2003 Oil 14.5 x 24in

When I have a subject in mind to paint, it is usually my normal practice to seek out a viewpoint of my own — often spending much effort researching maps and exploring on foot to find just the right spot. In this way, the views painted and claimed by other artists are avoided. However, there are some irresistible scenes that have been painted time and time again by every artist and his dog, and have become 'classic views'. These 'classics' have appeared so often on calendars, post cards and — dare I say it — chocolate boxes, that no one need feel guilty of poaching them. The picture here of Burnsall is one of those. Of course I still did my homework, researching and tramping the area to find an alternative, but had to concede in the end that there was no better view.

To show how Burnsall nestles and harmonises with its surroundings, a more panoramic picture than usual was produced. Passing cloud shadows were emphasised to vary the tones in the fields and hopefully introduce an element of movement through time.

A restricted palette of cobalt blue, cadmium red, cadmium yellow and titanium white was employed until the painting was almost complete, then to finish, ultramarine and raw sienna were used sparingly. This method of limiting the colours has served me well in many pictures, and is one that I fully recommend. It needn't be the same choice every time.

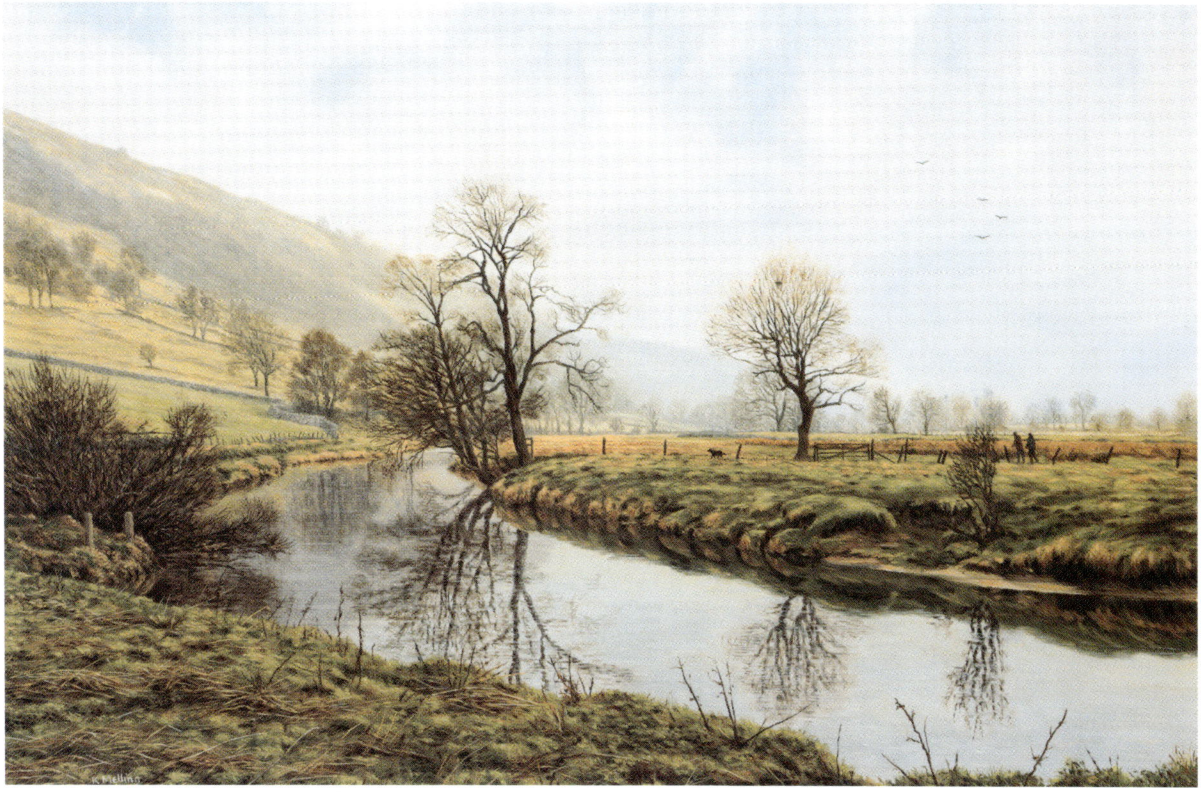

The River Wharfe near Starbotton

1989 Oil 14.25 x 19.5in

Generally the Wharfe is quite a fast flowing river in the upper reaches, so I was surprised to find this calm quiet stretch. Looking upstream, the location is between Kettlewell and Starbotton on the 'Dales Way' footpath. The figures and dog on the opposite bank are imaginary and probably trespassing — positioned there to add a little life to the composition. I remember having great difficulty with them, painting them in and wiping them out about six times before being satisfied. It's not easy to include figures and to make them seem natural. Constable was a master of it, much more convincing than Turner. Some seventeenth century Dutch landscape painters employed specialists to paint their figures. I don't really approve of that but can well understand the reason.

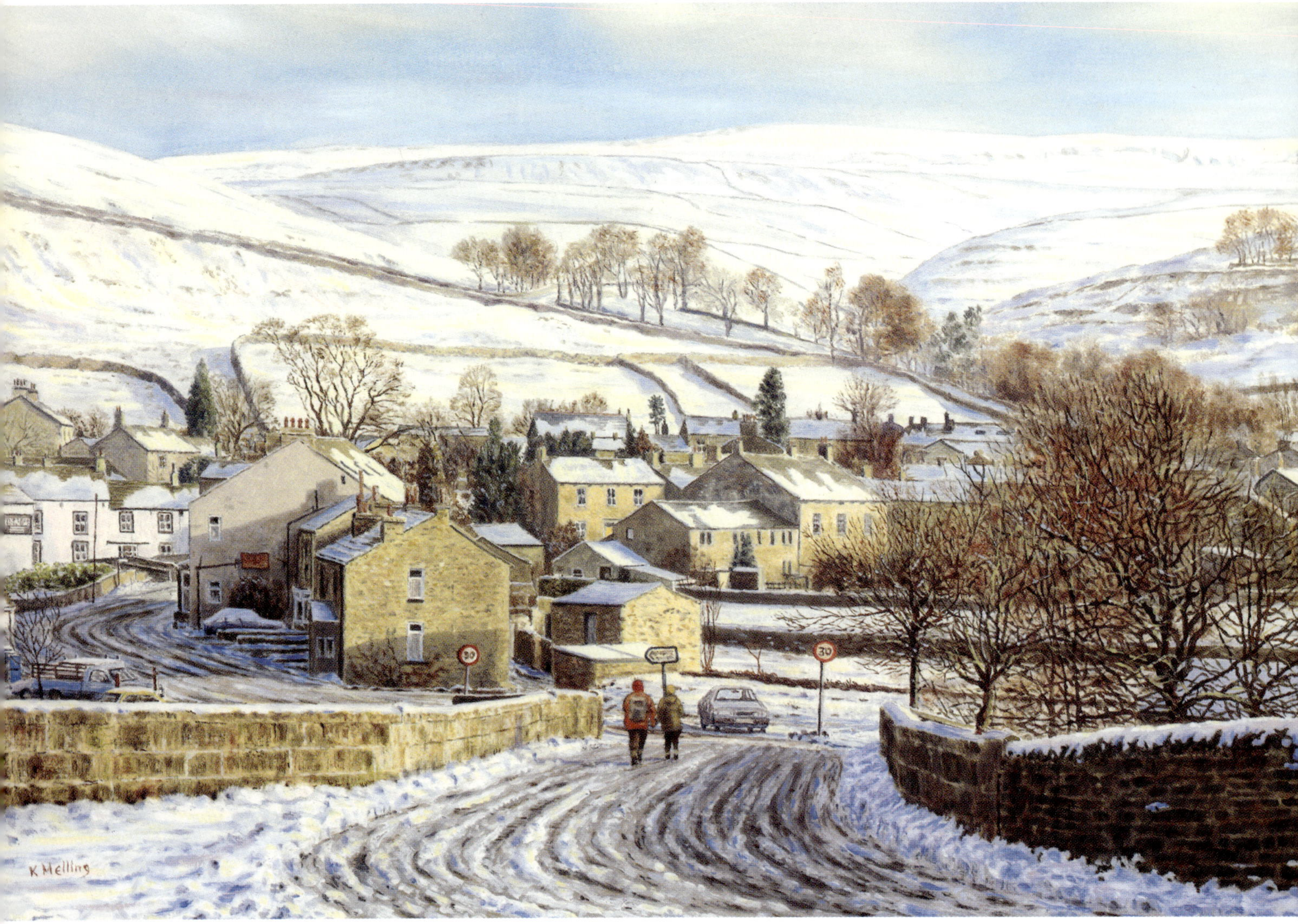

A Dales Winter, Kettlewell

1995 Oil 8 x 12in

A charity Christmas card company had asked me to paint a snow scene of a Dales village for the following year. Although it was winter there hadn't yet been any snow and as there'd been very little in the previous few winters I thought the possibility pretty slim. Then I heard on the radio that there was snow on high ground in the Dales.

Setting off immediately in our Citroen 2CV, I took the shortest route. At Bolton Abbey there wasn't a snowflake in sight. Neither was there at Burnsall, or at Grassington. Just where was this snow? Approaching Kilnsey, a little sprinkling appeared on the hills but hardly enough for my purpose. Would I be resigned to faking the snow as I'd done in one or two pictures before? Following my nose I turned left into Littondale. Happily for me the landscape became whiter, until at Halton Gill the snow was four inches deep with hardly a blade of grass showing.

After completing a couple of sketches I decided to take the Stainforth road, hoping to see Pen-y-ghent draped in white. 2CVs are surprisingly good in winter conditions — a light car with large wheels and high chassis. As the old faithful chugged up the steep fell road, a few ice patches were encountered. Still, they were only small so on we went, further and further up, with just a little skid now and then. Pen-y-ghent beckoned — it would be spectacular. Inevitably the ice patches became more frequent and the snow here was frozen solid.

It dawned on me that to continue would be foolish. I must turnaround and go back. Unfortunately, the road was too narrow for a three-point turn and there was a deep icy camber on the road's edge. It would be impossible to get back onto the road once off it. So there was no choice. The brave little 2CV had to be reversed down the steep frozen road for a very long half-mile. Slipping and sliding sideways, still traveling with the brakes full on and trusting to large dollops of luck — the treacherous lane was negotiated in reverse little by little, until, what seemed like an eternity later, the valley bottom was reached. 'That's certainly enough drawing for today' I thought.

On arrival home an hour later in the sunshine with not an iota of snow in sight — it seemed unbelievable that having set out searching for snow, I almost ended up getting stuck in it.

Resuming my task some days later at Kettlewell, I worked on the painting shown here. The low winter sun conveniently shines horizontally; enhancing the features of Great Whernside in the background and throwing the buildings into greater relief. The scene was used successfully for the Christmas card and raised quite a sum for charity.

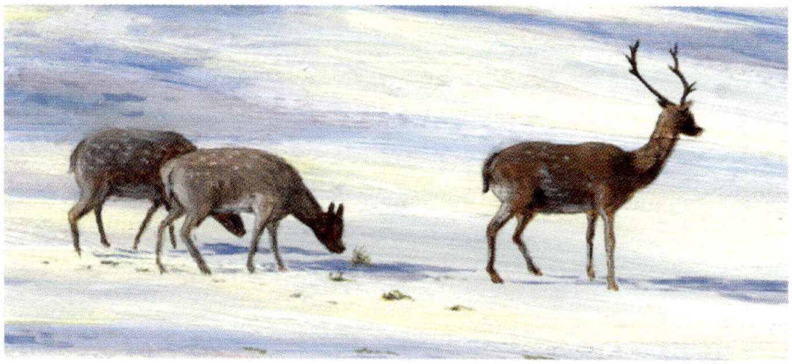

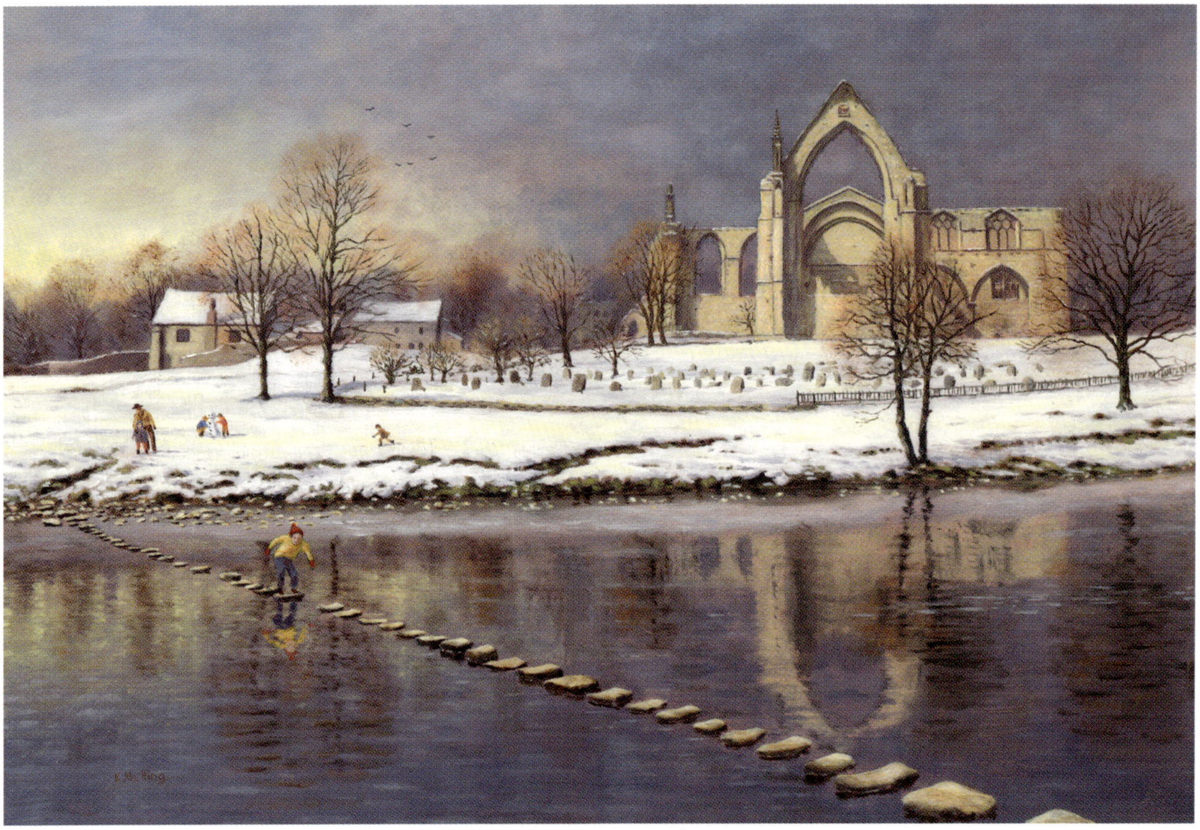

Bolton Priory, Winter
1994 Oil 8.75 x 13in

The viewpoint here was chosen solely because the painting was commissioned to be used as a Christmas card, and the card company wanted the stepping stones to feature in the picture. Every time I visited the spot in winter, there was so much water flowing that the stones were submerged and could not be seen. I had to paint the scene without the stepping-stones then return later in the year when the water level was lower.

Originally I painted two figures crossing the river, which actually appeared on the card, but was never really satisfied with the second figure so later painted it out. In time, when the oil paint becomes a little more transparent, the figure might come back to haunt me as it starts to show through like a ghost!

The nave of the magnificent Augustinian priory survived the dissolution because the local people used it as a place of worship. Today it still serves the village as a rather grand parish church.

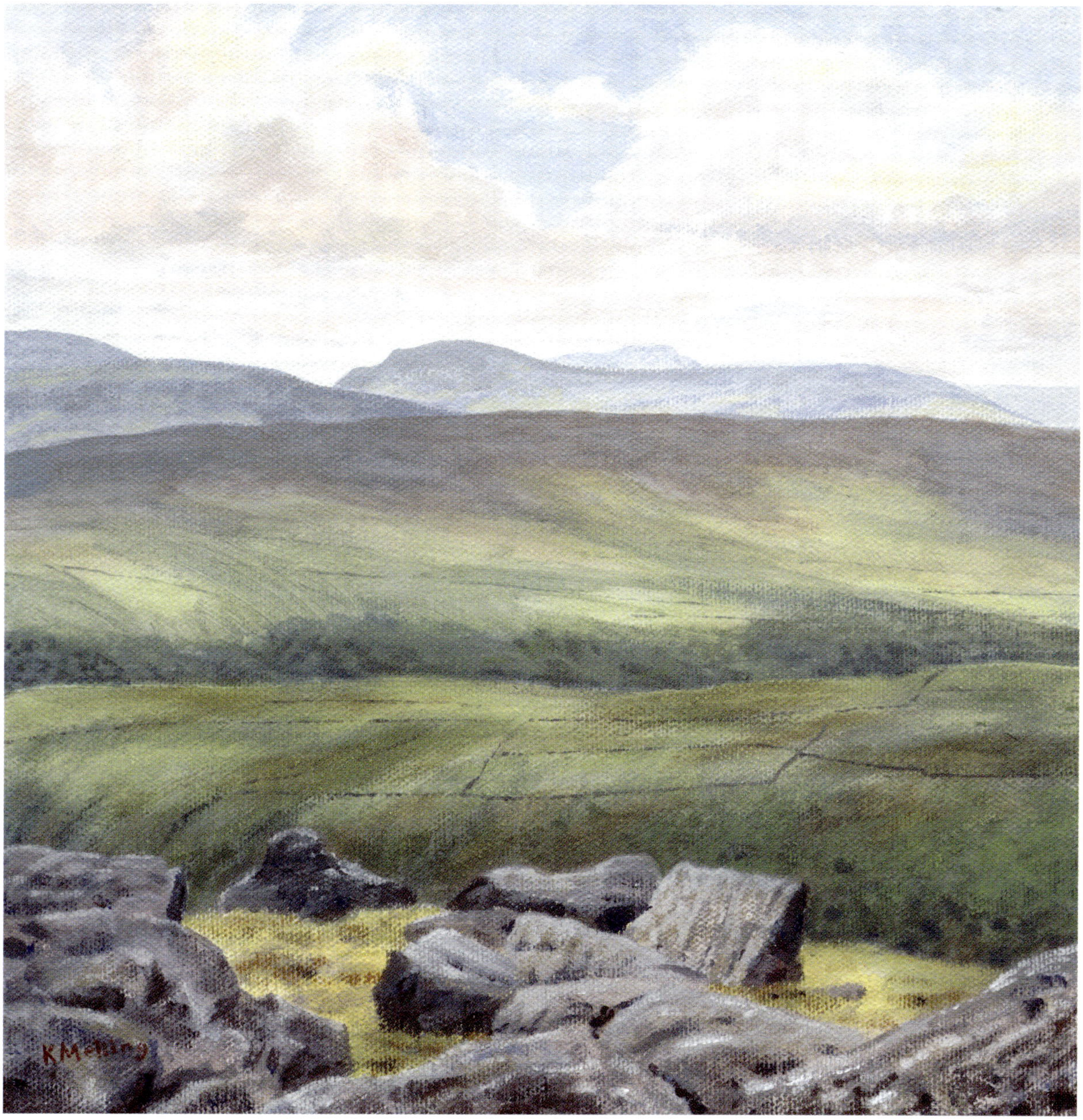

Across Wharfedale to Penyghent and Ingleborough from Great Whernside
2006 Acrylic 10 x 10in

The Yorkshire Dales covers a very large area, yet it is possible from many of the highest fells to see most of the other lofty fells. This painting shows a blinkered view towards two of the distant Three Peaks, which I felt would fit the square format of the canvas. If we remove the blinkers there is a wonderful 360-degree panorama from Great Whernside's boulder scattered summit to, amongst others, a spellbinding view southwest to the hazy Pendle Hill in Lancashire's 'Witch Country'.

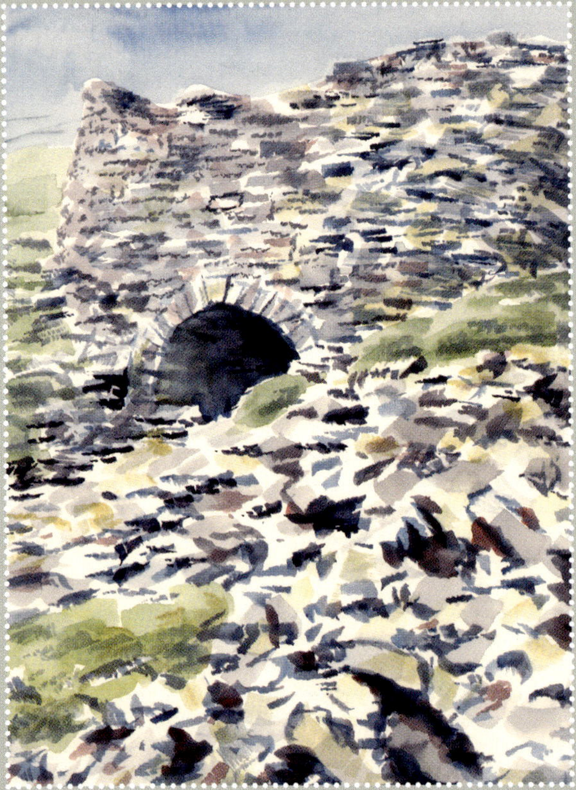

Limekiln

1996 Watercolour 8.5 x 6.5in

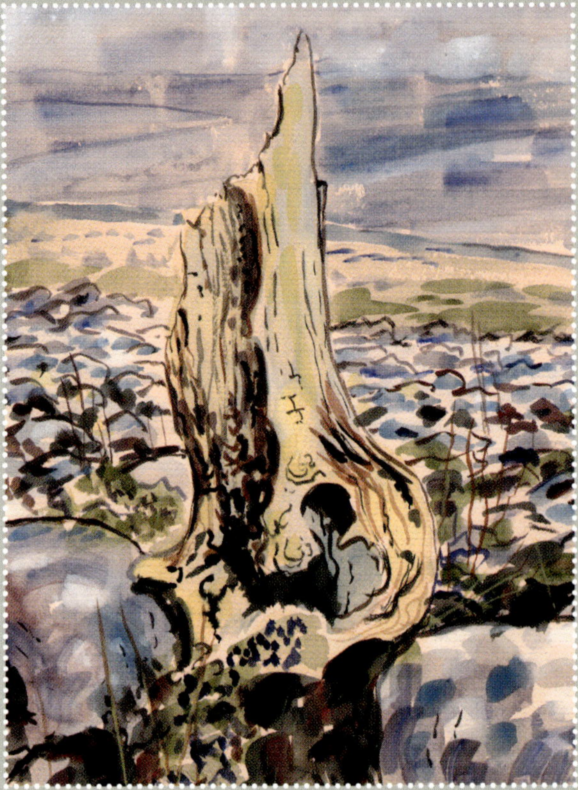

Tree Stump Between Clints

1996 Watercolour 8.5 x 6.5in

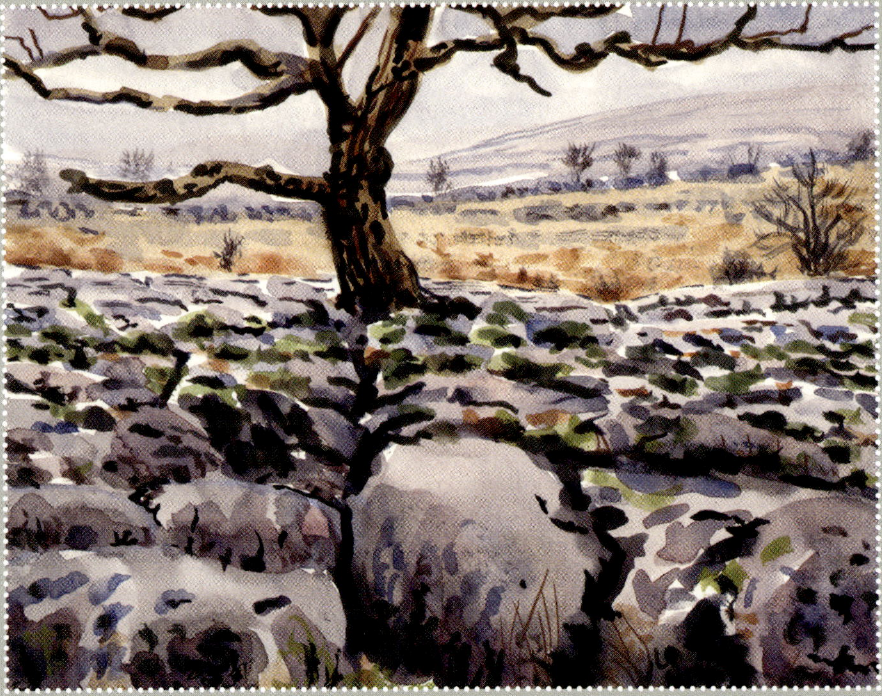

Limestone Pavements

1996 Watercolour 6.5 x 8.5in

All five pictures here were painted around the Limestone pavements above Conistone Dib

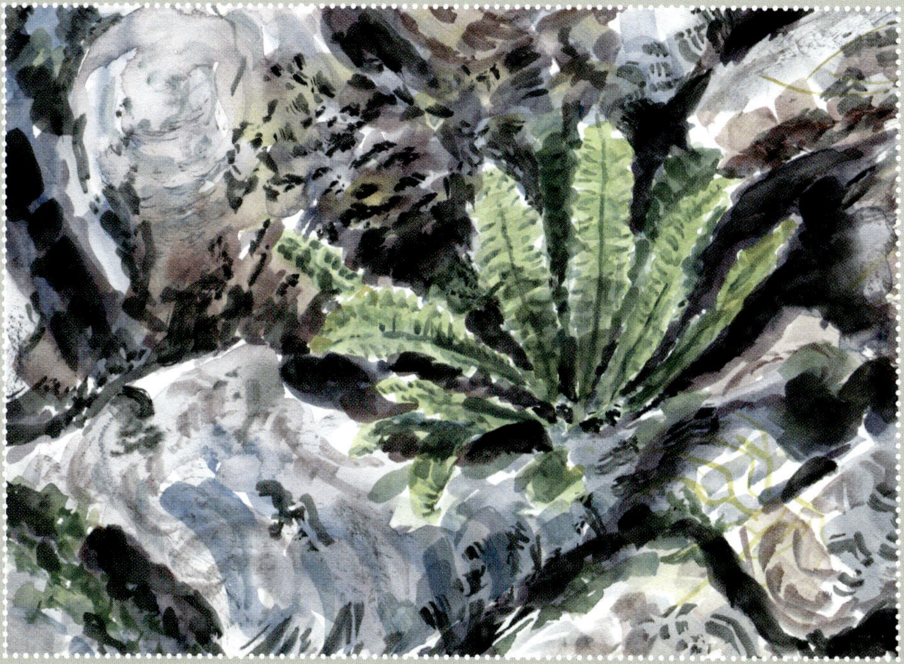

Harts Tongue Fern

1996 watercolour 7 x 10 in

Towards Buckden Pike

1996 watercolour 7 x 10 in

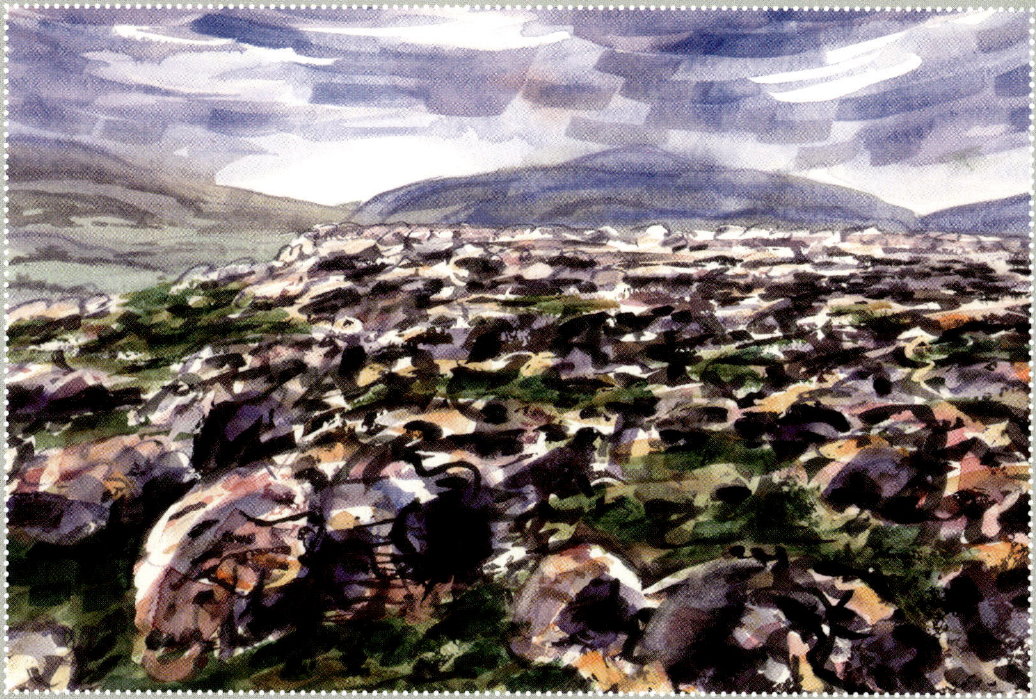

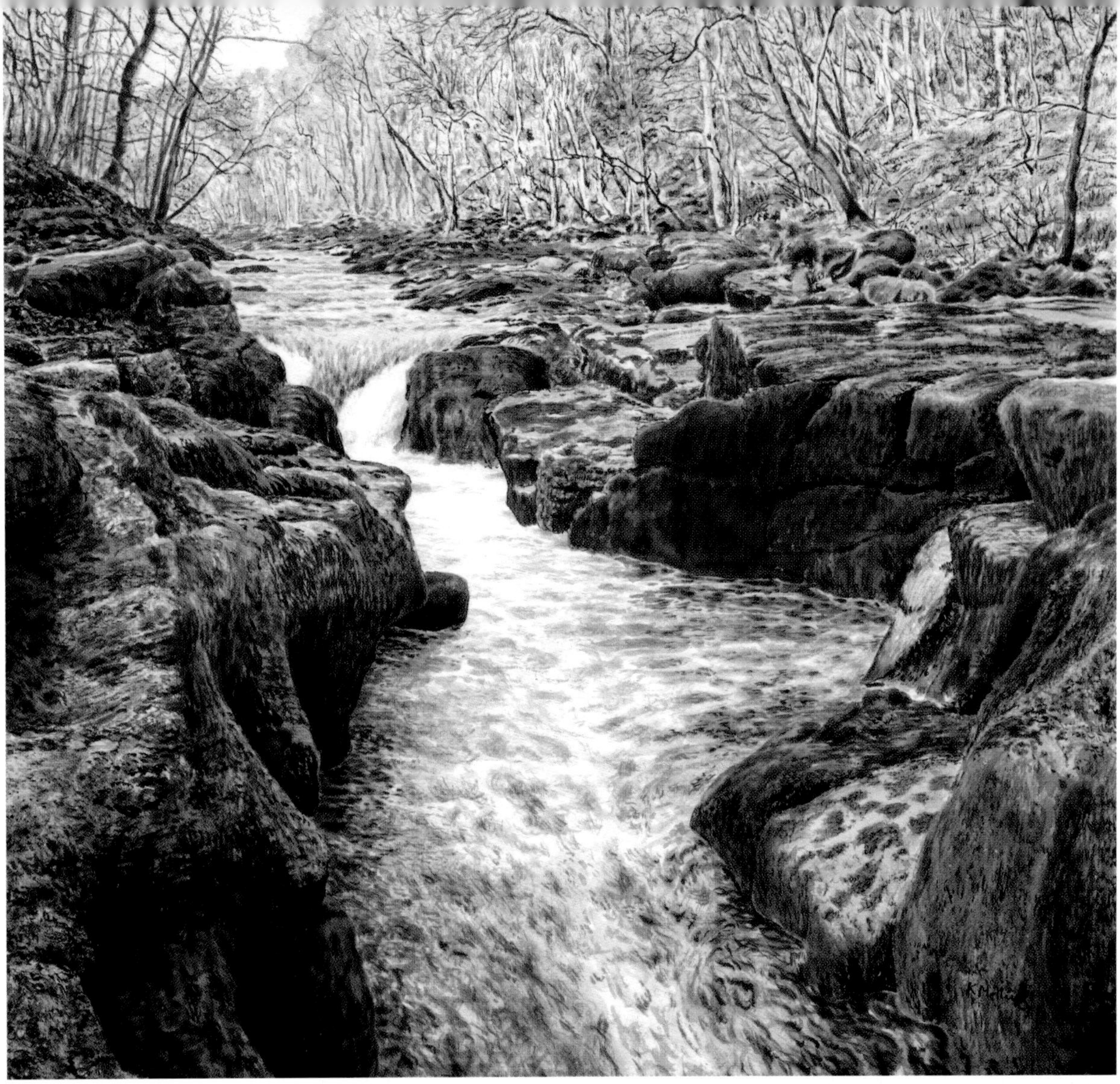

The Strid at Bolton Abbey

2005 Ink 11.8 x 11.8in

The River Wharfe changes character dramatically as its waters rush and roar through the notorious narrow channel of the Strid. This rocky ravine at one point appears to be narrow enough to jump across, but unless you have the spring of a champion kangaroo, it is definitely not to be recommended. Lives have been lost here. The swirling torrent, which is 30 ft deep, drags its victims down without mercy, below the dark underwater ledges and crevices. There is the ancient legend of the Boy of Egremont who plucked up courage to try the leap, only to be foiled by his dog, which, still on leash, refused to jump and tragically pulled him back into the boiling cauldron of foaming water. His mother, Lady Alice Romilly, was so stricken with grief that she gave some land to the Augustinian order of monks in 1155 to build a priory in her son's memory. Actually, historical records show that the boy was one of those who signed the deeds, so part of this story cannot be true.

This picture shows the Strid in early spring before the trees burst into leaf. The recession through the trunks and branches helps to give a feeling of space. Often, when trees are in full leaf they have the effect of restricting the view and closing up this type of composition.

Although this drawing is rather elaborate, I still attempted to be more spontaneous in rendering the rapidly flowing white water. I'll leave it for you to judge whether I've been successful or not.

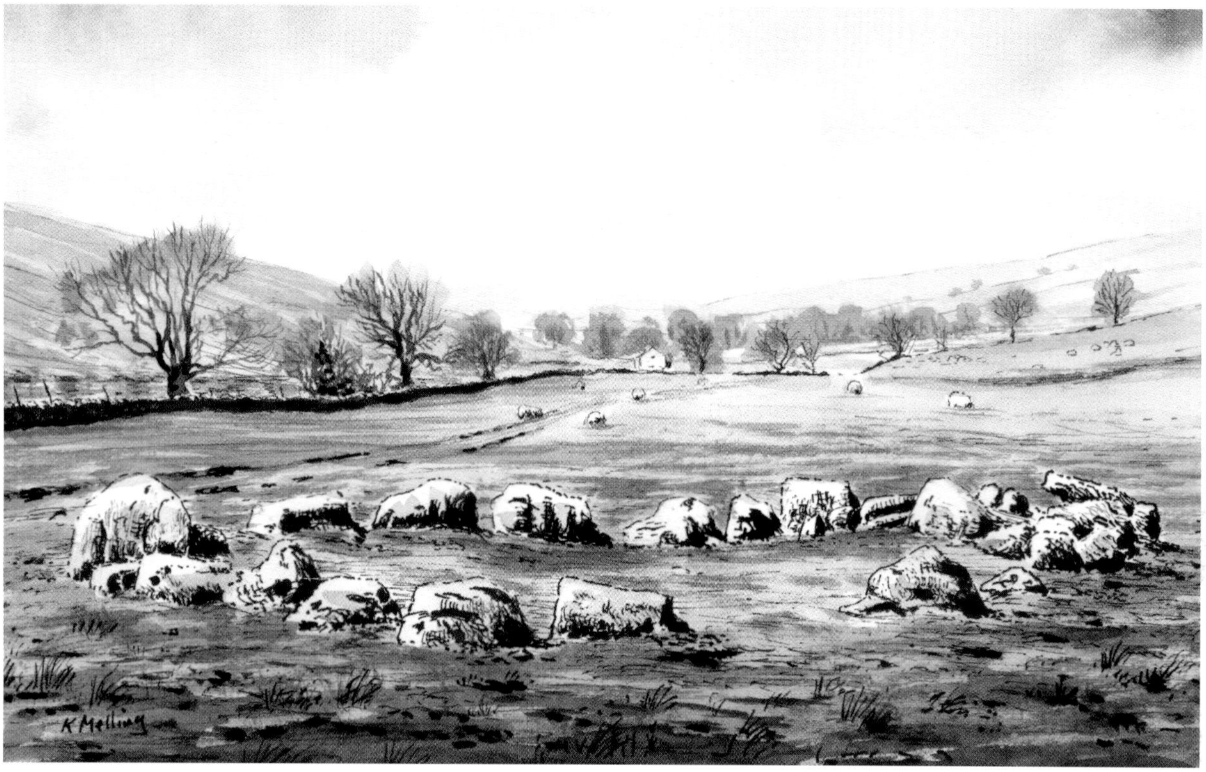

Yokenthwaite Stone Circle

2006 Ink 8 x 10in

This ring of rock is certainly no Stonehenge and there is little mystery of how the boulders were transported here, yet the sense of wonder evoked whilst in its presence is equally rewarding or more-so, for we can if we choose, sit peacefully in the circle and ponder its long lost secrets alone, in solitude and in silence, save for birdsong, bleating sheep and the cheerful gurgling of the nearby beck. It stands modestly as a timeless testimony to the Bronze Age people who built it some 3500 years ago.

The drawing was done on one of those nondescript overcast days when everything is bathed in an even silvery light. Days like these can be quite beautiful.

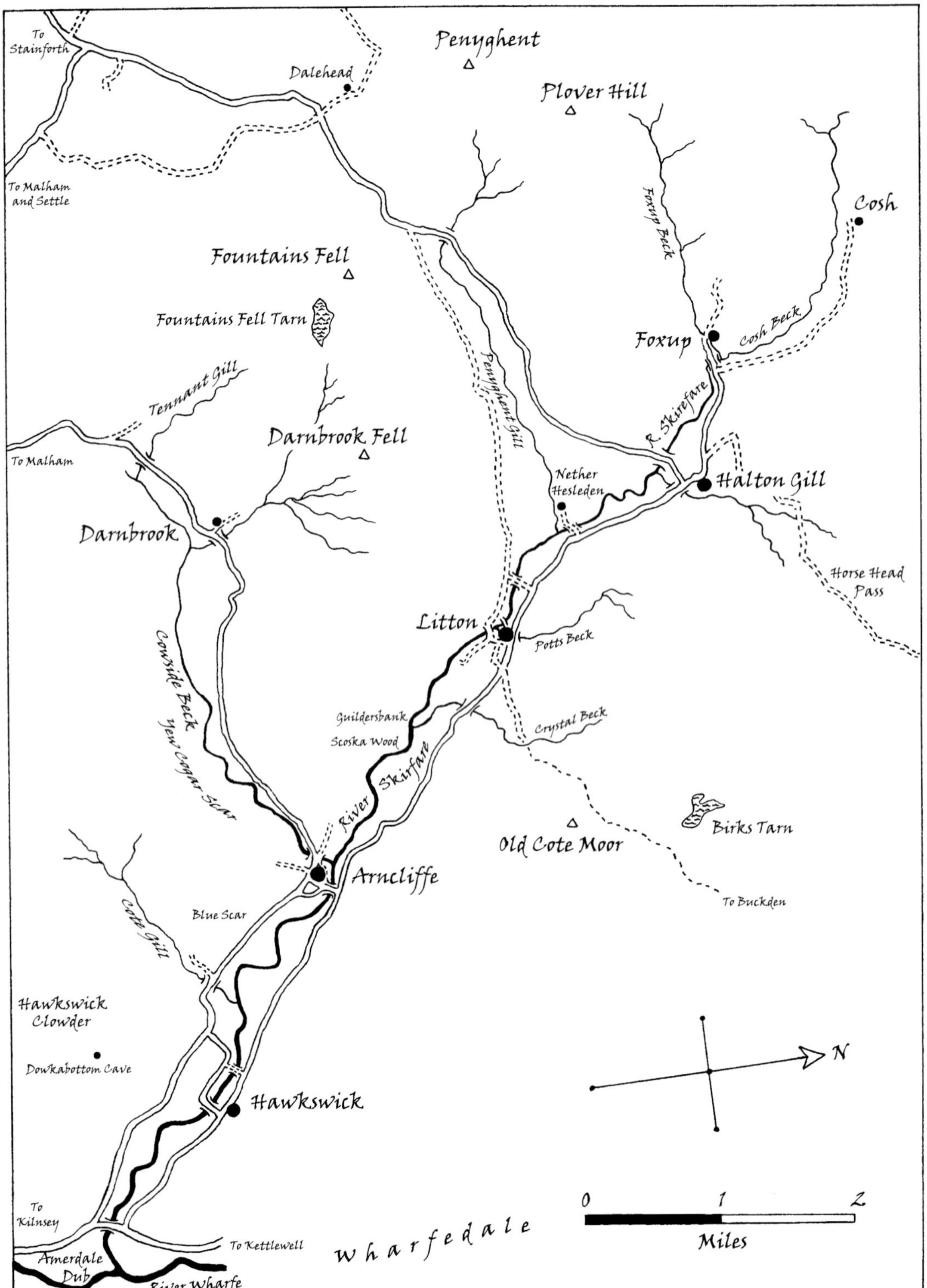
To Stainforth
Dalehead
Penyghent
Plover Hill
To Malham and Settle
Cosh
Foxup Beck
Fountains Fell
Fountains Fell Tarn
Foxup
Cosh Beck
Tennant Gill
Penyghent Gill
R. Skirfare
Darnbrook Fell
To Malham
Nether Hesleden
Halton Gill
Darnbrook
Horse Head Pass
Litton
Potts Beck
Cowside Beck
Yew Cogar Scar
Guildersbank
Scoska Wood
Crystal Beck
River Skirfare
Birks Tarn
Old Cote Moor
Arncliffe
To Buckden
Blue Scar
Cote Gill
Hawkswick Clowder
Dowkabottom Cave
N
Hawkswick
To Kilnsey
0
1
2
Miles
To Kettlewell
Wharfedale
Amerdale Dub
River Wharfe

Littondale

Littondale

This lovely secluded dale, which is only 8 miles long, is really a side valley or tributary of Wharfedale, yet it is separate and distinct from the parent dale and contains between its enveloping hills such individuality, variety and charm that it demands recognition and equality with the larger dales.

The artist is spoilt for choice here, for every step of the way there is something of interest and worthy of a picture. Writers too have found this valley appealing — it is 'Kingsley's 'Vendale' and 'Wordsworth's 'Amerdale', also it was the location for some of the early television episodes of 'Emmerdale Farm'.

The River Skirfare is formed where Cosh Beck and Foxup Beck meet at the remote hamlet of Foxup — thereafter meandering a varied course through the dale's length to join forces with the Wharfe near Kilnsey at Amerdale Dub.

Foxup (valley of foxes) has some curious stone bridges which connect individual buildings to the little road opposite the beck; the most attractive of these at the aptly named Bridge Farm. A track leads up to the wildly situated Cosh House, which at 1,450 ft above sea level must be one of the remotest dwellings in England.

Halton Gill, (at 1,000 ft) lies tucked beside the rising mass of Horse Head Moor; its weathered grey buildings harmonising completely with the backdrop of fells. An ancient packhorse route 'Horsehead Pass' zigzags up the steep fellside on the way over to Raisgill, and as it ascends, a wonderful panorama opens out; Fountains Fell, Plover Hill, Penyghent and the distant Ingleborough compete for attention. I have loitered on this green track on more than a few occasions, trying to fathom the illogical field patterns on the opposite hillsides and in the valley below.

Penyghent — one of the Three Peaks, is usually associated with Ribblesdale, but Littondale also stakes a claim, for the 'Hill of the Winds' is very dominant in the upper reaches of this dale. A fell road from Halton Gill to Stainforth climbs Hesleden Bergh to skirt around the mountain's wilder south side — Back o' Penyghent. Here in this treeless wilderness, the feeling is one of true timelessness.

In Littondale on the whole, trees are very plentiful; the wealth of woodlands on the lower slopes and beside the river give the impression of lushness in summer, and in winter contribute to the valley's tawny look, which is unlike that of any other dale.

The whole area is rich in early Iron Age and Bronze Age settlement sites, particularly around Penyghent Gill. If anyone has ever had their curiosity stirred by seeing sites of antiquity marked in archaic lettering on an Ordinance Survey map, only to be disappointed later to find nothing but a slight bump on the ground — well, here you will surely have more joy, for the remains are quite prominent and more obvious.

In several places between Nether Hesleden and

"The artist is spoilt for choice here, for every step of the way there is something of interest and worthy of a picture"

Guildersbank, the Skirfare does a vanishing act as it disappears underground. This trick, thankfully, prevented the valley from becoming a reservoir.

Litton, which gave the dale its name, is a tiny village with a slight air of importance. All who journey through the valley must pass through some part of it, as it stands by the entrance of the narrowest section where road and river run close together, nipped between the fell's jaws. The old packhorse route from Wensleydale to Ribblesdale also passes through, and it must have been a wonderful sight for the local inhabitants to see the approaching packhorse trains descending Ackerley Moor. What a subject to paint!

Between Litton and Arncliffe the dale widens again and the fellsides flecked with limestone gaze down into pastoral perfection. A mosaic of hay meadows pattern the flat valley floor, their irregular shapes edged with drystone walls and randomly spaced trees.

Scoska Wood, a botanist's dream on the southwest side of the dale is probably the largest rowan and ash wood left in the county. This National Nature Reserve managed by English Nature displays a remarkable array of wildflowers, especially in spring or early summer, including; early purple orchid, wood crane's-bill and baneberry. Also in the adjacent field below the wood, field scabious and lady's bedstraw grow in profusion, and the scarcer birds-eye primrose may be spotted.

The largest of Littondale's four small settlements, Arncliffe (eagle cliff), is situated in the very heart of the dale. Creeper-covered cottages are set around a large traditional village green, street lighting is absent and the Falcon Inn serves ale from ceramic jugs in the old way. Nothing appears to have changed much here; it's like stepping into a bygone age (if we ignore the Range Rovers). Hidden in trees by the riverside, St Oswald's church which dates from the 12th century has a memorial to local men who fought at the Battle of Flodden Field in 1513.

Various routes radiate from Arncliffe like spokes of a wheel. One ancient monastic path to Malham — Monk's Road, traverses the impressive limestone etched Yew Cogar Scar on a broad natural ledge. The drunken wanderings of Cowside Beck can be followed far below and peregrine falcons might be seen quartering the air. This is a magical place to be, especially on one of those lovely days when cloud shadows gently roll over the shoulders of the fells, changing limestone walls from light to dark to light again, revealing the land's form and structure.

Two roads now escort the winding river downstream from Arncliffe; one on either side of the dale. The accompanying stonewalls are draped in a tapestry of velvet lichen and moss, a sure sign that the air is pure. Along this stretch, a curious natural phenomenon can be seen: the profile of the first Duke of Wellington complete with his distinctive noble nose has been hewn accurately in the rock by glacial action, and honed to perfection by the elements high on the edge of Blue Scar cliff.

Hawkswick is a tiny village with its single line of grey cottages strung along the narrow lane on the north side of the river. Apparently, from long ago there has been a settlement here, for Saxon cultivation terraces are in evidence on the hillsides nearby, and above them even older Celtic lynchets (fields).

Littondale, as other limestone dales, has its secret subterranean world. A notable cave, Dowkabottom, has a chamber known as 'The Cathedral' where Neolithic human remains and various artefacts from the Romano-British period have been unearthed.

The dale draws closer to Wharfedale now, and with the scars of Conistone rearing up and appearing to block the way directly ahead, the River Skirfare bids a bubbly farewell to Littondale and merges merrily with the Wharfe.

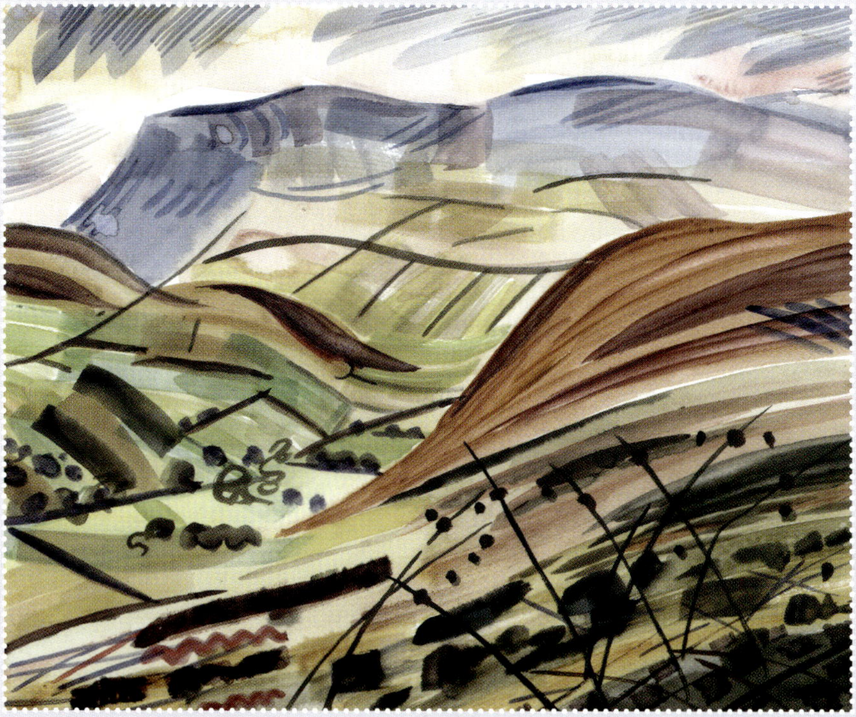

Penyghent from Akerley Moor

1995 watercolour 7 x 8 in

Yew Cogar Scar

1996 watercolour 7 x 8.5 in

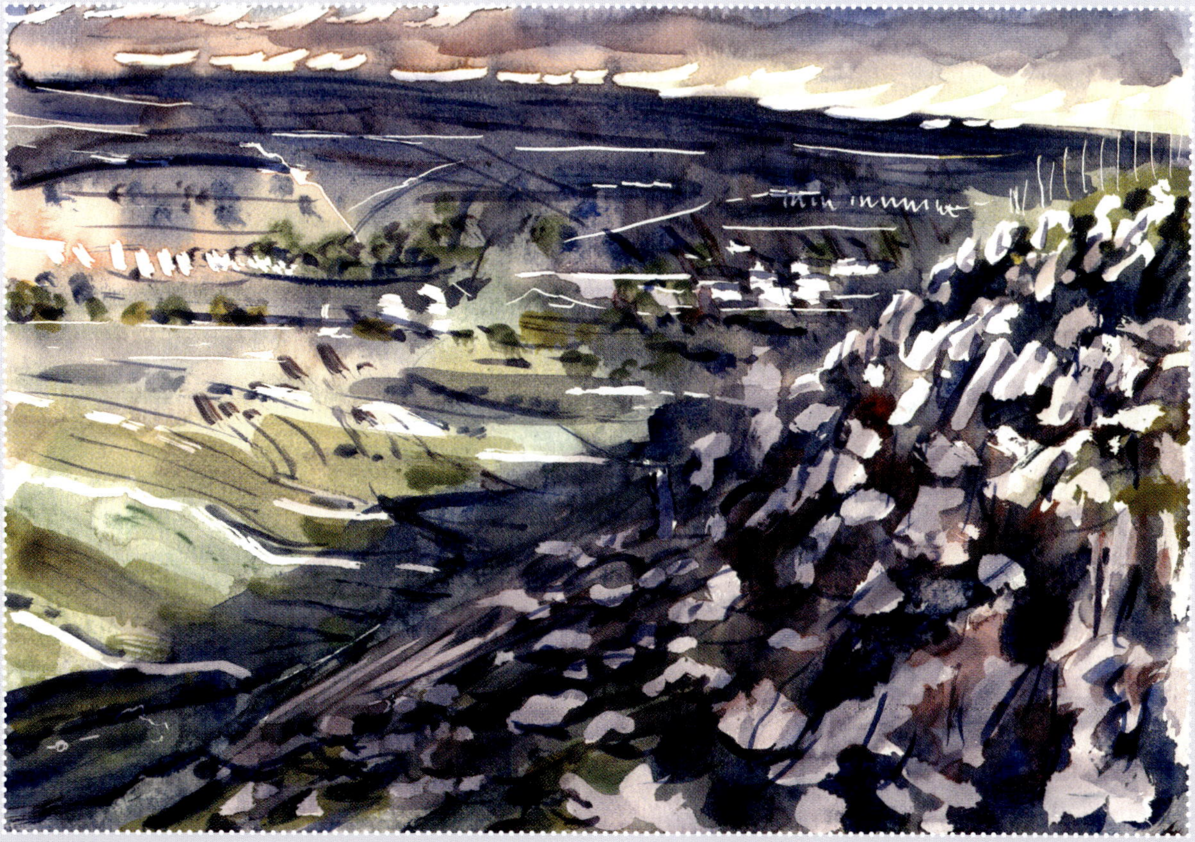

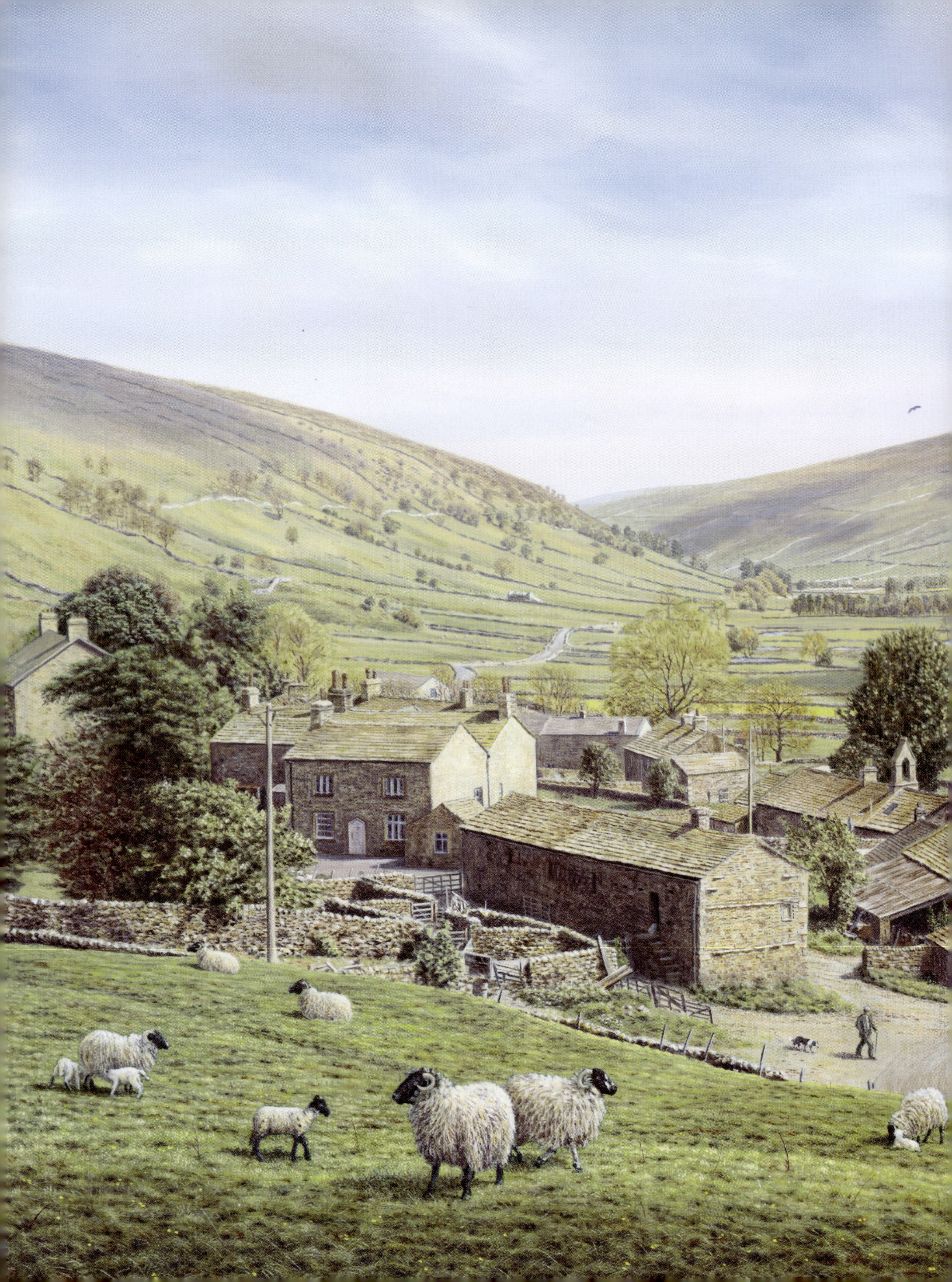

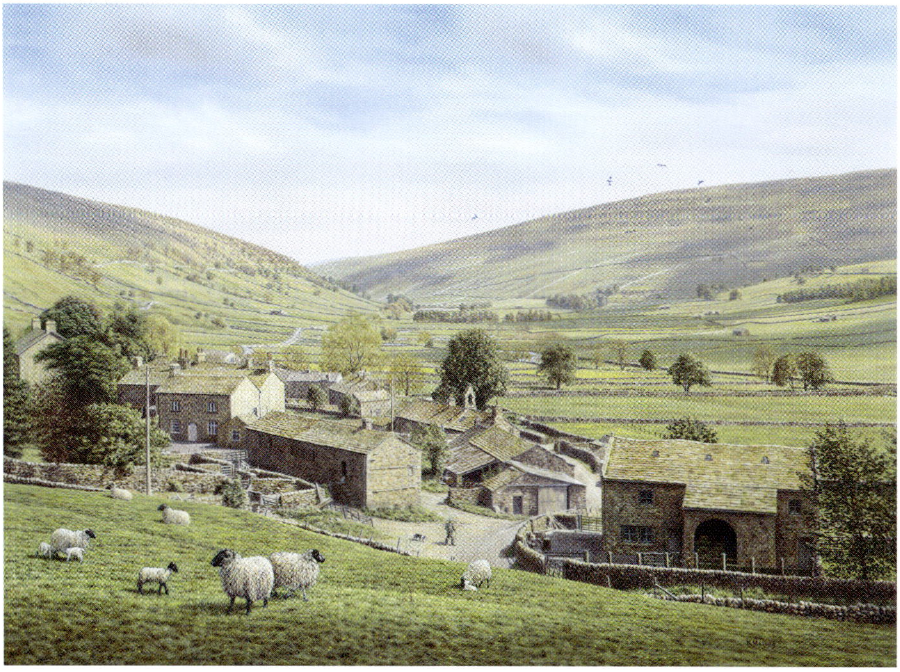

Halton Gill, Littondale

1994 Oil 14.5 x 21in

Some years ago, I had the idea to paint all the major Yorkshire Dales. In each case I would find the view that would encapsulate the individual character and essence, a scene that would sum the dale up in one go. Obviously, in reality this is an impossible task, there are many facets to a dale's character, and they are not all going to be revealed from one single fixed point. However, this self-inflicted project was most enjoyable and did give me a better understanding of each individual dale.

Choosing a suitable viewpoint proved to be difficult in Littondale, not because good viewpoints are scarce, but because they are very abundant. After many excursions, much walking and exploring the valley and fellsides, a final choice was settled upon. It is the one shown here — situated a little way up Horsehead Pass, looking over the hamlet of Halton Gill.

Needs change in farming, and the barn on the right now has a large extension with corrugated roof. I used part research, guesswork and imagination to portray it how it might once have looked. Apart from this one little alteration, the scene probably hasn't changed much in 200 years.

Lapwings are performing their aerobatics over the meadows, usually a common sight here. Curlews, dippers, wagtails and surprisingly oystercatchers are other birds often seen in this green valley.

Peace and tranquility reign, though one day when I was sketching on Old Cote Moor, a platoon of young soldiers came charging over the hill carrying two telegraph poles. A red-faced sergeant running in their wake was cursing and screaming abuse at them, he seemed to be expending more energy than they were. The ground vibrated as they thundered within inches of me, and my water jar, which was finely balanced, tipped and spilt some of its murky contents over a drying ink sketch. I joined in the cursing (under my breath of course).

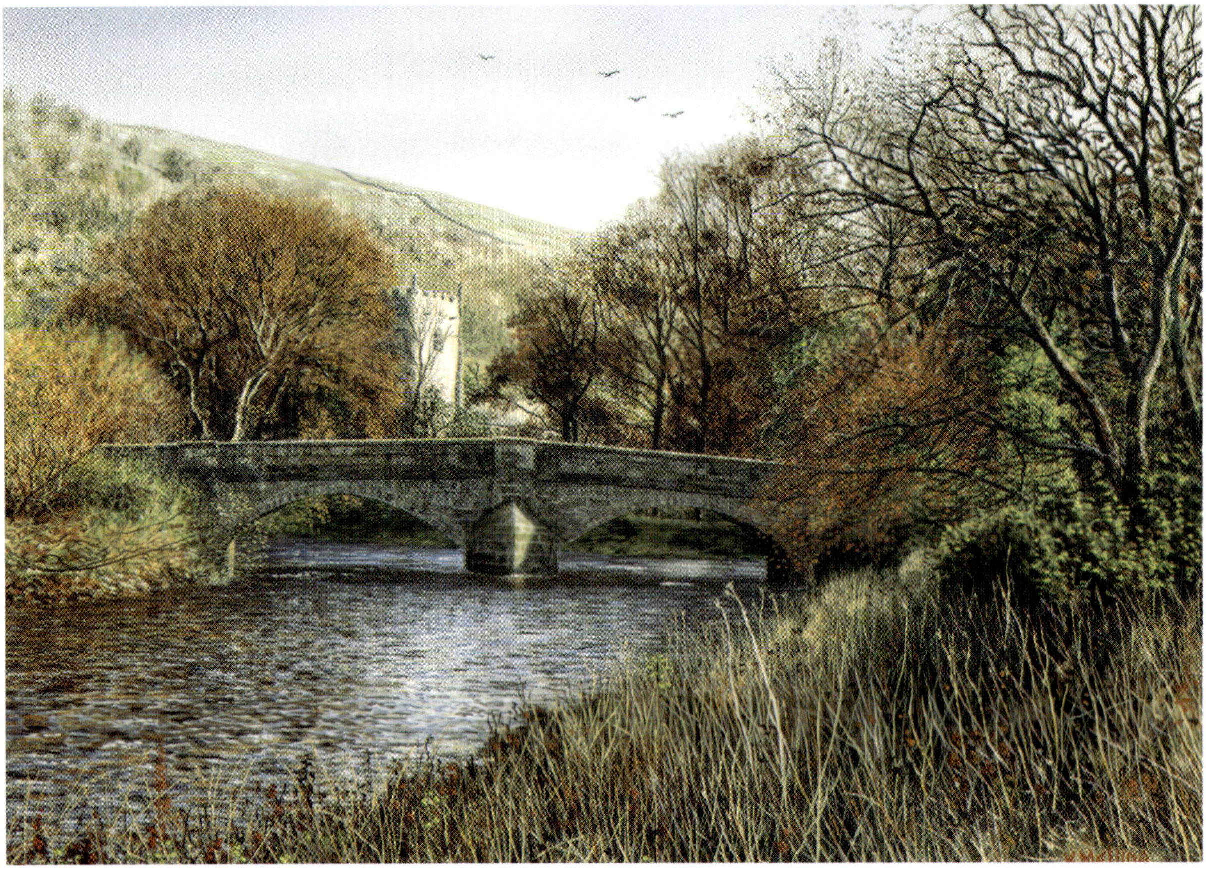

The River Skirfare at Arncliffe
1991 Gouache 5.75 x 8in

The bright clear waters of the Skirfare skirt around the north edge of this beautiful unspoilt village and is accompanied in part by a delightful little back lane. The banks here and below the fine old bridge are very popular spots for painters to set up their easels, and even if little work is done, the experience of just being there, observing and soaking up the scene is enriching. Charles Kingsley was inspired to write his famous book 'The Water Babies' whilst staying in the village at Bridge End.

Arncliffe is lovely in any season, but its profusion of lofty sycamores makes it especially attractive in autumn. My chosen viewpoint looking downstream shows both the fine stone bridge and the ancient church tower in the mellow afternoon sunlight. The fell in the background is Old Cote Moor, which separates Littondale from Wharfedale.

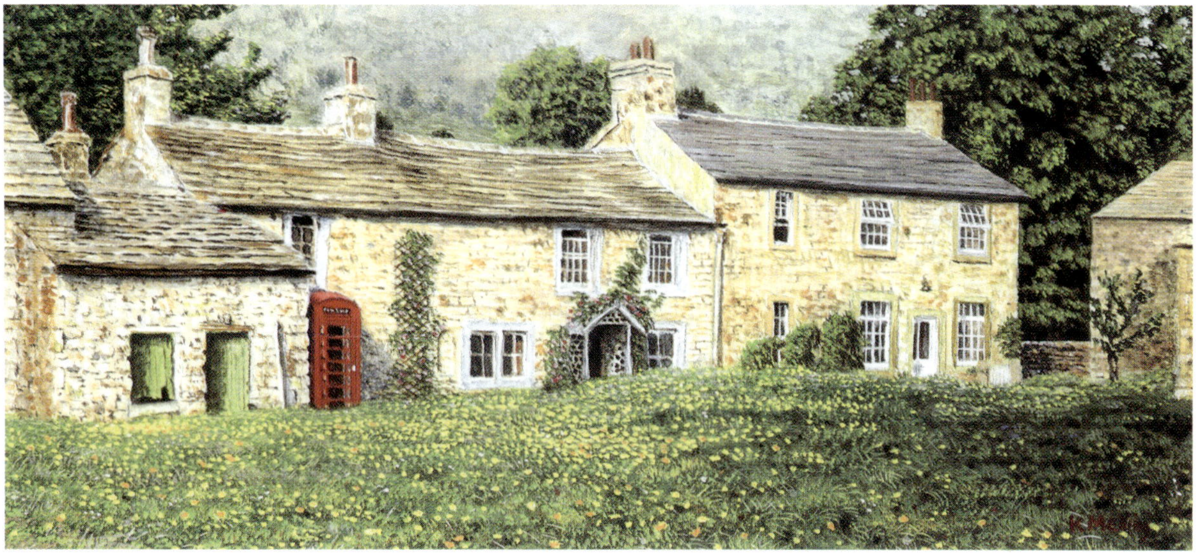

Arncliffe Cottages
1992 Gouache 3 x 6.5in

The various buildings around Arncliffe's peaceful village green without exception exude olde-worlde charm. I was inevitably drawn to the vivid red telephone box which complemented so perfectly the lively greens and bright yellows of early summer. This picture was painted with gouache on a very small scale, in fact approximately the size shown here.

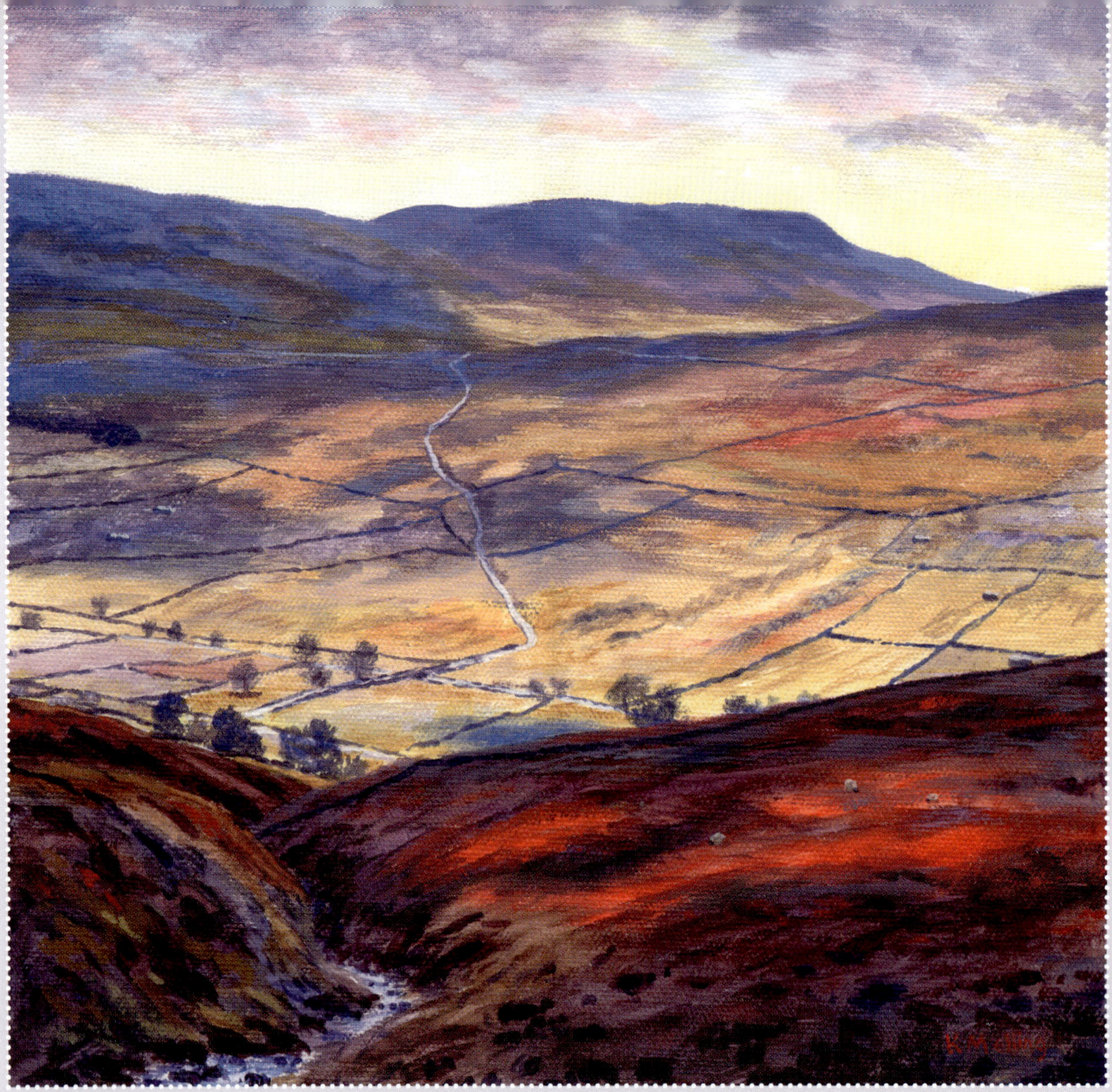

Fountains Fell from Horsehead Pass
2006 Acrylic 10 x 10ins

Outshone by its more illustrious neighbour Penyghent, this reclining fell with no dale to call its own except the hanging valley of Silverdale, is happy after years of exploitation to remain relatively anonymous. The monks of Fountains Abbey had mining rights here, hence the name and from which the broad summit plateau is still pitted and scarred.

This view from above Halton Gill looks across the head of Littondale to the shadowy escarpments of Penyghent Gill and the lithe contours of Fountains Fell itself. The narrow Silverdale road climbs stubbornly over the broad shoulders of Hesleden High Bergh (where I once nearly got stuck in ice and snow and had to reverse my car all the way back down). The blotchy lines of drystone walls slice the fellsides and valley awkwardly. These seemingly arbitrary wall patterns invariably pose a puzzle for me. Why does that one not join this? Why does that one change direction? And so on.

One of a series of paintings from this spot on Horse Head Pass, the colouring is a subjective response and not the actual colour we see. I find myself returning to the way I painted as a teenager — bright, bold, colourful and a little more abstracted.

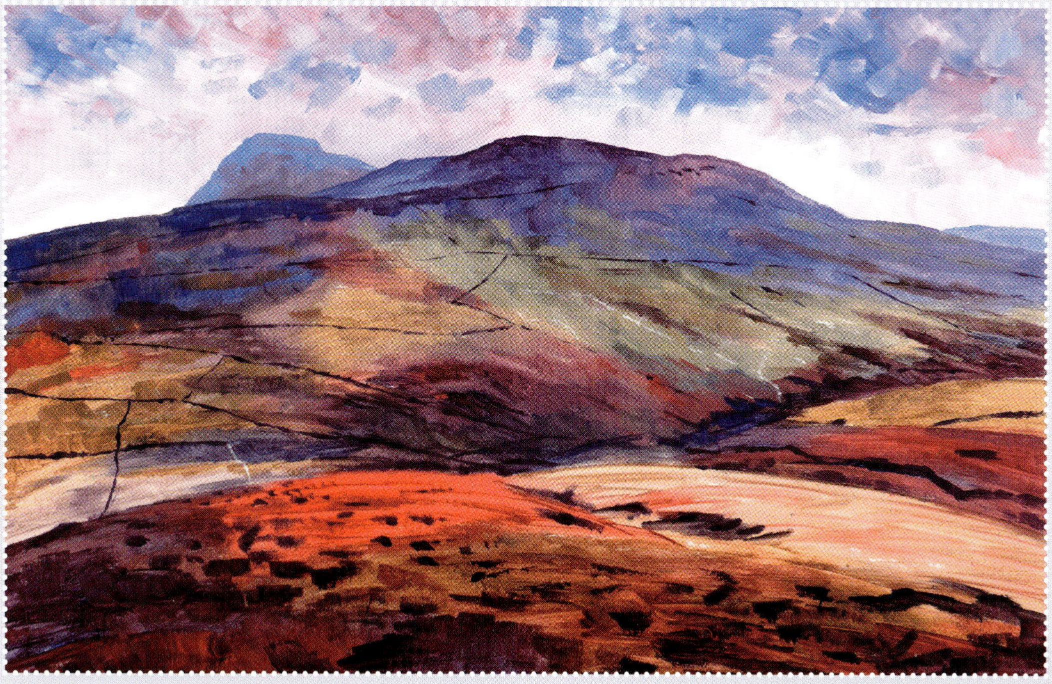

On Horsehead Moor looking to Plover Hill and Penyghent
2003 Acrylic 9 x14in

This and the triptych below were painted from virtually the same spot as the previous picture. The unusual back view of Penyghent peeping over Plover Hill is more akin to the profile of Ingleborough — a little confusing!

Distant Ingleborough from Horsehead Pass
2005 Acrylic 13 x 28in

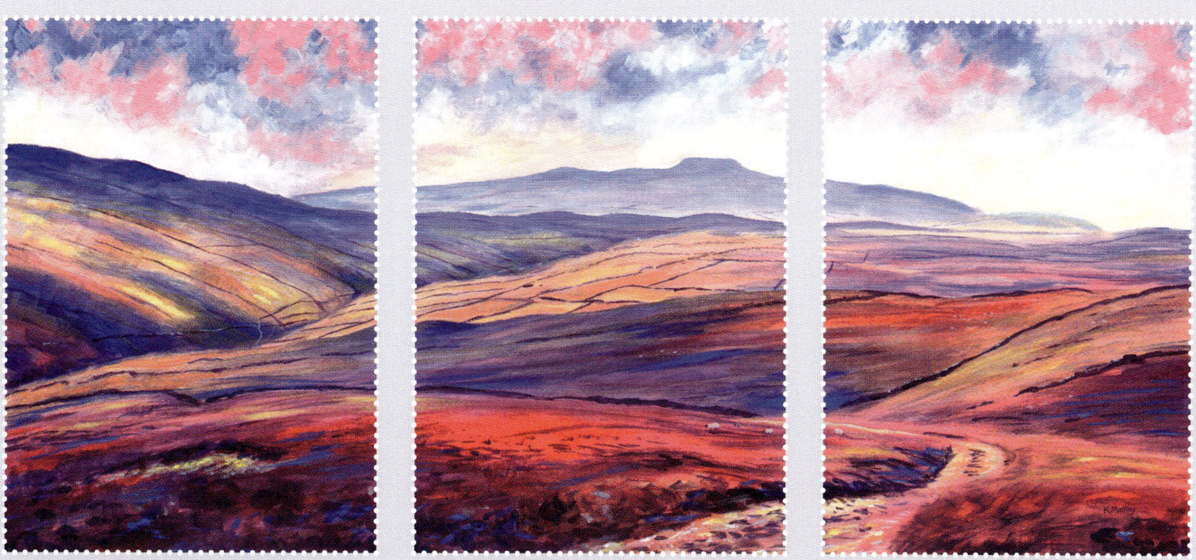

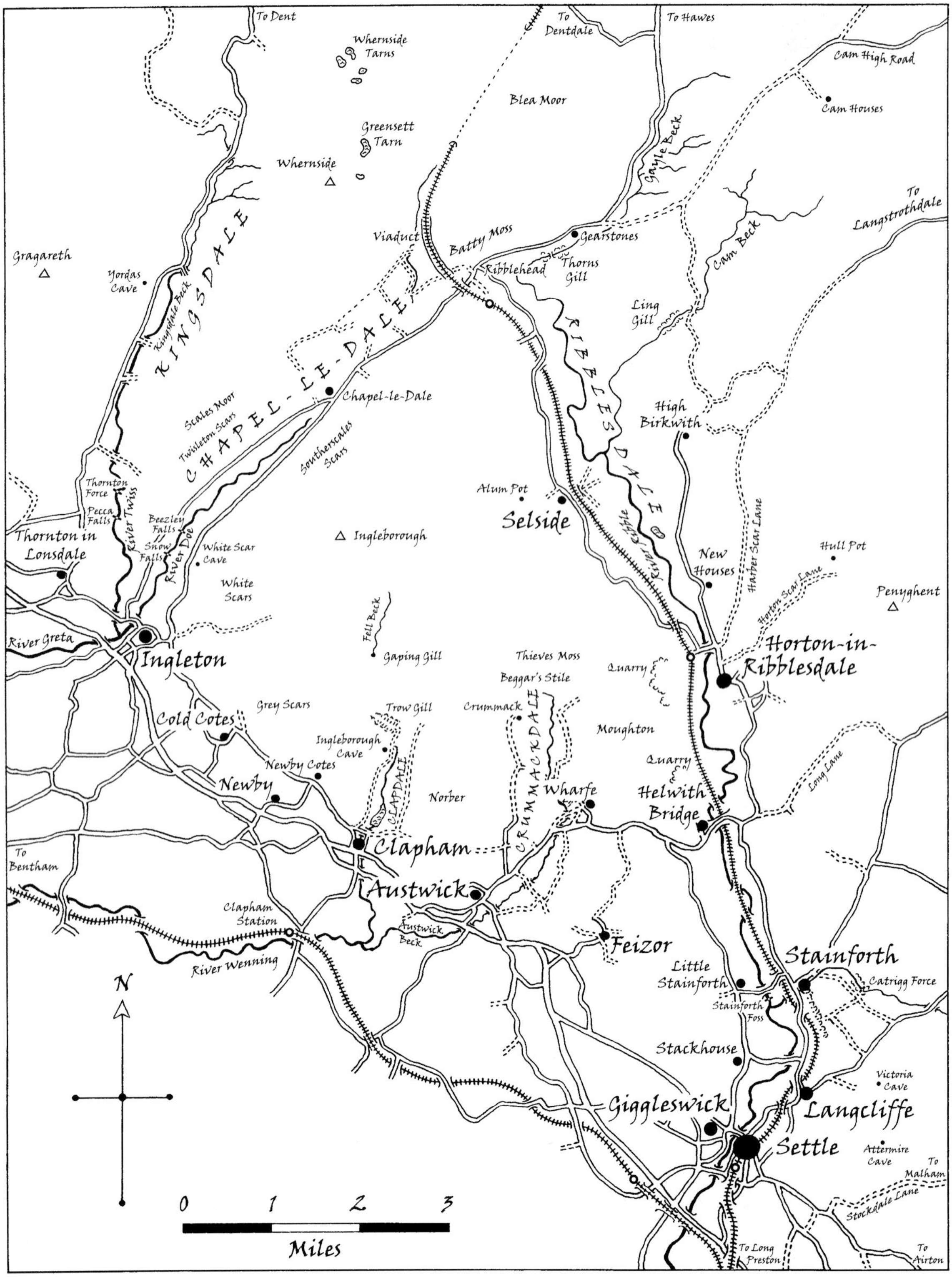

Three Peaks and Ribblesdale

Three Peaks and Ribblesdale

The Ribble is the black sheep of Yorkshire's rivers, for it is the only principal river to navigate southwestwards to the Irish Sea. It pays no heed and cares naught for political boundaries, flowing for the greater part of its length through Lancashire. This waywardness has caused some Yorkshire writers a little consternation: Phyllis Bentley says of the Ribble — 'it has the audacity to enter Lancashire'. Alfred J Brown says — 'the worst that can be said against it (Ribblesdale) is that its guardian river slips away ultimately over the border', and similarly Ella Pontefract remarks — 'its river may forsake the country at its end, but its beginnings are on Yorkshire's fells'.

Being a Lancashire lad, I see no fault in the Ribble's meandering; it continues to be a grand river despite crossing an imaginary line on the ground. In truth, from source to sea, the Ribble remains sublime, and retains its own name, unlike other Dales rivers that merge and eventually defer to the Ouse. However, Ribblesdale is the most dramatic and spectacular section, and is entirely in Yorkshire. When the boundary is breached it becomes 'Ribble Valley', and although very beautiful, is of a different nature; gentle, lush and pastoral.

Where the Ribble begins is a matter of choice. Several tributary streams starting high on the moors have been claimed to be the source; of which, Gayle Beck and Cam Beck are the main candidates. Where Ribblesdale itself begins there is no doubt; it is firmly marked on the map as 'Ribblehead', a wild desolate place, famous for its Victorian railway viaduct. This mammoth structure of 24 arches is a quarter of a mile long and 105 ft high. It carries the Settle Carlisle line over the notorious Batty Moss, where, during the viaducts construction, there was a huge shanty town to accommodate thousands of 'navvies'. The viaduct was designed and built of course to serve a purpose, but it also can be seen on a different level — aesthetically, as architecture or art: in fact, a work to rival any from any era. The soaring functional construction may be appreciated not only from close quarters, but also from mountain summits, where, the snaking curvature of its layout appears far below like a model railway.

The windswept treeless landscape, seemingly barren, has a strange attraction, and actually abounds with hidden features. The rocky gorge of Ling Gill with its natural hanging gardens of wild flowers and rowan is only revealed after a short hike. Similarly, the intimate Thorns Gill, containing perhaps the most appealing packhorse bridge in England is reached after a brief walk from Gearstones. This area, like most of Ribblesdale, has a secret dark world of potholes and caves, and whilst this might be out of bounds to most artists, the individual entrances when found can be interesting subjects to draw.

At Ribblehead, the Ribblesdale road meets the Hawes to Ingleton route that runs through Chapel-le-Dale between the elevated Ingleborough and the sprawling Whernside. Whernside is the highest of the Three Peaks, but deceptively so. When standing on its airy summit, looking to

Ingleborough, I have tried to compare heights using the artist's visual method of measuring with outstretched arm and pencil — a kind of point to point or dot to dot, which is primitive yet effective. Most definitely Ingleborough seems higher. This is usually explained as an illusion, but why then does Whernside appear lower when viewed from Ingleborough, is this an illusion too? Could it be that the official heights are wrong, or is it just a case of mountains and mathematics not mixing very well?

> "Being a Lancashire lad, I see no fault in the Ribble's meandering; it continues to be a grand river despite crossing an imaginary line on the ground."

While the two mountains staring at each other across the glacial valley are quite close, their characters are very different. Whernside is an introvert; the long slow incline from Twisleton Scar renders its quiet profile almost unnoticeable, the collection of tarns (Norse for tear drops) on the northern slopes, gives a solitary sad feel. Ingleborough on the other hand is extrovert, displaying its towering tabletop proudly to all and sundry, and easily recognisable from afar. Evidence of an Iron Age fort can still be seen around the summit plateau. Whole books have been written about this intriguing fell. The region has large areas of limestone scars and pavements, and these features have held a great fascination for me as an artist. I've wandered endlessly over the clints and grykes of this moonscape, and tried various visual interpretations of its surreal appearance.

Ingleton, located where Chapel-le-Dale and Kingsdale converge, is a pleasantly unpretentious village, popular with cavers and ramblers. The spectacular series of waterfalls there, which cascade and leap down the wooded glens of the Twiss and Doe have made Ingleton famous: and deservedly so. The dynamic four miles of the waterfalls walk is a feast for the eyes, delightful in any season and awesome when in spate. I find it hard to believe that before the 1860s local folk including farmers and quarrymen hardly knew of the falls' existence, but apparently they didn't. A chap named Joseph Carr brought the area to the public's attention — so much so, that the Ingleton Improvement Society was formed. Walkways were constructed through the glens for public access and word soon spread of the dramatic 'Glens Walk'. Special trains brought hordes of day-trippers and Ingleton boomed as a tourist attraction. Local people cashed in by digging out wild orchids and lilies of the valley to sell to visitors. Unfortunately these once profuse flowers have not returned although the flora of the woods is still very rich and varied. The walk remains popular and painting here is quite trying in summer. You can bet someone will say in an Australian accent 'can ya tell what it is yet', and dogs may mistake the easel for a lamppost. It's not easy to concentrate.

From Ribblehead the Ribble flows southwards, accompanied by road and railway. Alum Pot near Selside is yet another remarkable hidden feature. The water from Alum Beck plunges and free falls 200 ft into a spine chilling sinister chasm. After coming up for air at Footnaw's Hole a mile away, the water disappears again and heads for the Ribble. Curiously, the water does a subterranean loop the loop and re-emerges at Turn Dub on the hillside beyond the opposite bank.

Horton-in-Ribblesdale is a Mecca for walkers; it is the start and finish of the gruelling Three Peaks walk, where Penyghent, Ingleborough and Whernside are bagged in one day. The Pennine Way and Ribble Way also pass through here. The green tracks of Horton Scar Lane and Harber Scar Lane both start from the village and are brimming with interest. The latter, that boasts a string of notable potholes on either side, is a favourite of mine. Near this rough lane, above High Birkwith, I've sketched a particular derelict field-barn many times; on certain days an exceptional light seems to emanate not only from the sky but also from the valley below, illuminating the building softly in a peculiar way.

Penyghent is the smallest of the Three Peaks, yet its pleasing shape has a huge presence and dominates this part of the dale. The mountain's outline is sometimes used in emblems and logos on outdoor equipment; it has become almost an icon. The lovely lilting Celtic name 'Pen-y-ghent', apparently meaning 'hill of the winds' is very apt, as the exposed summit ridge is often very breezy — and I can vouch for that. Working here once on a gusty afternoon, a half finished drawing detached itself and became airborne. I watched helplessly as the tumbling white sheet flew off in the direction of Penyghent Gill, where it could still be lodged, soggy and dog-eared as a piece of litter. Sensibly, I prefer to take properly bound smaller sketchpads to such high places now.

Ribblesdale could well do without the huge unsightly quarries that sadly blight one side of the valley near Horton. On second thoughts, perhaps this opinion is too idealistic. The Dales area is not only a leisure park but also a working environment, just as it was during the lead mining days. We tend to look back at those bygone operations with nostalgia and affection now, even though much land was spoilt and men died prematurely from lead poisoning. If the quarries become obsolete and nature re-established, we might look back with admiration. Maybe artists and photographers ought to be making a visual record of these workings, as they have done with the coal mining industry.

A narrow road diverts from Helwith Bridge towards Wharfe, Crummackdale and Austwick. Crummackdale is a small side dale, encircled by fells with more than their fair share of interesting geological features. On the west side, stands Norber, with its crowded field of famous erratic boulders. These

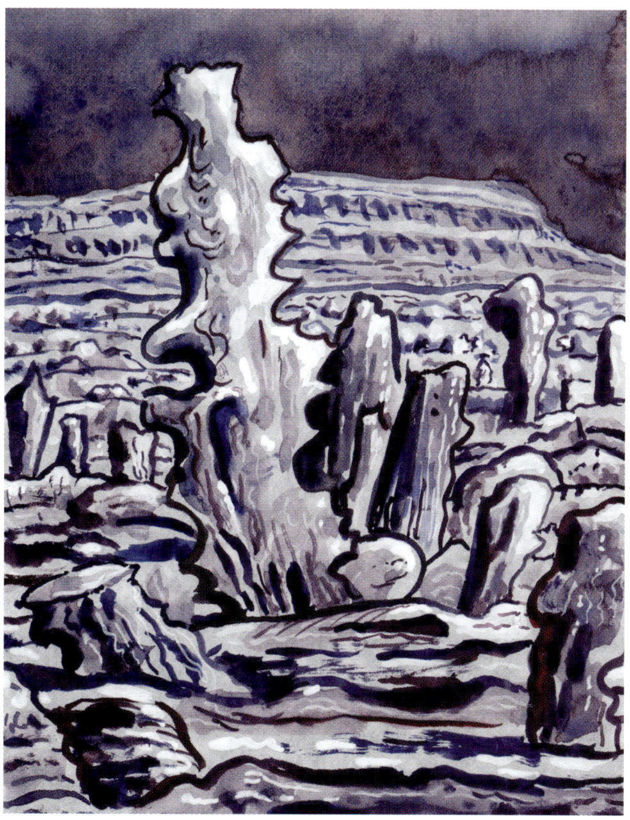

Thieves Moss, Moughton

large gritstone boulders, perched comically upon limestone pedestals were carried up here by glacial ice, and like any piece of sculpture that is raised on a plinth, they demand attention. The theory is that the boulders have acted as umbrellas and sheltered the limestone directly underneath from erosion. The exposed area has been eroded away, leaving the protected parts proud.

"The curlew was desperately trying to drive a hungry fox away from its chicks. I watched in amazement until the fox could stand no more bombardment and nonchalantly slunk off along the rim of the scars."

Directly opposite, across the foot of Crummackdale, the grey cluster of cottages at Wharfe snugly nestles under the scars of Moughton. Moughton (pronounced Moot'n) is an appealing limestone fell that completely encloses the east side of Crummackdale and abruptly cuts off the dale-head. Above Beggars Stile, Thieves Moss is a beguiling, entrancing place; a wild plateau of clints and bog, shielded by a crescent shaped escarpment where eerie echoes can be quite startling. I remember vividly an afternoon sketching here, when the distressed calling of an alarmed curlew reverberated all around. The anxious bird was repeatedly swooping down at something on the ground. Curiosity got the better of me and I decided to investigate. The curlew was desperately trying to drive a hungry fox away from its chicks. I watched in amazement until the fox could stand no more bombardment and nonchalantly slunk off along the rim of the scars.

Seen from the nearby A65, Austwick looks an inviting village with a wonderful backdrop of craggy fells. I've often passed here and thought it would make a splendid picture. Alas, after exploring the surrounding fields and lanes for a suitable viewpoint, the promised composition has so far eluded me. Sorry Austwick. Clapham is another very picturesque village off the A65, made all the more attractive by an abundance and variety of trees, mostly planted by the Farrer family who had a great influence in the district. A babbling brook divides the village and a collection of bridges enhances the setting. A small admission fee gives access to a colourful nature trail through Clapdale, passing a secluded lake and Ingleborough Cave. Further, a path en route to Ingleborough visits the dry gorge of Trow Gill and the frightening black hole of Gaping Gill, where supposedly, the enormous underground cavern could accommodate a cathedral. Fine landscape features abound for the artist; probably the most visually imposing at Trow Gill with its impressive limestone cliffs. The remote rural settlements of Newby, Newby Cotes and Cold Cotes are not without interest and complete the circuit of Ingleborough. I have enjoyed drawing on the bleak fellside above here at Grey Scars where nearby there is a spectacular series of potholes.

The hidden village of Feizor has covered its tracks of progress well; with a working farm at its heart it has undoubtedly moved forward into the modern age, but unnoticeably so; the lovingly preserved water pump on the small tidy green says it all. The crags of Pot Scar and Smearsett Scar rear up directly behind the huddle of houses. From the stony summit ridge, Penyghent and Ingleborough are prominent in a wonderful 360-degree panorama, but my eyes are drawn to gazing south through the haze to the whalebacked Pendle Hill, my home territory. I've made dozens of sketches and paintings of Pendle; some from near and others from Yorkshire's hills (maybe all material for a future book). Adjacent to Smearsett Scar, across a narrow green valley, is the strategically placed Celtic Wall. This mysterious fragment, 5 ft thick, 5 ft high and 65 ft long is constructed from rather large irregular limestone blocks and is reputedly 2000 years old. No one knows its purpose, and perhaps this only adds to its intrinsic attraction. The side facing the prevailing wind shows typical scalloped erosion. I've used close up studies of this wall as the basis for several abstract paintings.

Back in Ribblesdale proper now at Stainforth, the river, railway and road run in close proximity on different levels. Beloved by campers who have bathed and dived into the deep pools, this is probably the most impressive stretch of the Ribble. In October, salmon seemingly perform miracles as they leap the roaring falls. Painters and photographers have portrayed the shapely packhorse bridge built in 1670 countless times.

South of Stainforth the peaceful village of Langcliffe seems so idyllic. As in Feizor you half expect Postman Pat to trundle by in his little red van. Nearby at Victoria Cave, archaeologists have unearthed relics of Neolithic people, bones of grizzly bear, rhinoceros, hippopotamus and others. The entrance (much enlarged now) is in an elevated position and looks out to Warrendale Knotts; a kind of early room with a view. I once sheltered in this spacious abode and sketched

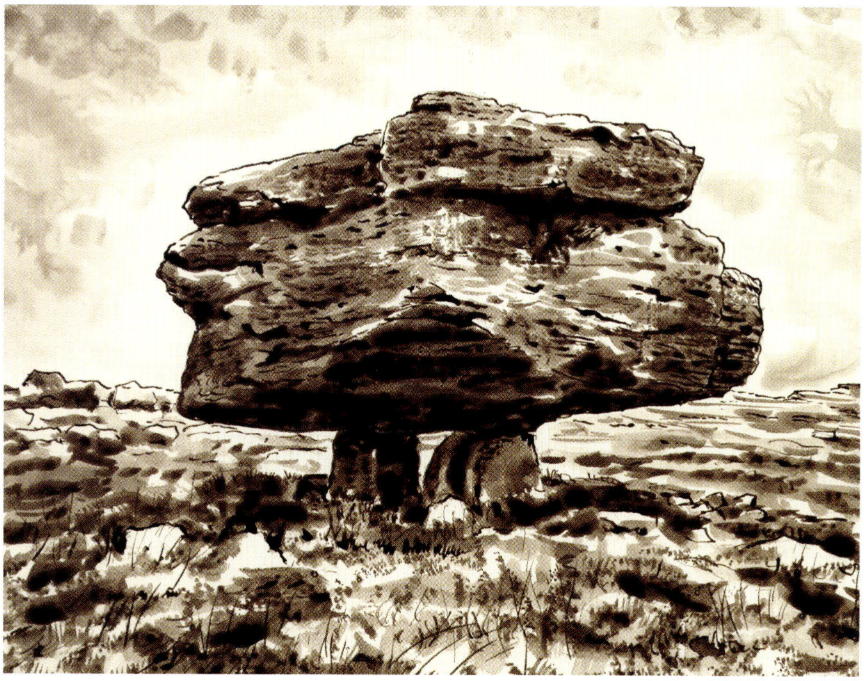

Norber Erratic Boulder

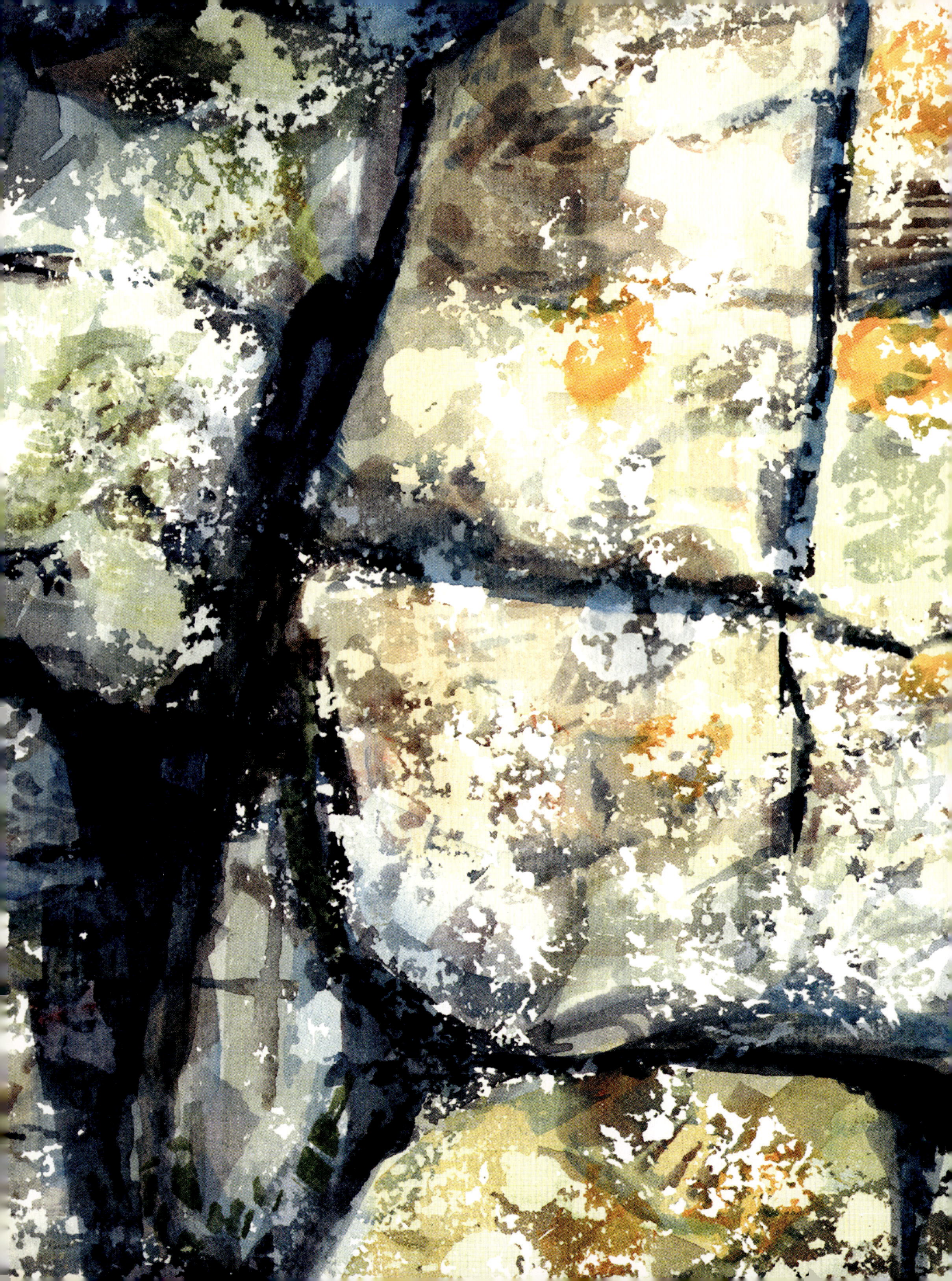

the hills opposite through a curtain of rain. The neighbouring Attermire Cave has an even better outlook, with views to Warrendale Knotts and Sugar Loaf Hill.

The market town of Settle and its quieter satellite village Giggleswick lie on opposite banks of the Ribble. Seemingly self sufficient they together make a very wholesome community where there is a little of everything. At the famous Giggleswick public school an unusual domed chapel appears a slightly incongruous landmark. This area of course lying on the South Craven Fault has natural landmarks aplenty: all to the east is limestone with its bright subtle hues, while all to the west is gritstone with the distant sombre fells of Bowland swelling on the skyline. An aerial prospect of Settle can be seen from the rocky Castleberg Knoll immediately behind and overlooking the town. This birds-eye view reminds me of those early cubist pictures by Picasso and his pal Braque, where from apparently random chaos they tease a carefully organised harmony.

The River Ribble flows serenely on to Long Preston where the low-lying fields are often flooded, then on to the Ribble Valley and the red-rose county of Lancashire.

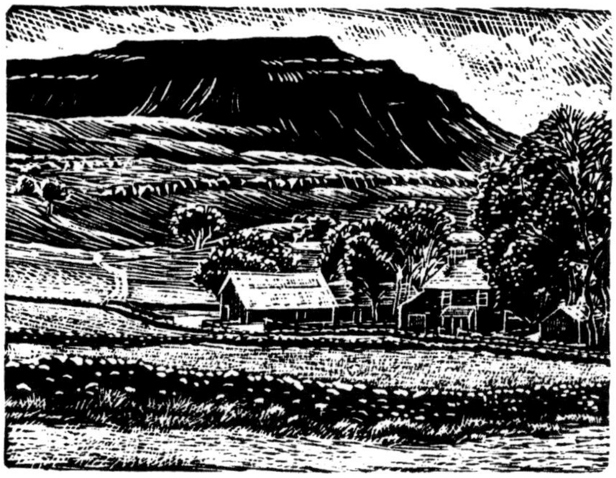

Ingleborough from Chapel-le-Dale

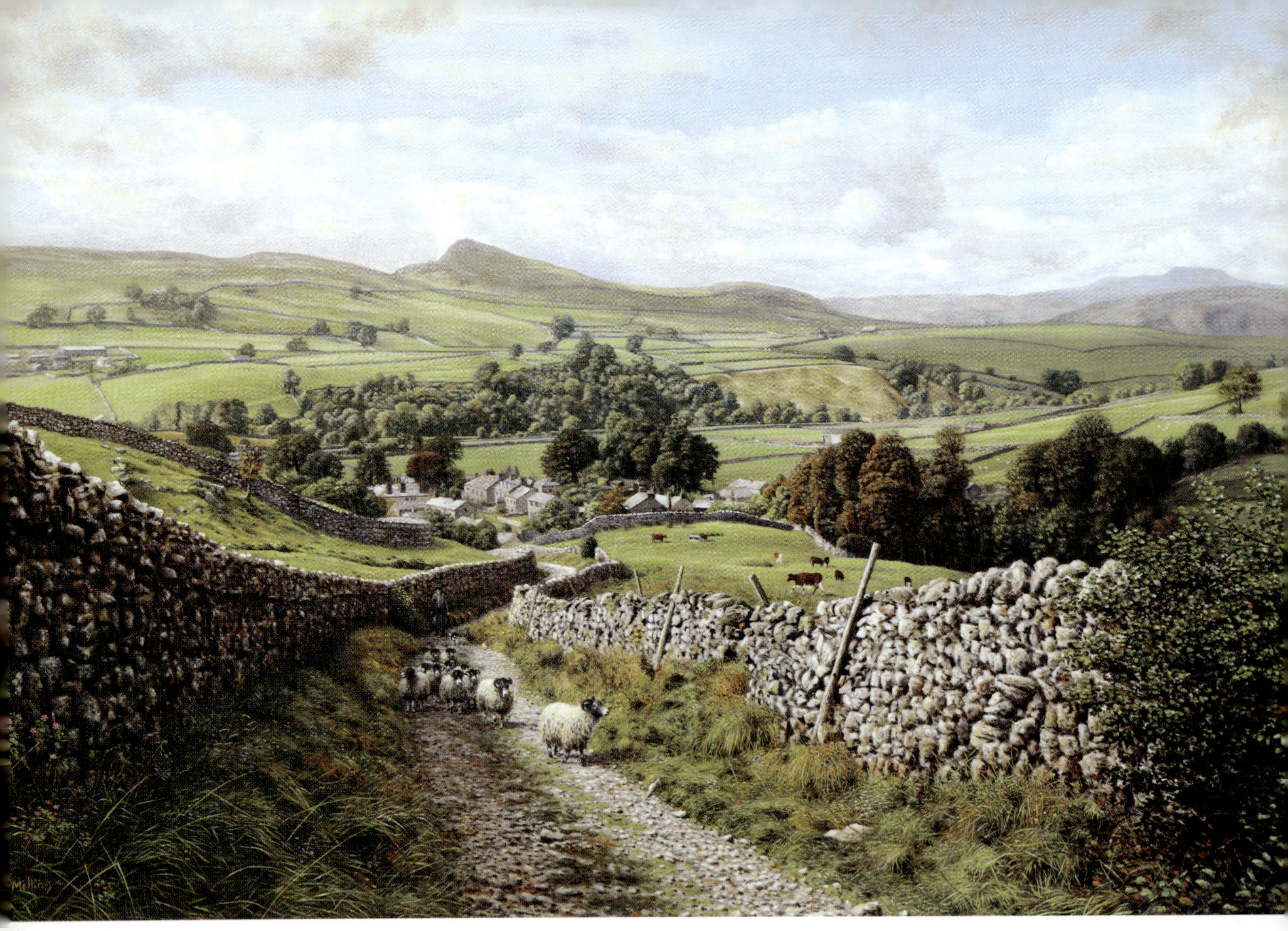

Above Stainforth, Ribblesdale

1991 Oil 15 x 22.25in

Strolling along Goat Scar Lane from Stainforth on one of those breezy late summer afternoons when anywhere would look lovely, I chanced upon this glorious view, and kept it in mind for several years before painting it. Revisiting many times to witness the varied effects of the seasons and to observe the changing light throughout the day, I decided finally to try and recreate my first impression, albeit with a slight difference.

The scene before me had all the ingredients required of a composition, but there was a problem. A tree half way down the lane obscured most of the village from view. Now, not being one to advocate the indiscriminate felling of trees, I reluctantly came to the conclusion that this one would have to go. So, I omitted it. Going to great lengths to see exactly how the village would look from here without it, I returned when the tree had shed its leaves, so as to see through it (with difficulty). This, combined with going to either side of the offending tree enabled me to render it invisible.

The lane with its impressive limestone walls rises steeply from Stainforth, and acts as a good lead-in to the picture, a favourite pictorial device of mine that gives the illusion of space and depth. Ingleborough makes an appearance on the far right, and the distinctive pointed hill in the centre is Smearsett Scar, which always appears bigger than its modest height.

Goat Scar Lane, Ribblesdale

1991 Gouache and watercolour 8 x 12in

I couldn't resist doing another picture featuring Goat Scar Lane. This time from higher up the track. The composition is a little unusual with the tree bang in the centre; something which art instruction books tell us to avoid. For some time it puzzled me why in this case the composition worked. It's rather a lengthy explanation so I'll just say that it is to do with the unequal dark and light masses in the foreground, which break the symmetry. If you turn the picture upside down to see it more abstractly, this becomes more obvious.

Ingleborough is in view again; its height exaggerated slightly to make it appear more as we experience it. This is an old trick that eighteenth and early nineteenth century painters overused, blowing their hills and mountains up out of all proportion.

The quarrying at Helwith Bridge (visible on the right directly behind the shepherd) is eating away the hillside of Moughton. Quarrying rights were given hundreds of years ago when methods of extracting stone were not mechanised and much less damaging to the landscape. It seems hideously crazy now to allow hills to be blasted out of our National Parks.

Whilst standing still here on the lane, concentrating on sketching, a strange thing happened. A young rabbit scampered towards me, stopped for a moment between my feet then dashed off through a hole in the wall. Seconds later a weasel followed — circled my feet twice and hurtled after the rabbit. I was dumbfounded. Then would you believe it? A few moments later, the rabbit came back through the wall pursued by the weasel and they both performed a similar party piece around my feet in the opposite direction. This was unreal, pure Bugs Bunny — was I in a cartoon? Some years later I was reading about weasels and discovered that rabbits are so terrified of them that they will seek the shelter of humans.

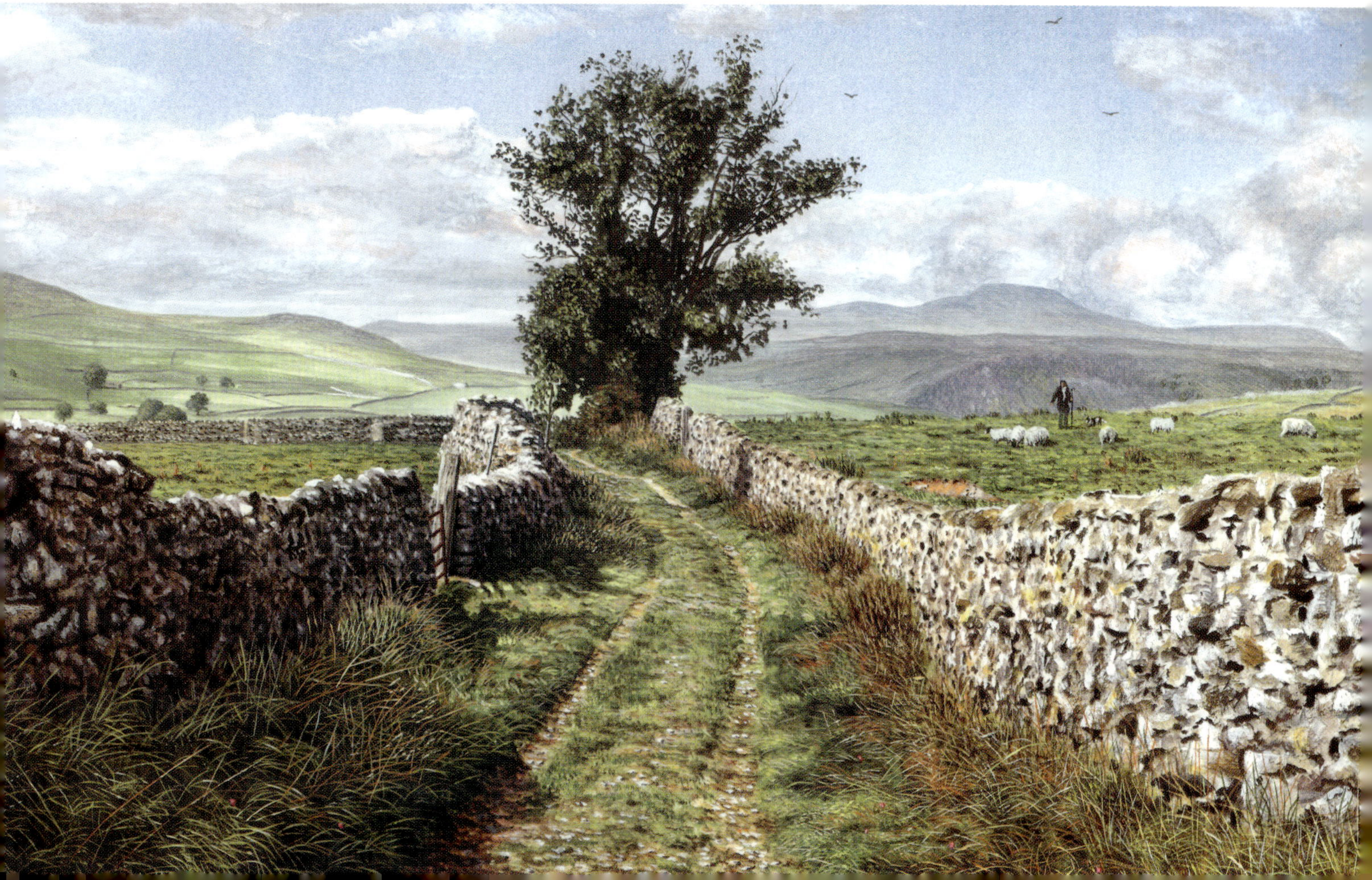

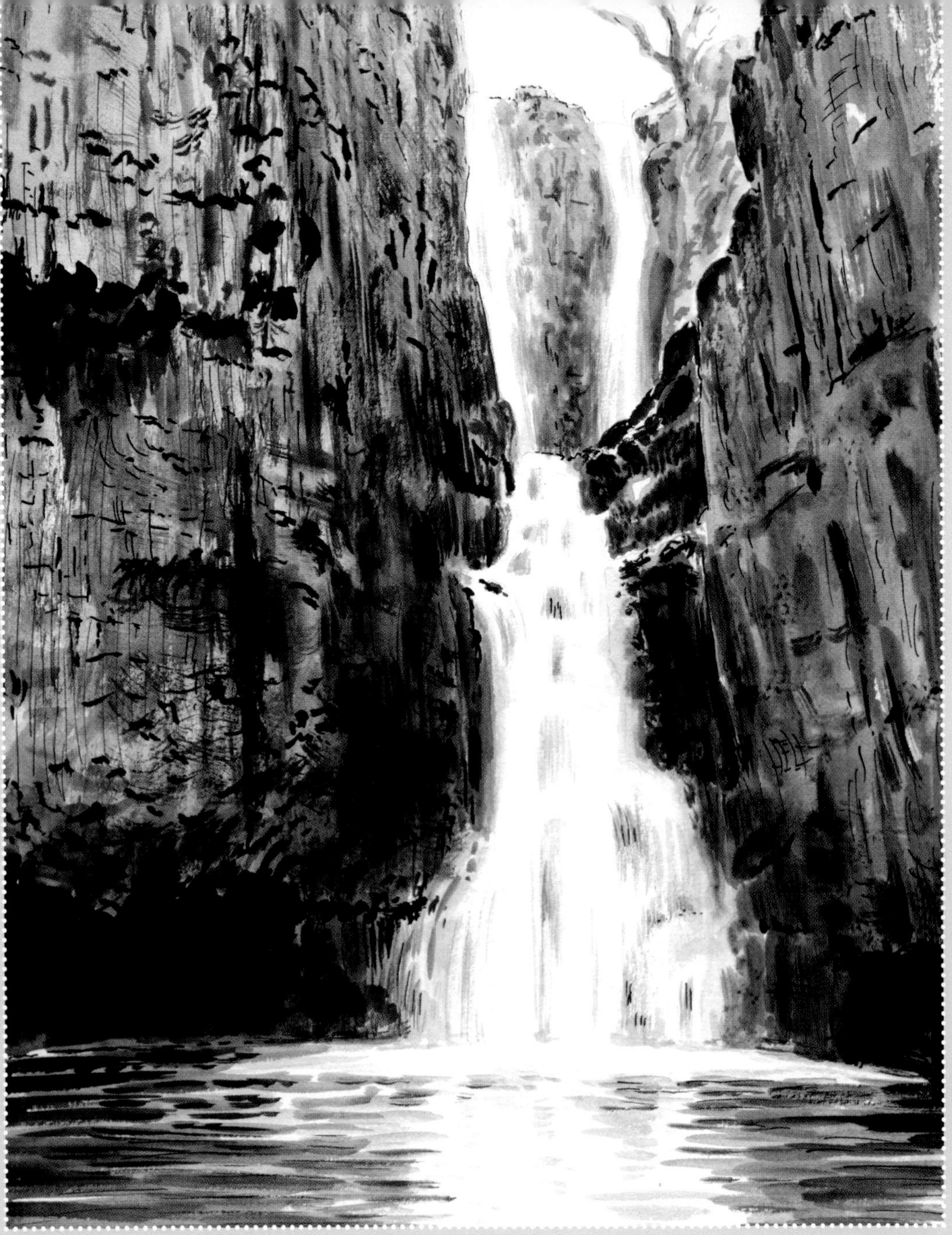

Catrigg Force
2005 Ink 11.8 x 9in

Cowside Beck is little more than a babbling moorland brook, uneventful and quite ordinary. That is until it reaches Catrigg Force (or Foss), where it suddenly plunges in two dramatic leaps down into the shadowy depths of a wooded gorge. The river reinvents itself here and is renamed Stainforth Beck. Downstream, a further series of lesser waterfalls are well worth exploring and are also excellent subjects for drawing.

Indian ink and water was the medium for this picture, applied with sable brushes and dipping pen.

After spending a couple of hours in the presence of the thundering cascade, I returned to the nearby quiet of Goat Scar Lane with faint ringing in my ears, as if I had just left a weaving shed.

Ingleborough from Grey Scars

2003 Iron gall ink 11.8 x 11.7in

The area of Newby Moss may be familiar to experienced cavers because of its range of fearsome vertical potholes, however it is less frequented by ordinary folk, possibly partly due to certain writers of walking books who persist in describing this terrain as dreary. It is true that the vast expanse of moorland is sombre, sparse and some might say featureless, but dreary it is not. A particular austere beauty dwells here, which defies description. Perhaps the attraction lies in simple minimalism, or conversely, in the complexity of its myriad parts. If we take time, observing carefully, we see an infinite variety of tone and richness of colour in the tussocky reeds and grasses; glowing bronze and golden where they catch the angled sun, or burnished russet and ochre under more leaden skies. We notice the ever-changing abstract shapes of light and shadow creeping over the hefty flanks of Ingleborough, and in the west, the hazy Bowland Fells.

On the occasion of this picture, the shattered outcrops of limestone shone brightly in the late afternoon sunlight, while the 'Big Blue Hill' remained constantly in shadow. Curlews recited their haunting melodies and invisible skylarks sang their never-ending song cycles (like the music of Philip Glass!).

I like to experiment with different materials and mediums, and had in my rucksack a little bottle of iron gall ink. This ink, made to a medieval recipe, is capable of producing a very intense black. I found that when let down with water the tints have a hint of warm brown, and when diluted further, the heavy pigment attempts to separate out, sometimes forming subtle kaleidoscopic patterns. A little patterning occurred here in the dark cloud above Ingleborough.

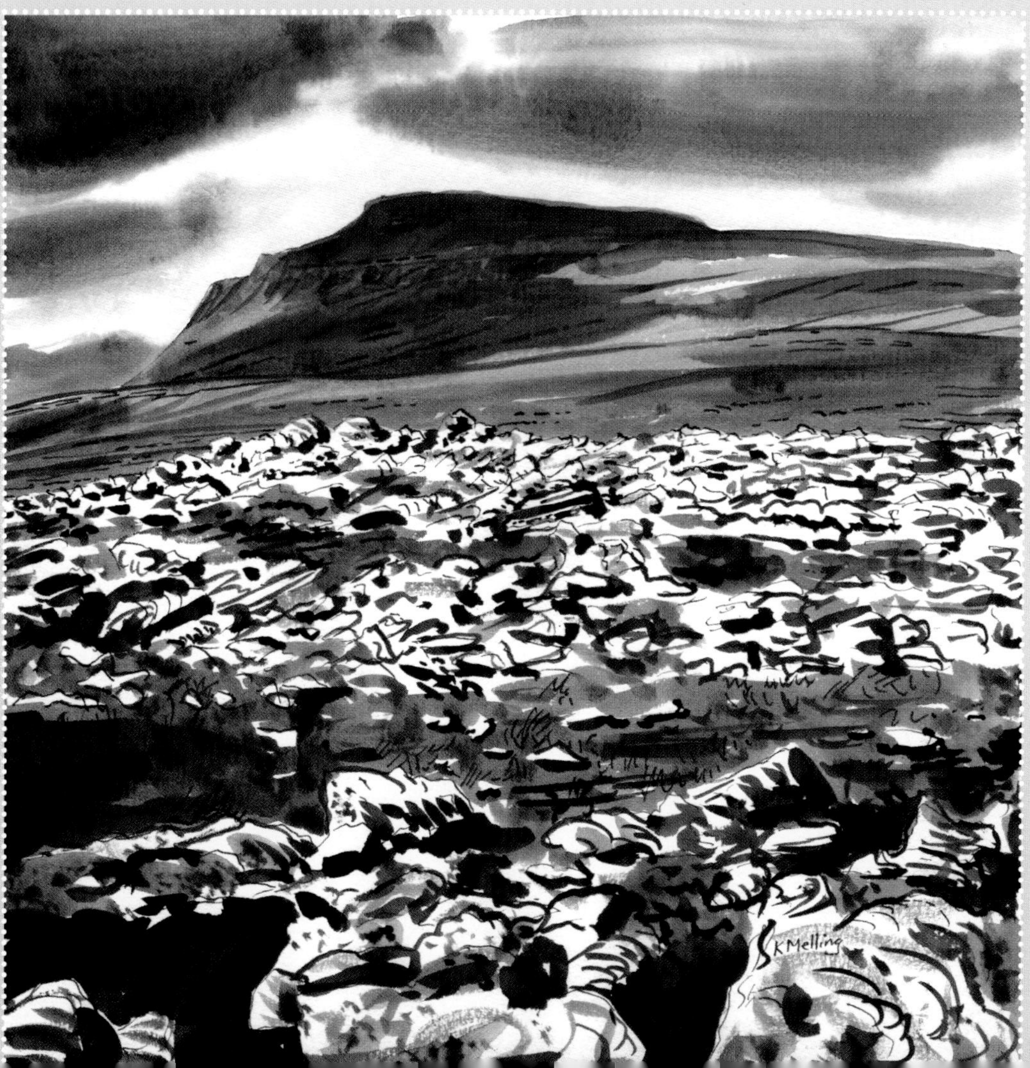

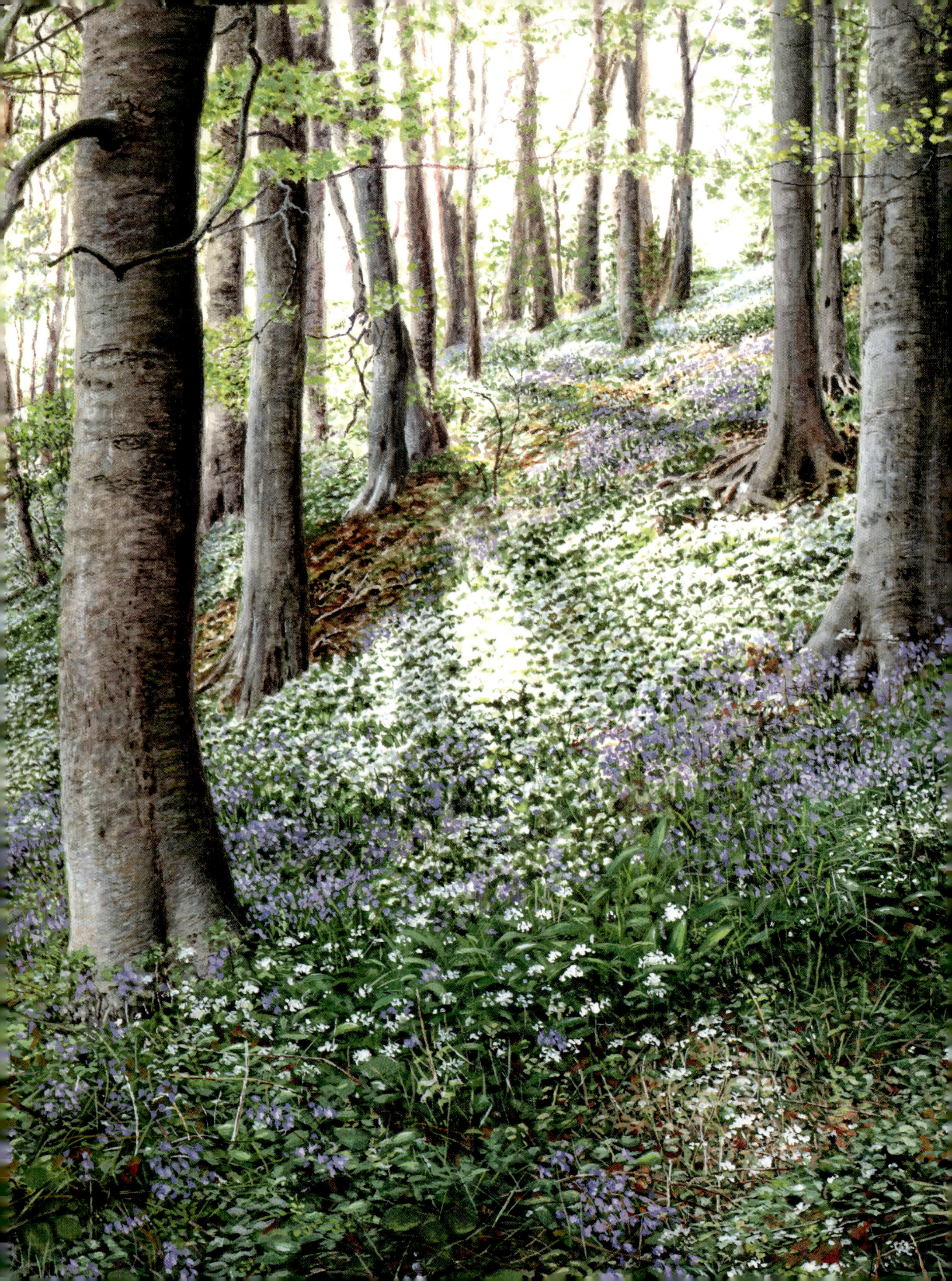

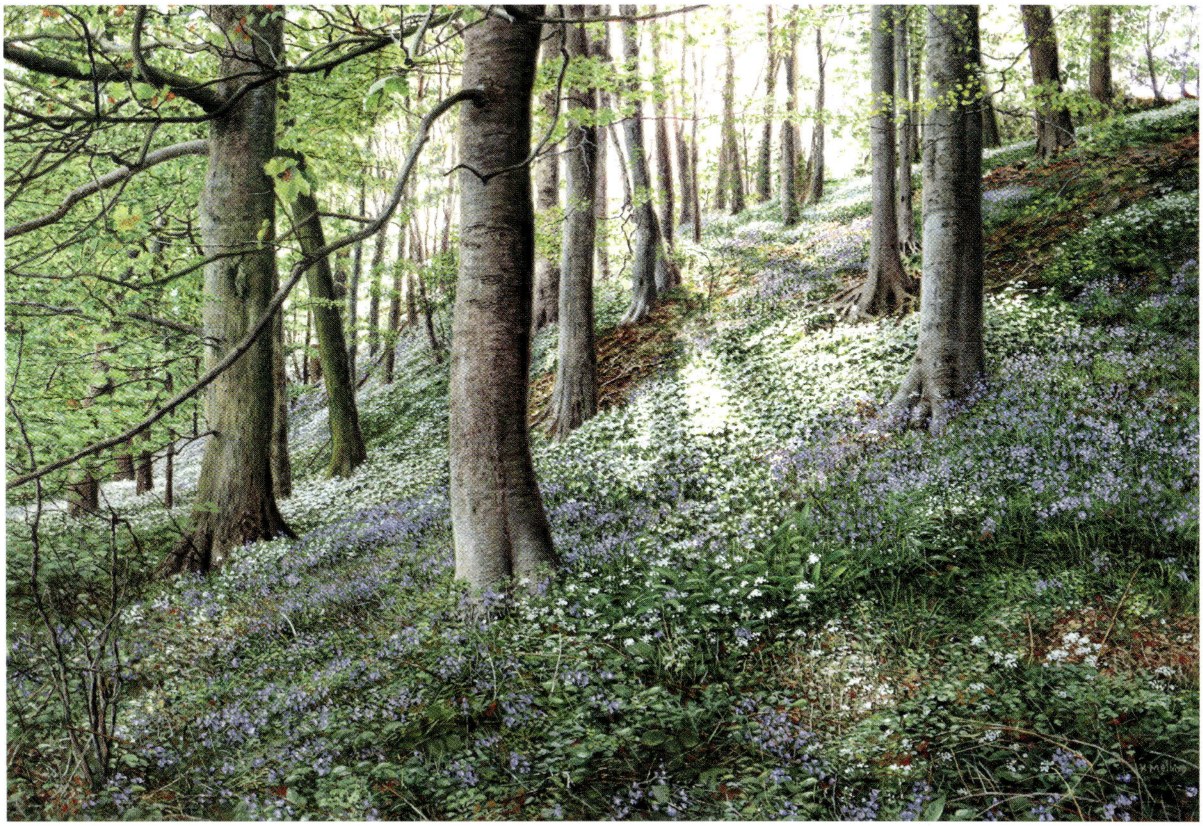

Bluebells and Ramsons

Homage to Heather and Robin Tanner
2004 Gouache and watercolour 10 x 15in

When thinking of springtime, the first vision to enter my mind is one of fresh leaved woodlands luxuriously carpeted with the purple-blue mist of bluebells. Yorkshire and indeed most of England is well endowed with them; it's no strange thing that many people have vivid childhood memories of these enchanting places, once seen, especially through a child's bright eyes, they are seldom forgotten. Who can say that as children they have never been tempted to pick great bunches of bluebells, and what harm did it do I wonder, compared to the devastation caused by road construction and other feats of so called progress?

Of course there are always other flowers growing amongst bluebells, though none strive for dominance except perhaps ramsons (wild garlic). When present in numbers, this beautiful plant, possessing delicate umbels of milky white stars, infects the atmosphere around with its outrageously pungent aroma. The senses could be almost overwhelmed by the foaming blue and white sea of these two flowers, the wood floods with a bittersweet fragrance and is made melodious by birdsong.

The wood in this painting, on the banks of the Ribble near Langcliffe, has no name as far as I'm aware. In any other season it would seem quite insignificant, having little of note to draw the eye. In springtime however, we are presented with a glorious exhibition of exquisite bluebells and ramsons.

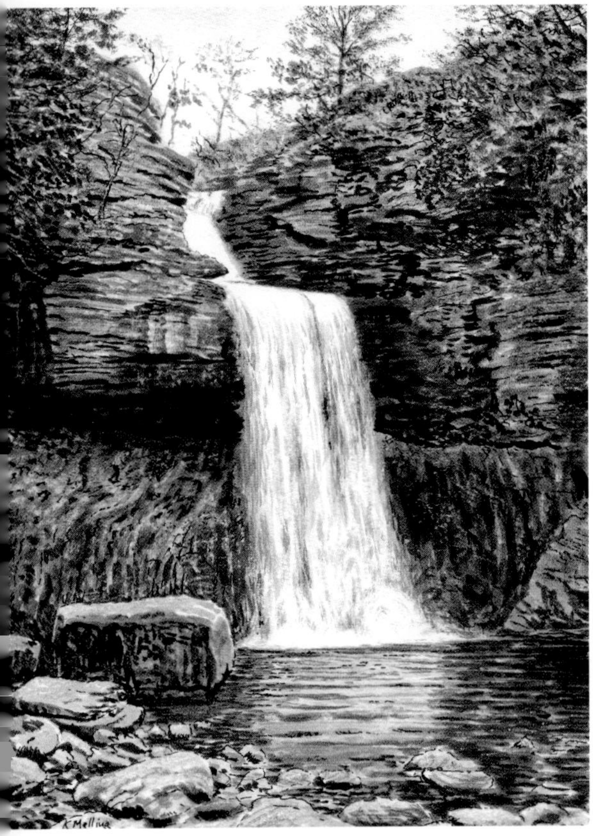

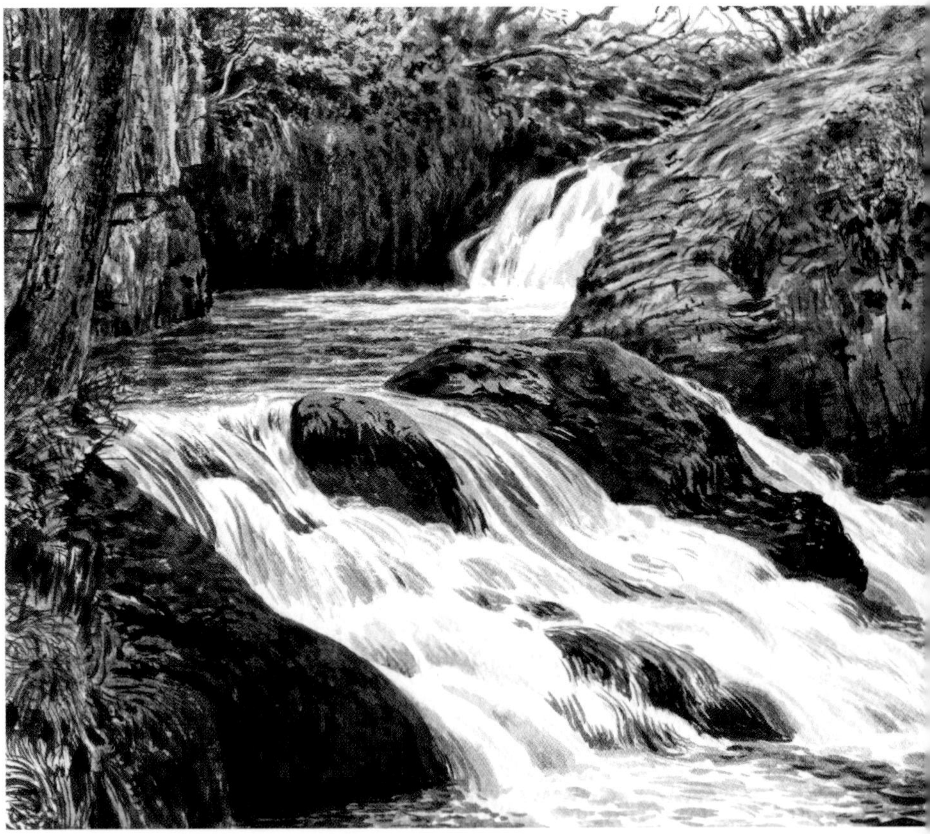

Ingleton Waterfalls
Left Thornton Force 2005 Ink 12 x 9in
Right Triple Spout 2007 Ink 5.75 x 7.5in

This amazing series of cascades in the deep wooded glens of the Twiss and Doe provide surprises galore. Just when you think there can't be another spectacular waterfall, you see an even better one, then another and another.... and so on. The expression 'over the top' doesn't normally apply to natural phenomena, but here nature has clearly been wonderfully self indulgent and we don't mind it being OTT.

I've chosen to illustrate only two waterfalls — one each from Twiss and Doe. Triple Spout on the River Doe is perhaps one of the less spectacular falls, but is beautifully situated in the mossy Beezley Gorge. Adorned plentifully with ferns and overhung with old oak and rowan, aesthetically this is my favourite. When I was here one hot summer's day, I witnessed semi-naked bodies falling out of the trees above the gorge and plunging into the cool dark pool below — very surreal. The upper parts of both glens are very popular bathing places in summer. Thornton Force on the River Twiss is the largest of the Ingleton Waterfalls and, geologically speaking, is very important. Carboniferous Great Scar Limestone 330 million years old sits upon rock 500 million years old belonging to the Lower Ordovician Group. This unconformity of rock strata enables you to span your hand across 170 million years. What a thought! Also it's possible here to scramble gingerly on the lower rocks behind the fall to contemplate the world through a thundering white screen of falling white water. I've included a couple of scrambling figures on the rocks in my picture but you'll have to look carefully, they're not easy to see.

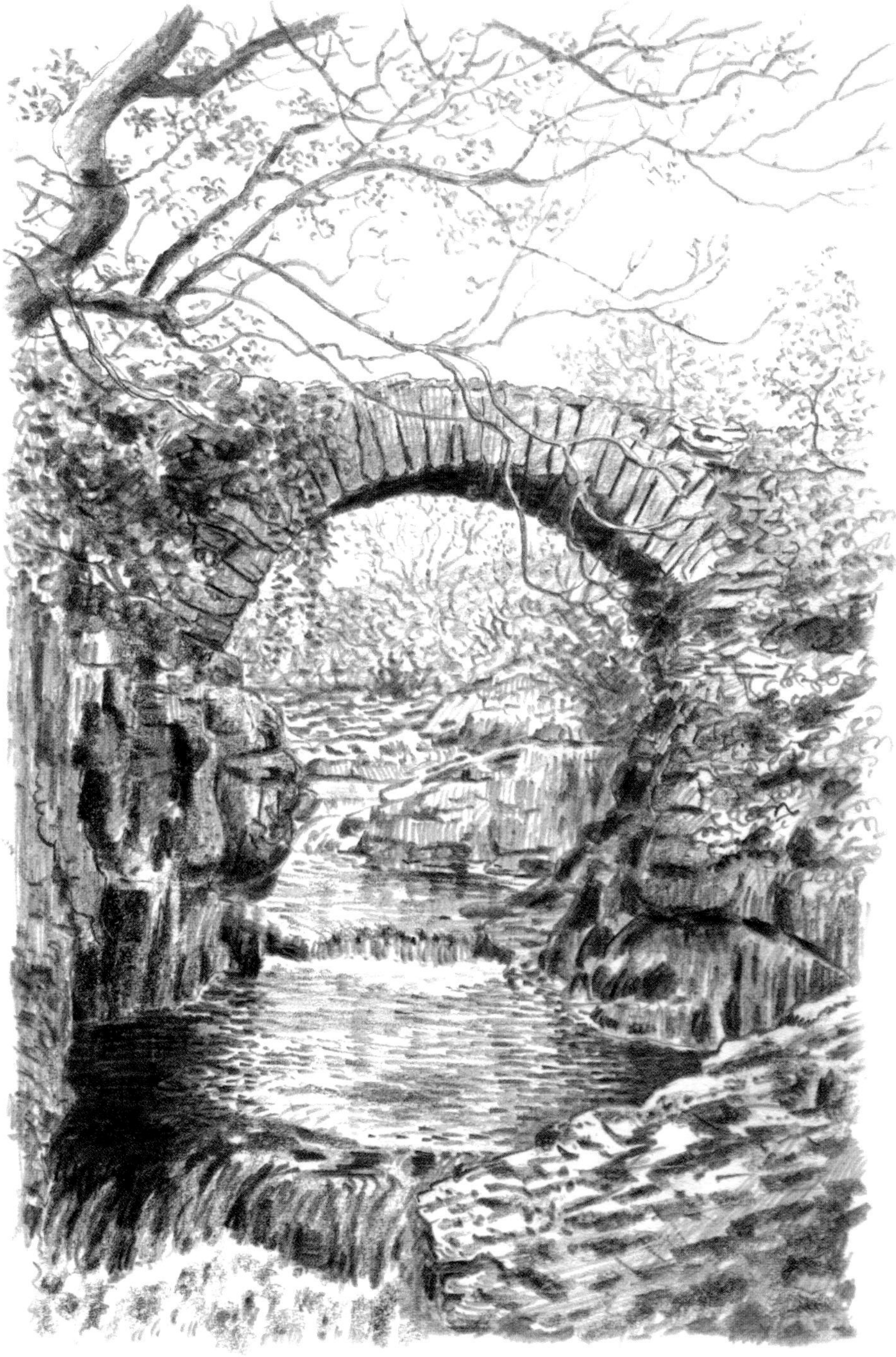

Packhorse Bridge, Thorns Gill

2007 Pencil 7 x 4.5in

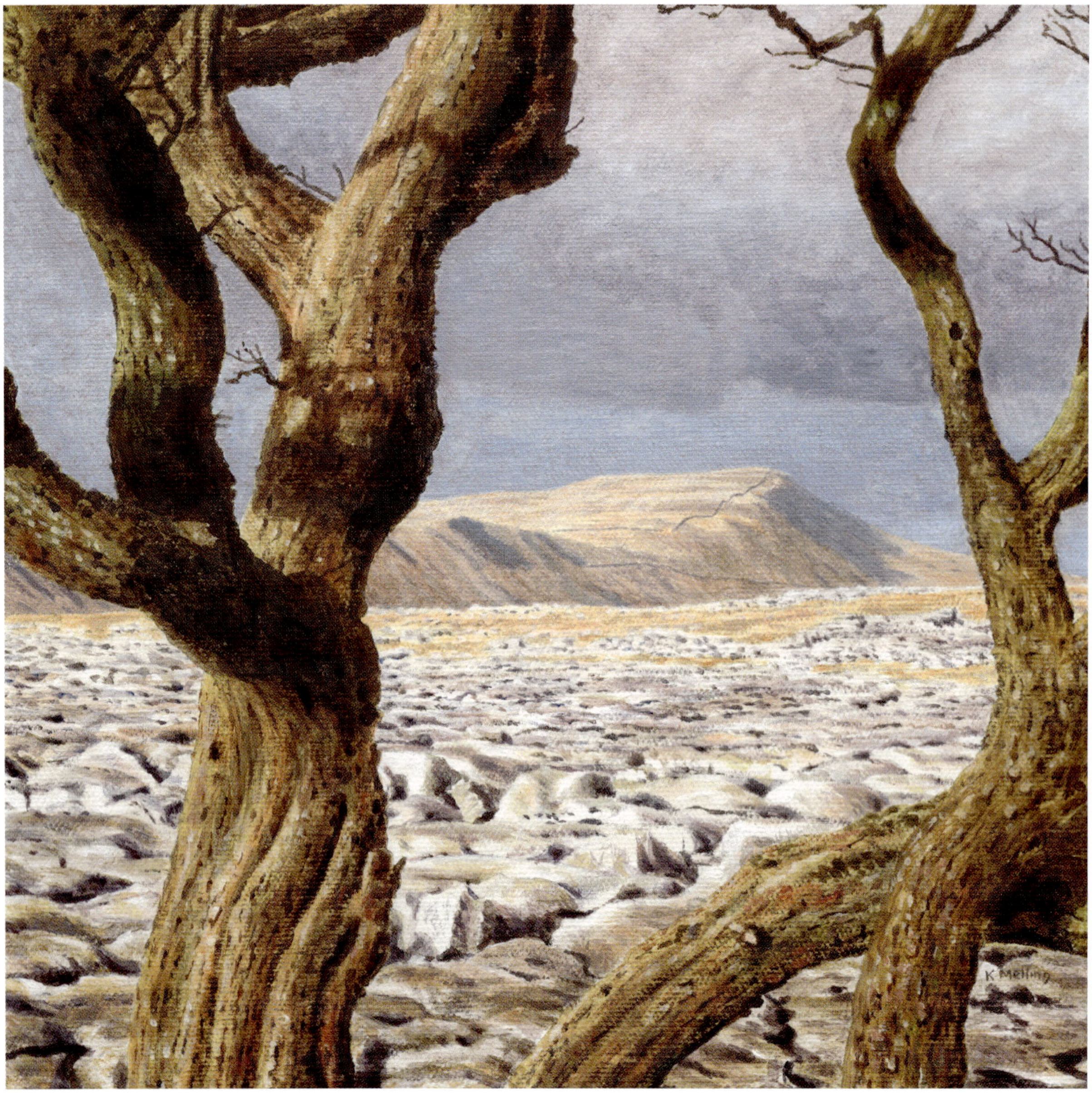

White Scars and Whernside

2005 Acrylic 10 x 10in

Whernside, the highest of the Three Peaks is not easily captured in a picture due to its rather ungainly profile. However, seen through the solitary hawthorn on the pavements below Ingleborough, the peak appeared quite dynamic. Of course the main subject of the painting is the foreground tree; the tangle of twisted branches dividing the picture plane conveniently into unequal segments and acting as a foil to the landscape behind, giving a greater sense of perspective.

From this surreal location it's not apparent that the lovely green valley of Chapel-le-Dale lies tucked between the edge of the scars and the steep slopes of Whernside.

Distant Pendle Hill from Norber

2007 Acrylic 10 x 10in

This view from the edge of Norber's summit plateau, gazes directly south over Bowland's green pastures to the sleeping lion of Pendle Hill. The huge gritstone boulders strewn on a sloping shoulder of Norber below — seem a little misplaced, as in fact they are. They were transported from further up Crummackdale and deposited here by glacial ice 12,000 years ago, they are known as 'erratic boulders' (kind of geological 'off-comed-uns'!). The pleasant village of Austwick is tucked just out of sight behind the dark line of trees — sorry again Austwick.

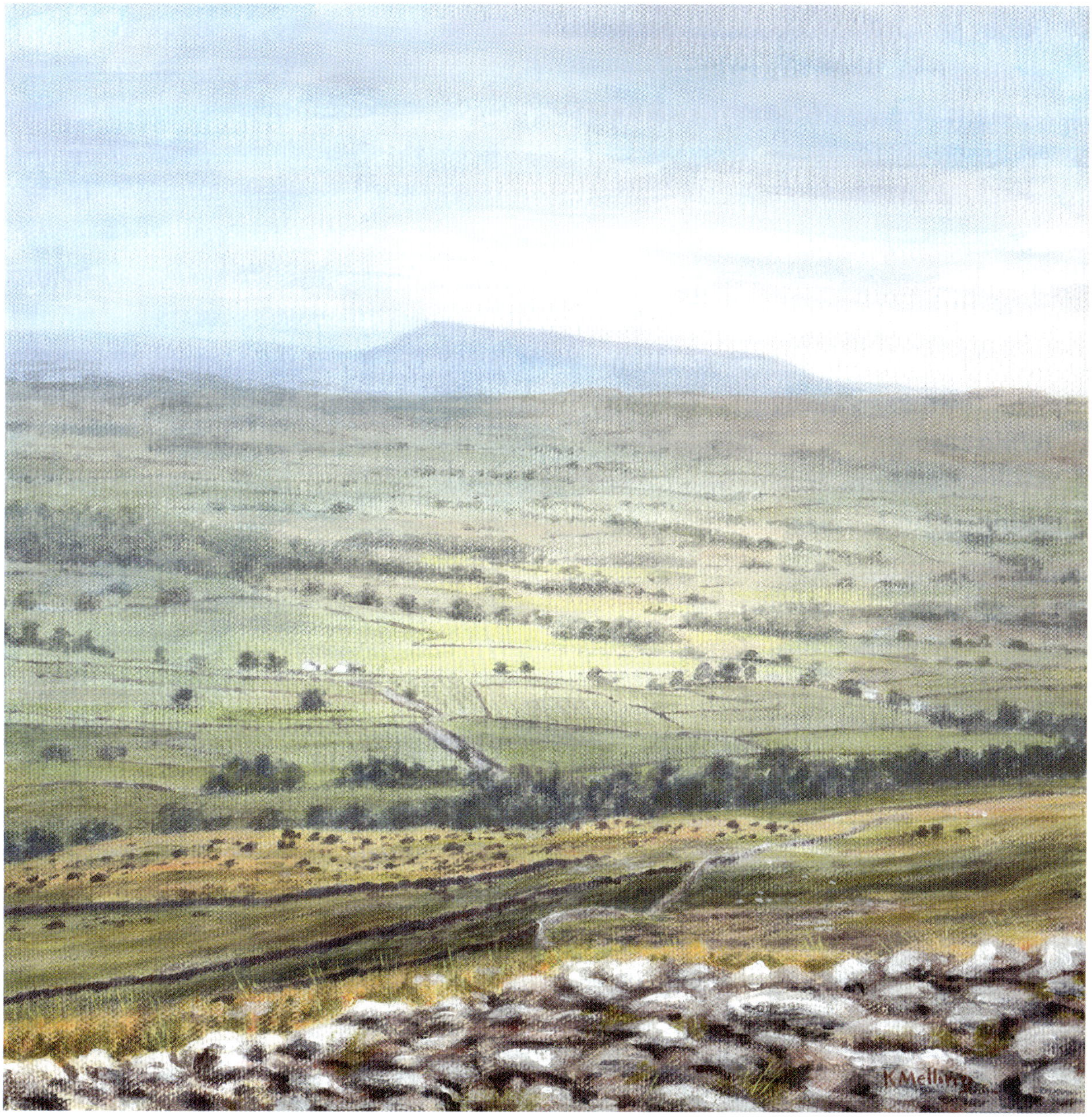

Drystone Wall, High Hill Lane, Settle

1996 watercolour 8 x 9 in

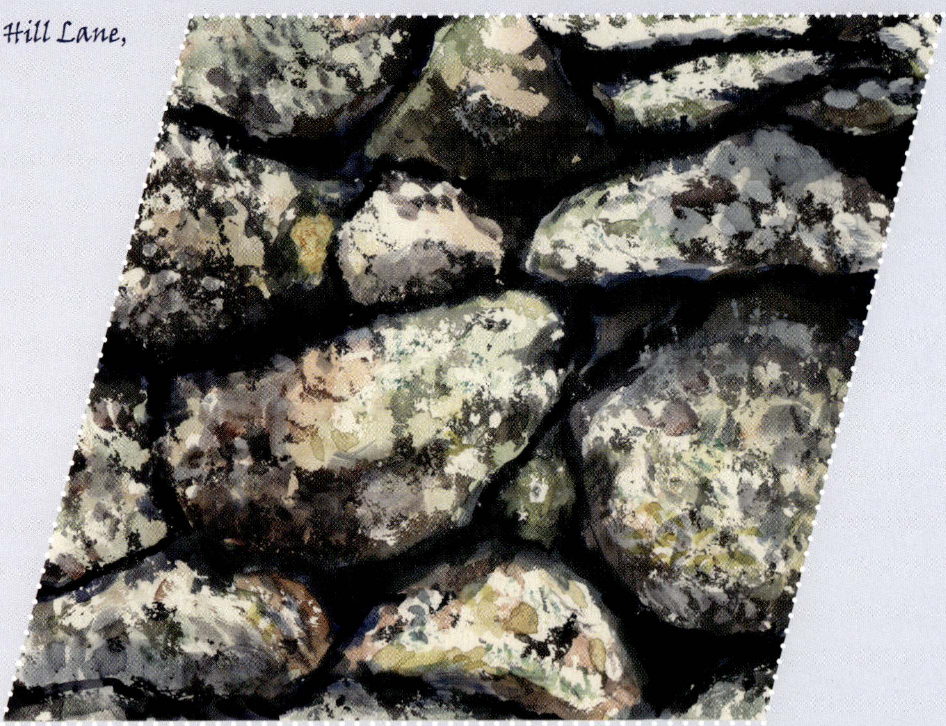

Hawthorn in Boulder Field

1996 watercolour 6.6 x 9.5 in

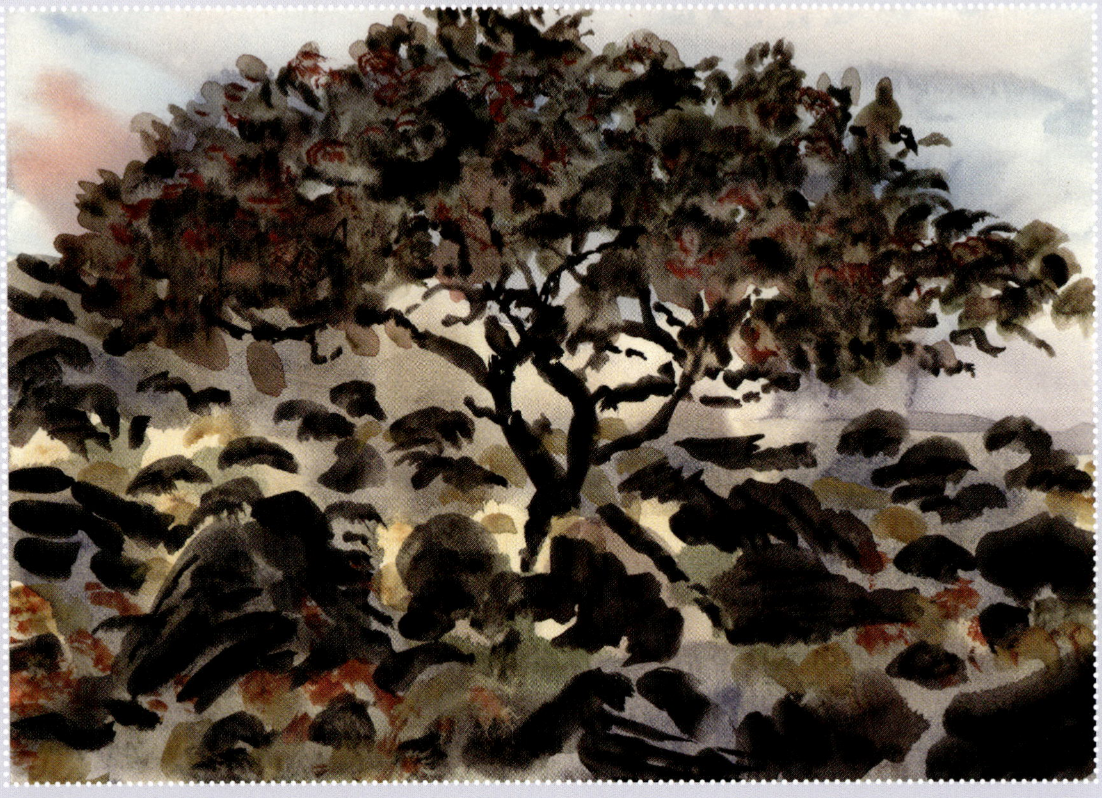

Catrigg Force, Dusk

1996 watercolour 10 x 7 in

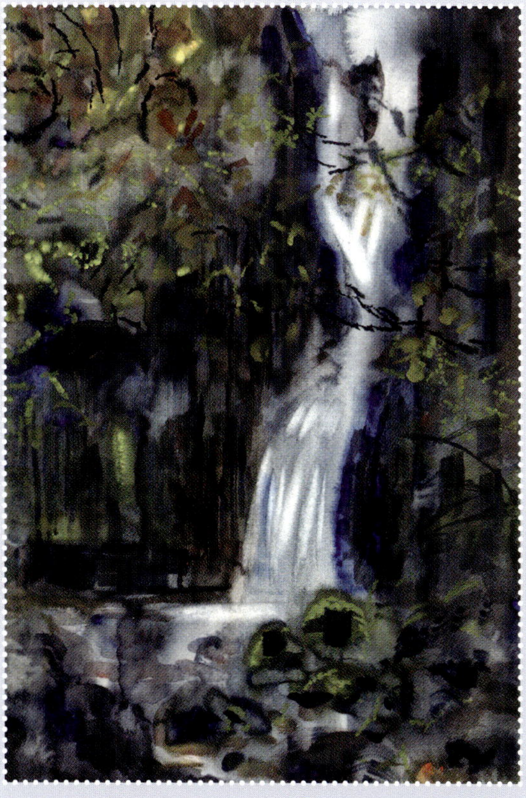

Sugar Loaf Hill and Warrendale Knotts from Altermire Scar

1999 watercolour and gouache 6.7 x 9.7 in

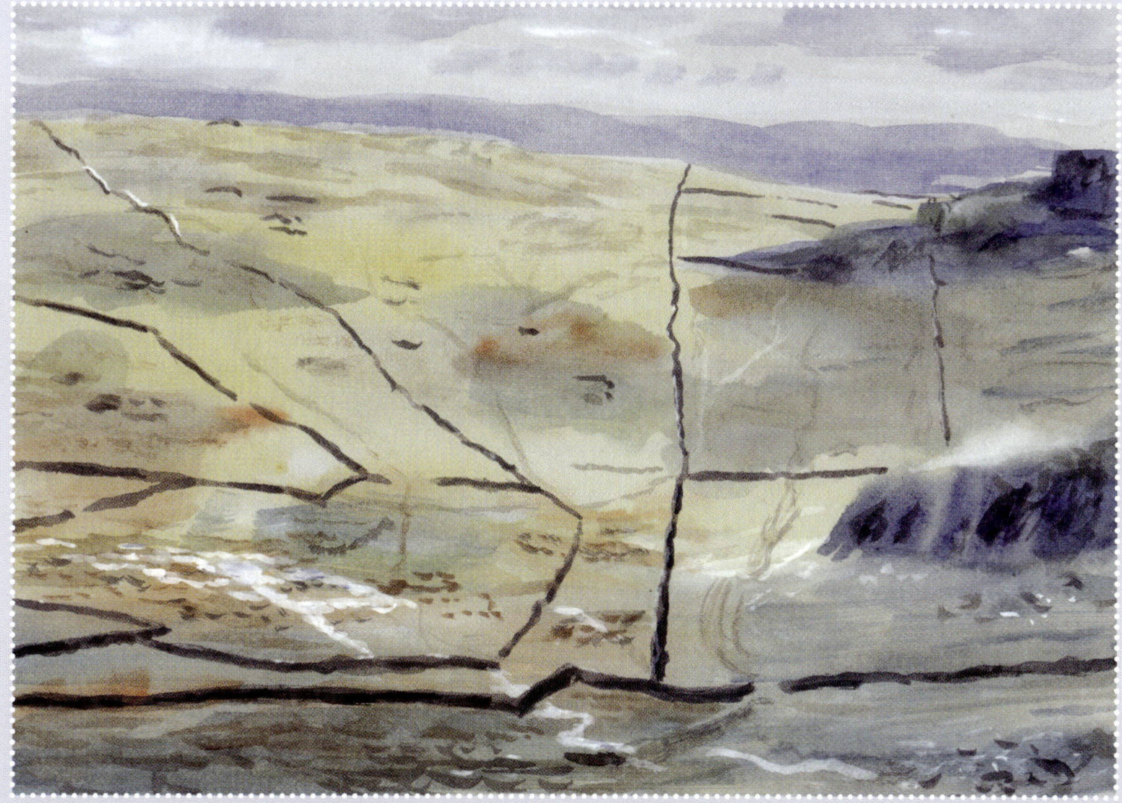

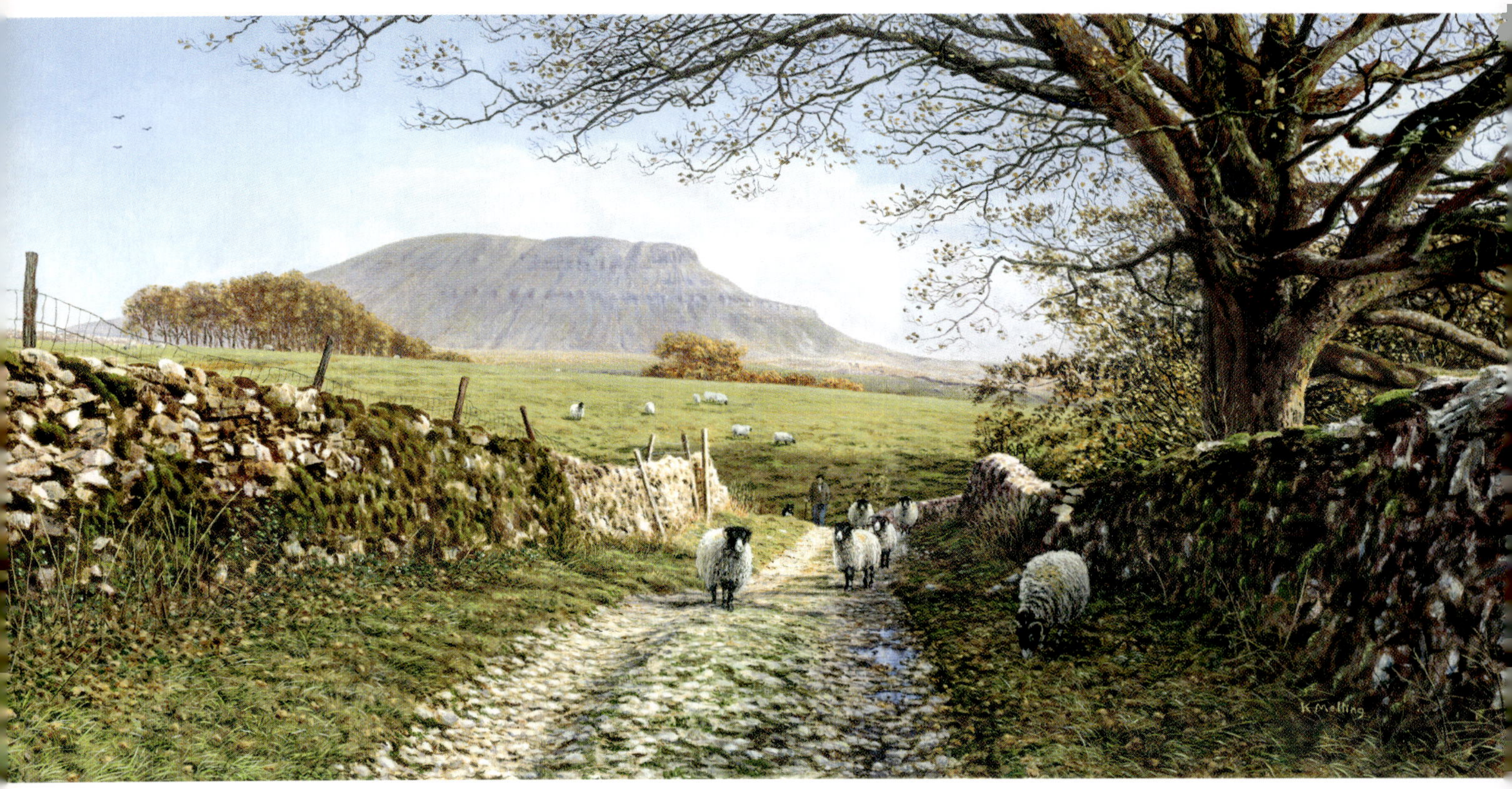

Penyghent from Horton Scar Lane
2000 Acrylic and Gouache 8 x 16.5in

The ancient makers of this fine green lane did not have artists in mind as they went about their work, but they certainly provided a very satisfying subject for them. The lane climbs, dips and turns dramatically upwards to the foot of Penyghent, and my chosen viewpoint is about the only place on it where the Peak's profile can be seen head-on. Another reason though for choosing this spot was that I couldn't resist painting the attractive sycamore with its profusion of spreading branches. The tree reaches conveniently over the lane and helps both to frame the composition and to create the feeling of depth and distance. Sky reflected in the puddle brings a little patch of blue down into the foreground, which helps to unify the whole. The mellow autumnal sun throws everything into relief, picking out the characteristic stepped layers of rock on Penyghent.

I didn't actually see any sheep on this track, but planned to include them from the beginning to add interest to the scene. Getting the right ratio between sheep and wall was a little tricky. I found myself returning in scientific mode, armed with tape measure and notepad to collect this vital data. The sheep in the adjacent field were not as cooperative as the wall, so I had to assess their average height from a few paces away. I tried to perform this comical task indiscreetly, but it took some time. Two puzzled ramblers who had seen my antics from a distance, stopped, and asked if I was from the Ministry of Agriculture.

Actually the result of my research was unusable, and I reverted to hazarding a guess at the correct scale, which I think worked out quite well in the end.

Rain Over Ribblehead, from Whernside

2005 Acrylic 10 x 10in

From Whernside's windy summit ridge we watched the rain gathering its spears like an army; assembling its cavalry far away in the north, over the elephant humps of the Howgills. A swirling disorganised detachment severed ranks and raced along a darkened Dentdale. Becoming light headed, light hearted and light filled, the now flimsy veil of rain frolicked freely in wild abandon above a bewildered Blea Moor. We lounged all the while in glorious sunshine, perched high and dry in our lofty eyrie, watching the vaporous party chase shadows in the valley below.

Clouds are not usually the main subject of a painting, yet there has been some notable precedents, starting with seventeenth century Dutch painters (they had so much sky). Then Constable whose studies included notes of wind direction and scientific cloud category, Samuel Palmer gave us a romantic interpretation and Turner pure atmosphere.

My picture shows a wild landscape where farmers battle against the encroaching moor. The massive Ribblehead viaduct hardly makes an impression; it appears as a small squiggle, a mere punctuation mark in nature's immensity.

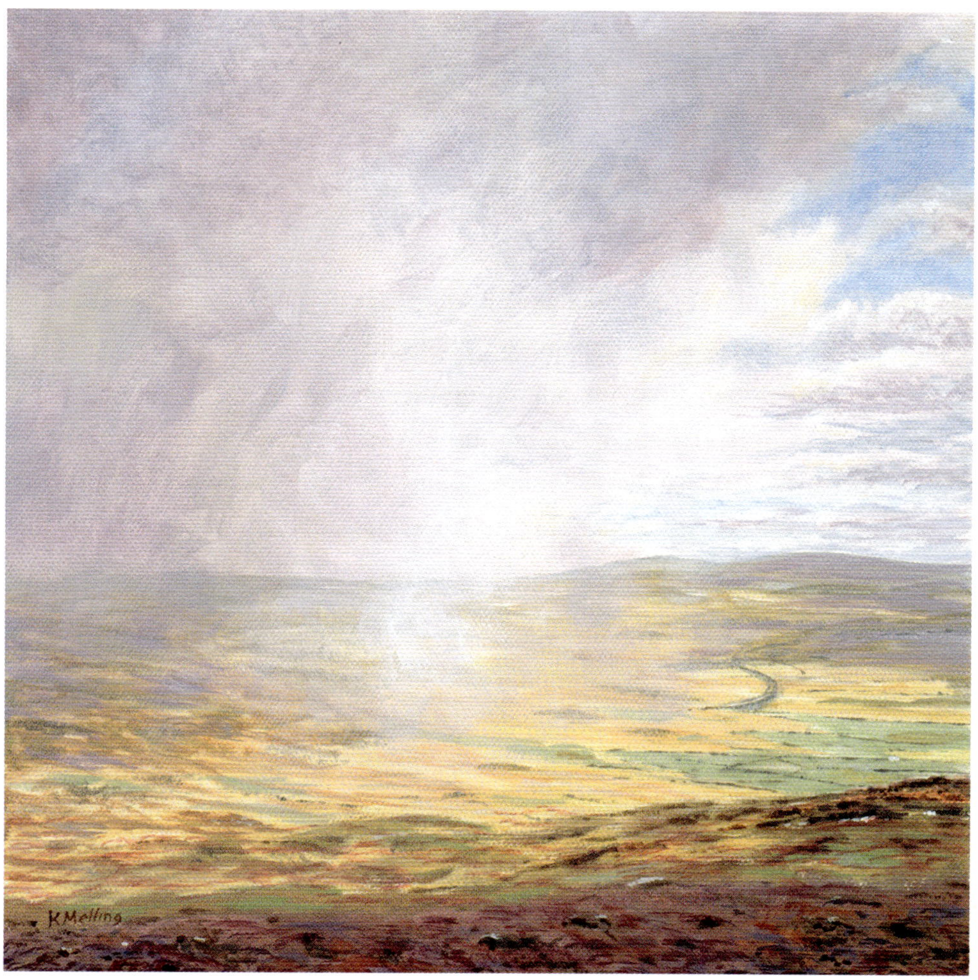

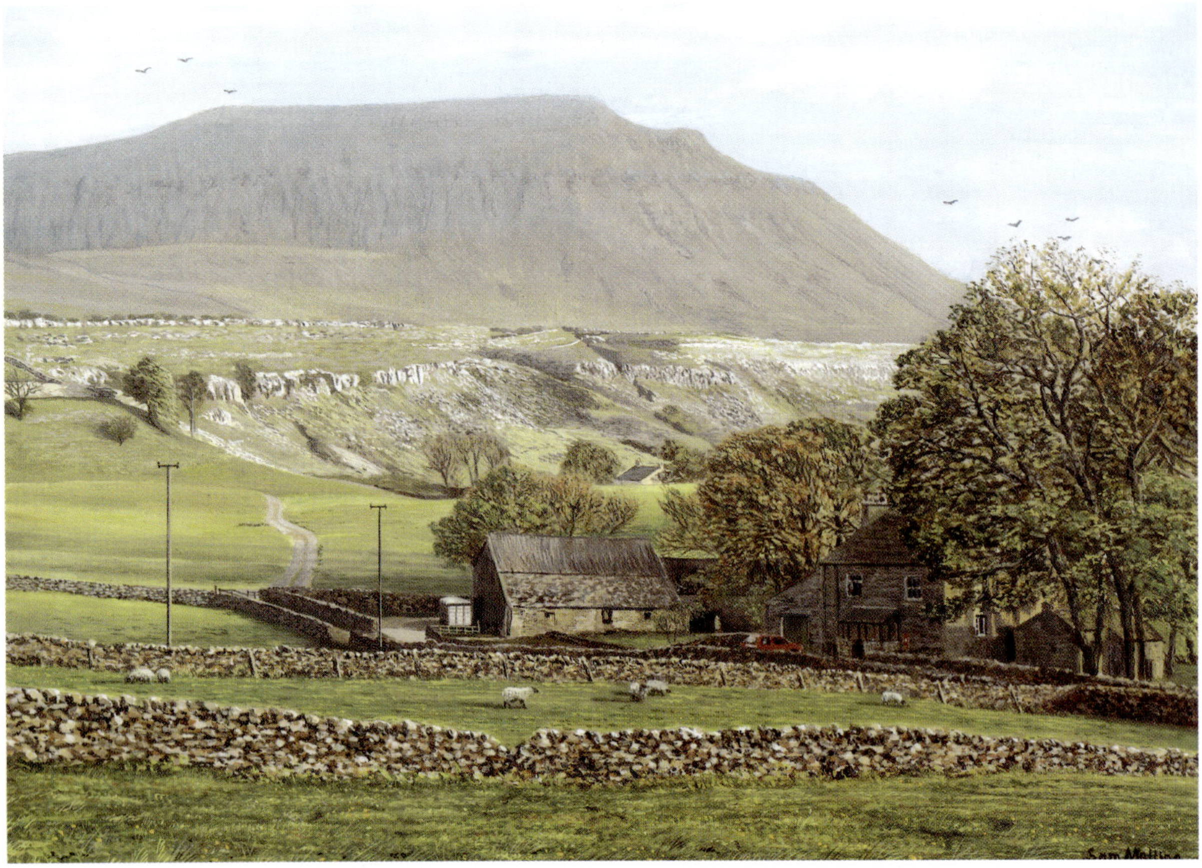

Ingleborough from Chapel-le-Dale
S.P. Melling 1999 Acrylic and gouache 8 x 10.5in

There are many good routes to the summit of this fine mountain but my personal favourite is from Chapel-le-Dale, not least because of the marvellous plateau of limestone pavements encountered above Southerscales Scars. This must be the most extensive system in Britain. When walking and sketching there, I've often been so fascinated that I've ventured no further.

This painting by my son Sam shows the location of the scars exceptionally well. Sam has accompanied me on numerous walking and sketching expeditions here.

The view from the camping ground at the Hill Inn makes an ideal composition, with the farm and leafy trees on the right acting as a foil to the main subject of Ingleborough.

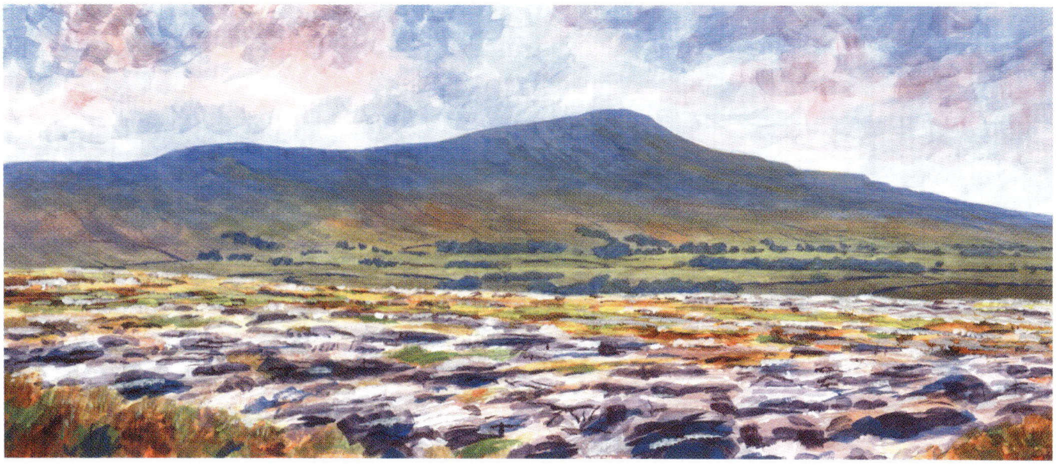

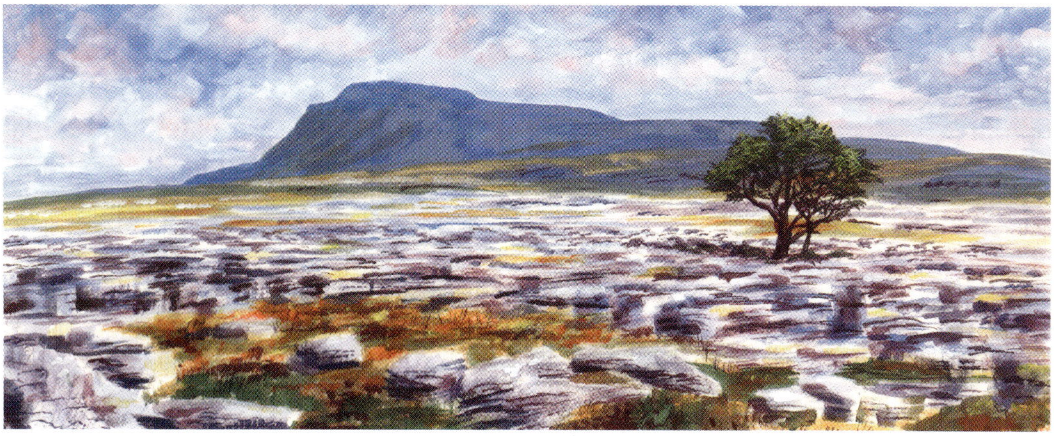

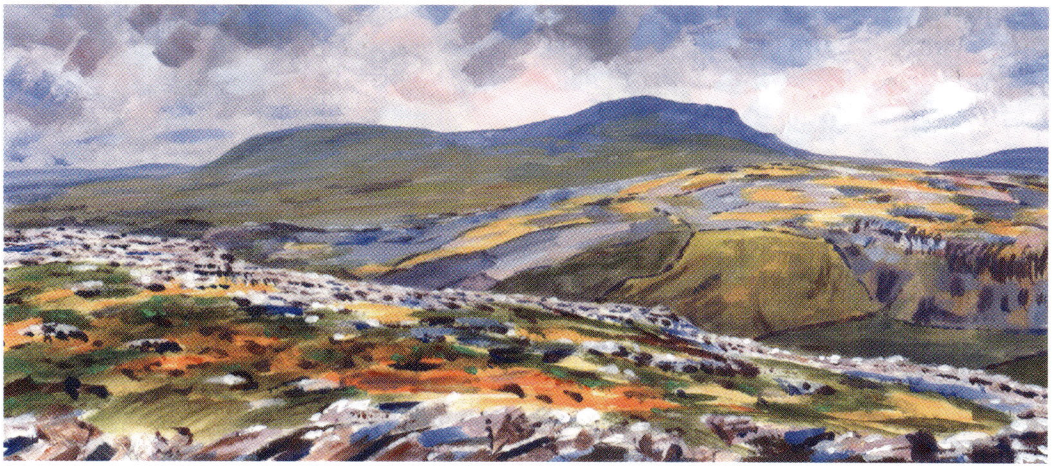

Three Peaks

Top: Whernside from Black Shiver Moss 2006 Acrylic 6 x 14.5in

Middle: Ingleborough from White Scars 2006 Acrylic 6 x 14.5in

Bottom: Penyghent from Norber 2001 Acrylic 6 x 14.5in

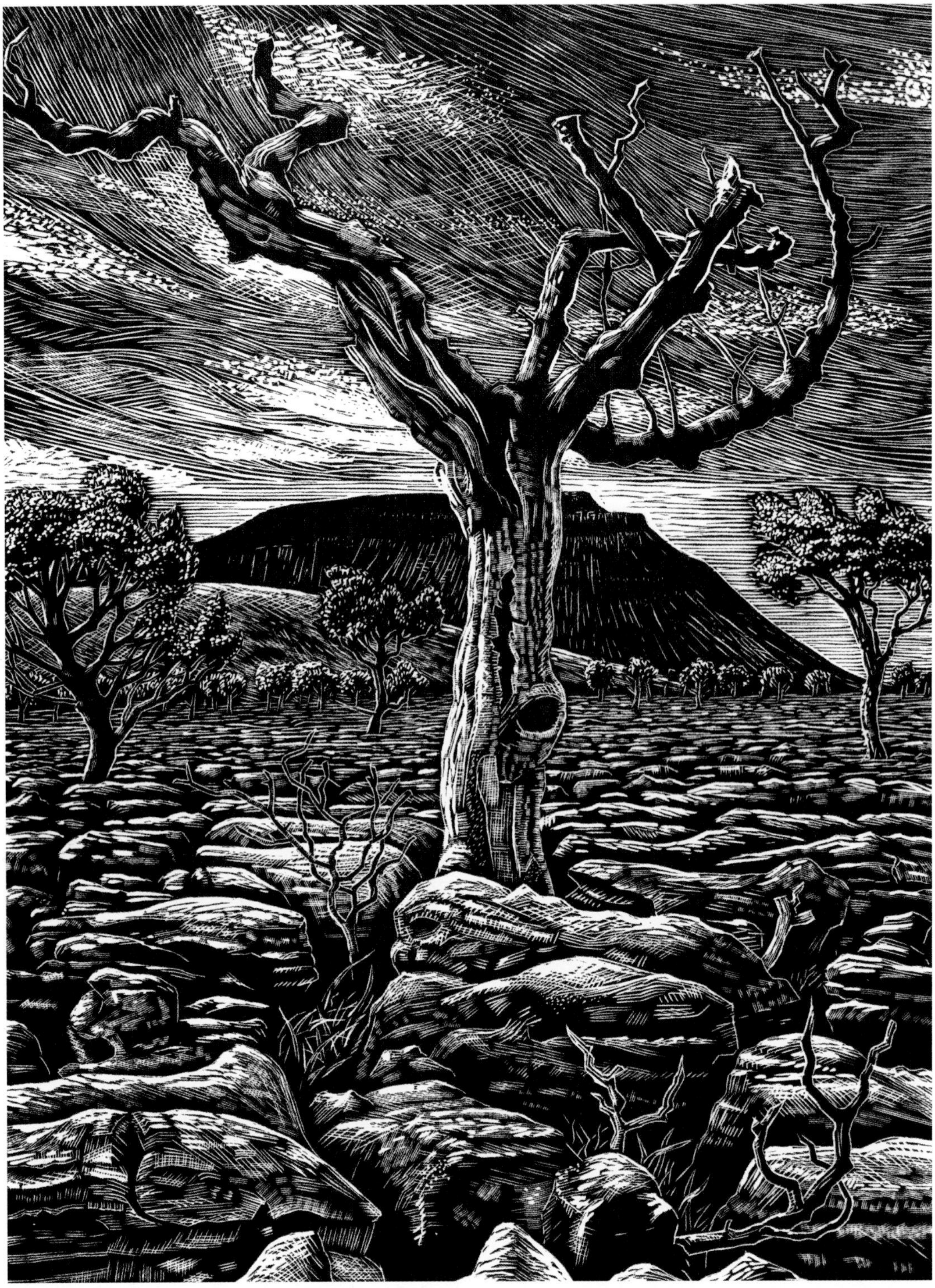

Ingleborough from Southerscales Scars

1995 Wood engraving 7.5 x 6in

Barn, Philpin Lane, Chapel-le-Dale

1995 Wood engraving 3 x 4in

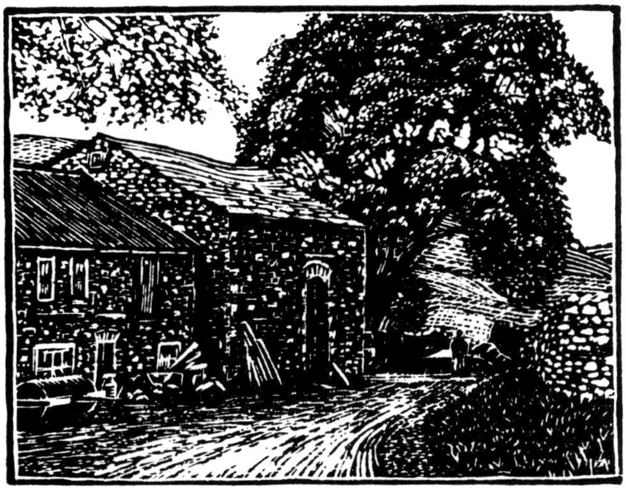

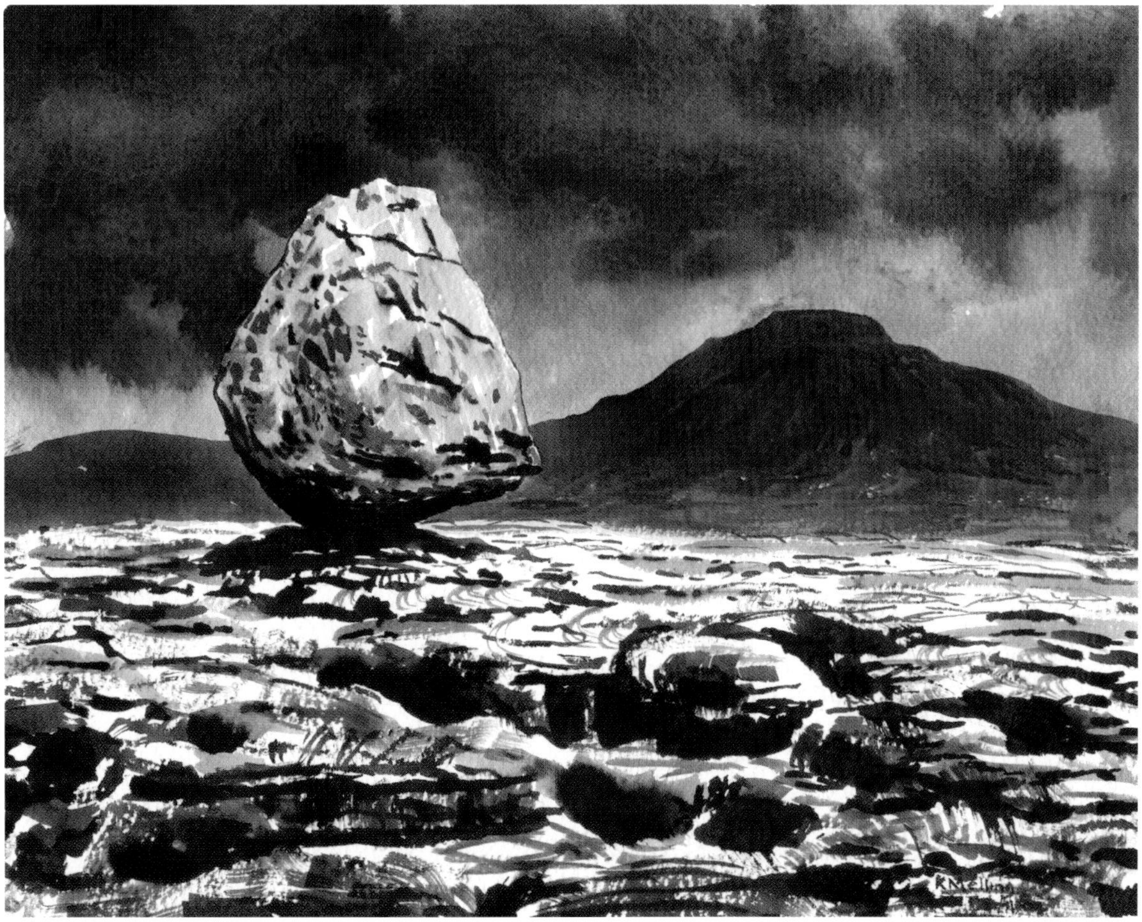

Scales Moor near Ingleton 2003

Iron gall ink 9 x 12in

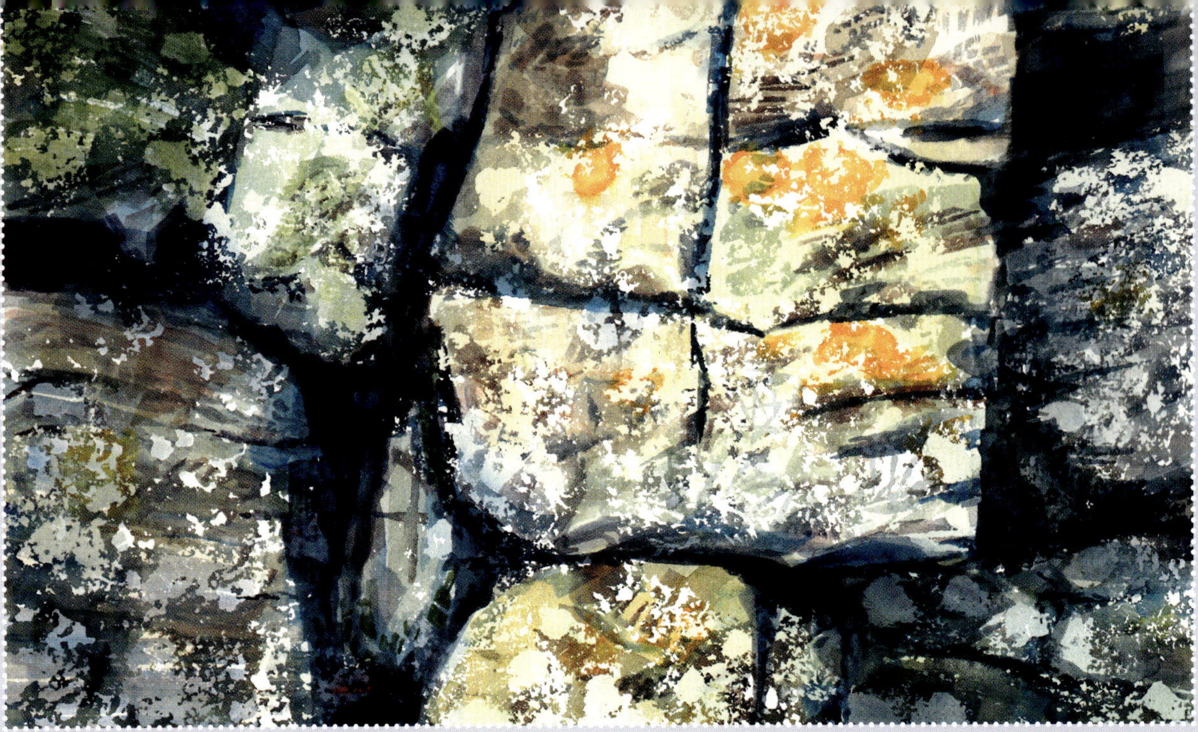

Drystone Wall, Moughton Scars

2002 Watercolour 11.7 x 16.5in

Across Crummackdale to Penyghent

2003 Acrylic and sand 9 x 14in

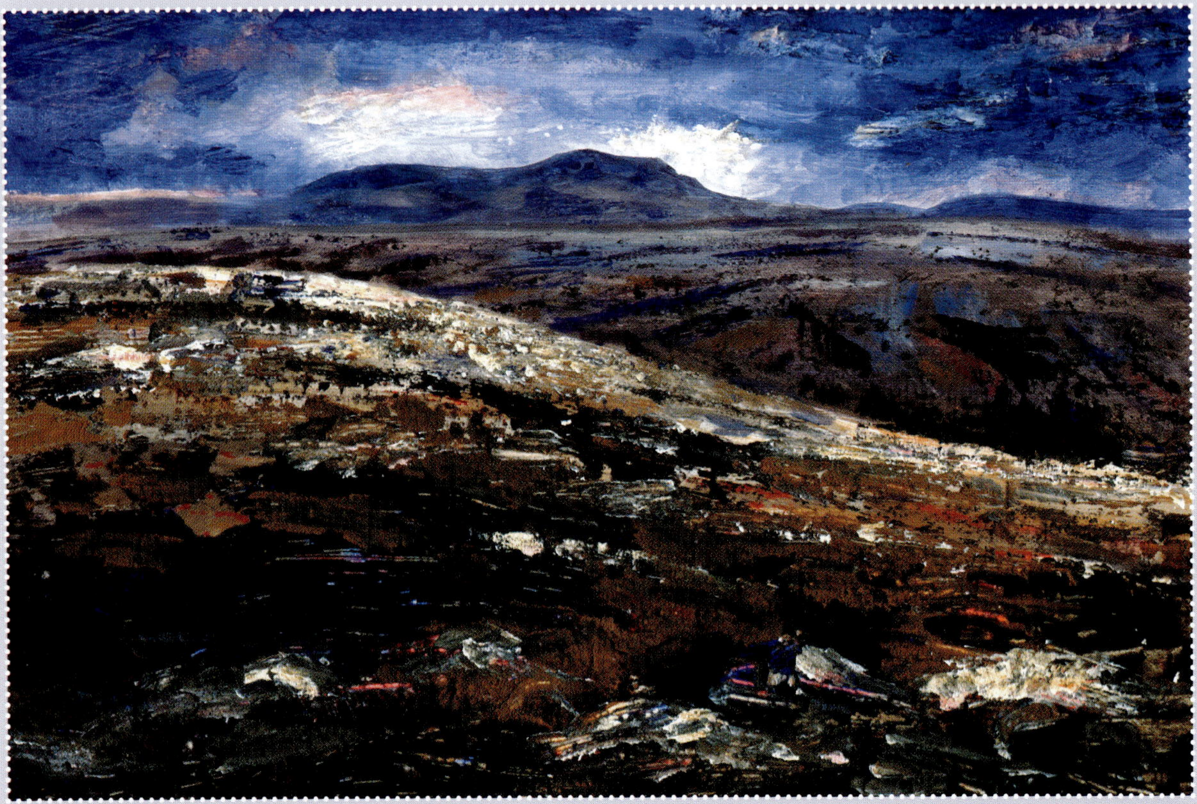

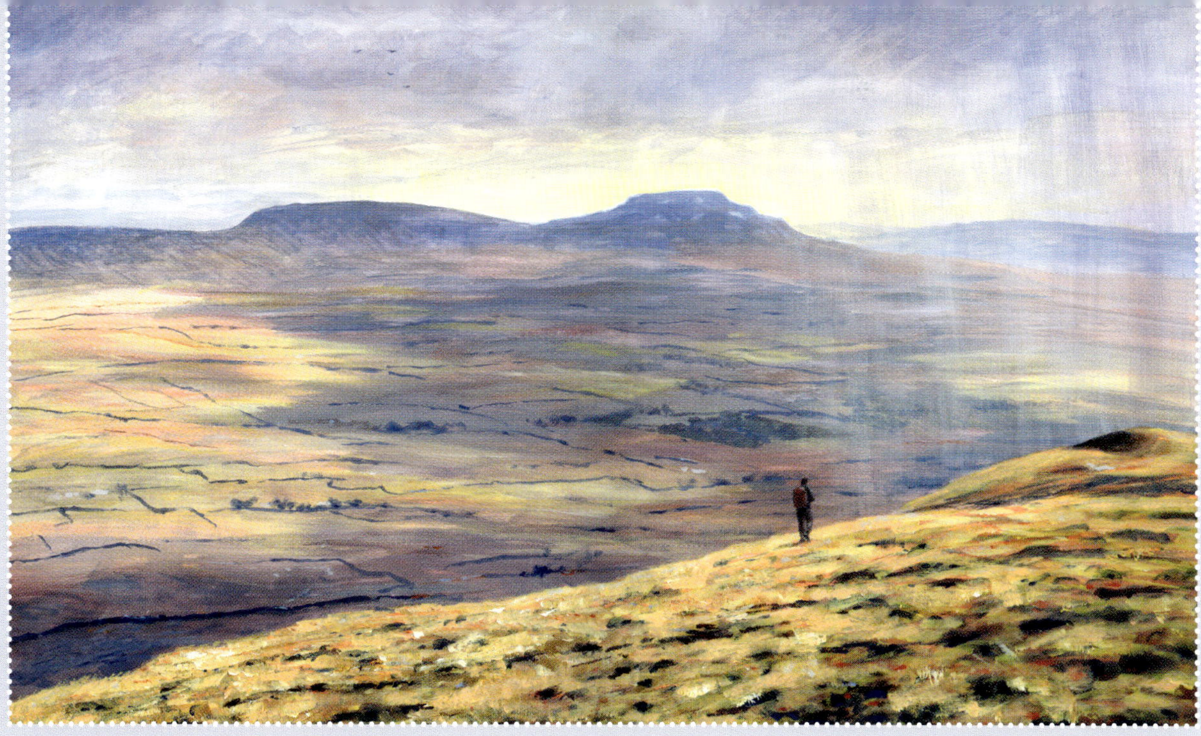

On Whernside, looking across to Ingleborough

2004 Acrylic 21.5 x 30in

On Penyghent, looking to Pendle Hill

2002 Watercolour 10 x 15in

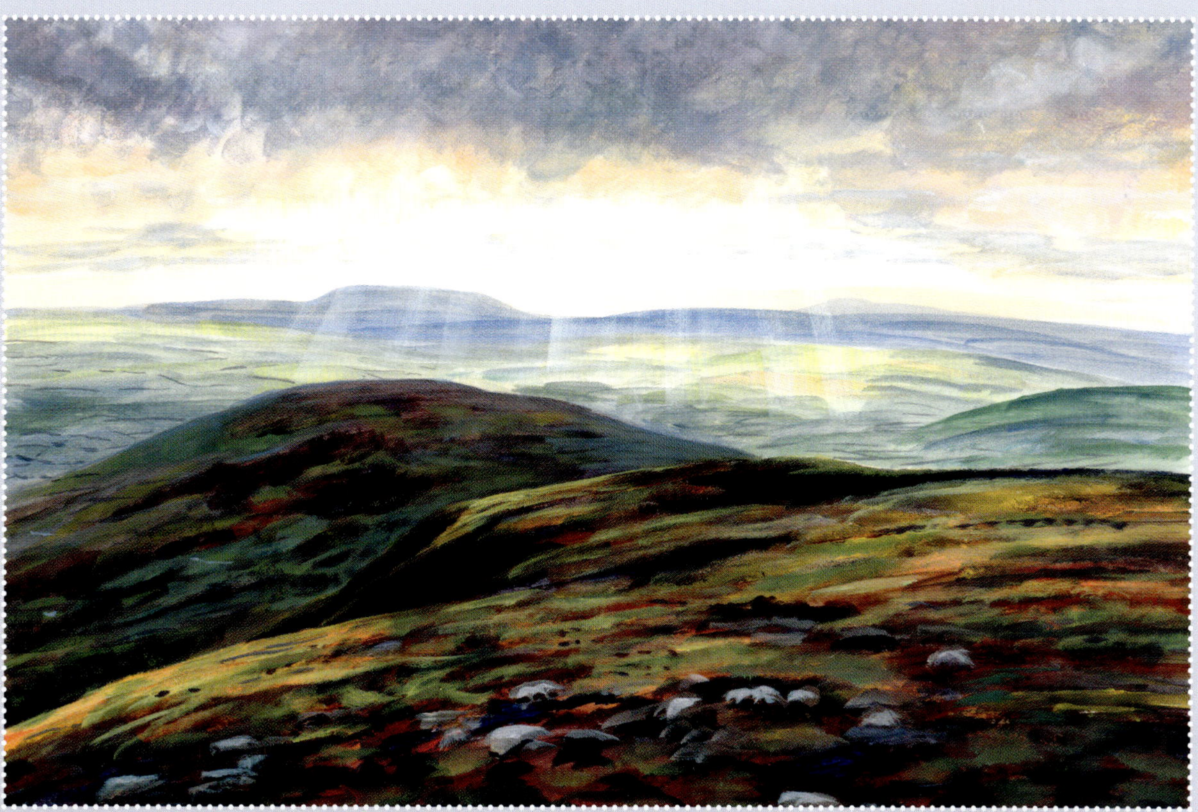

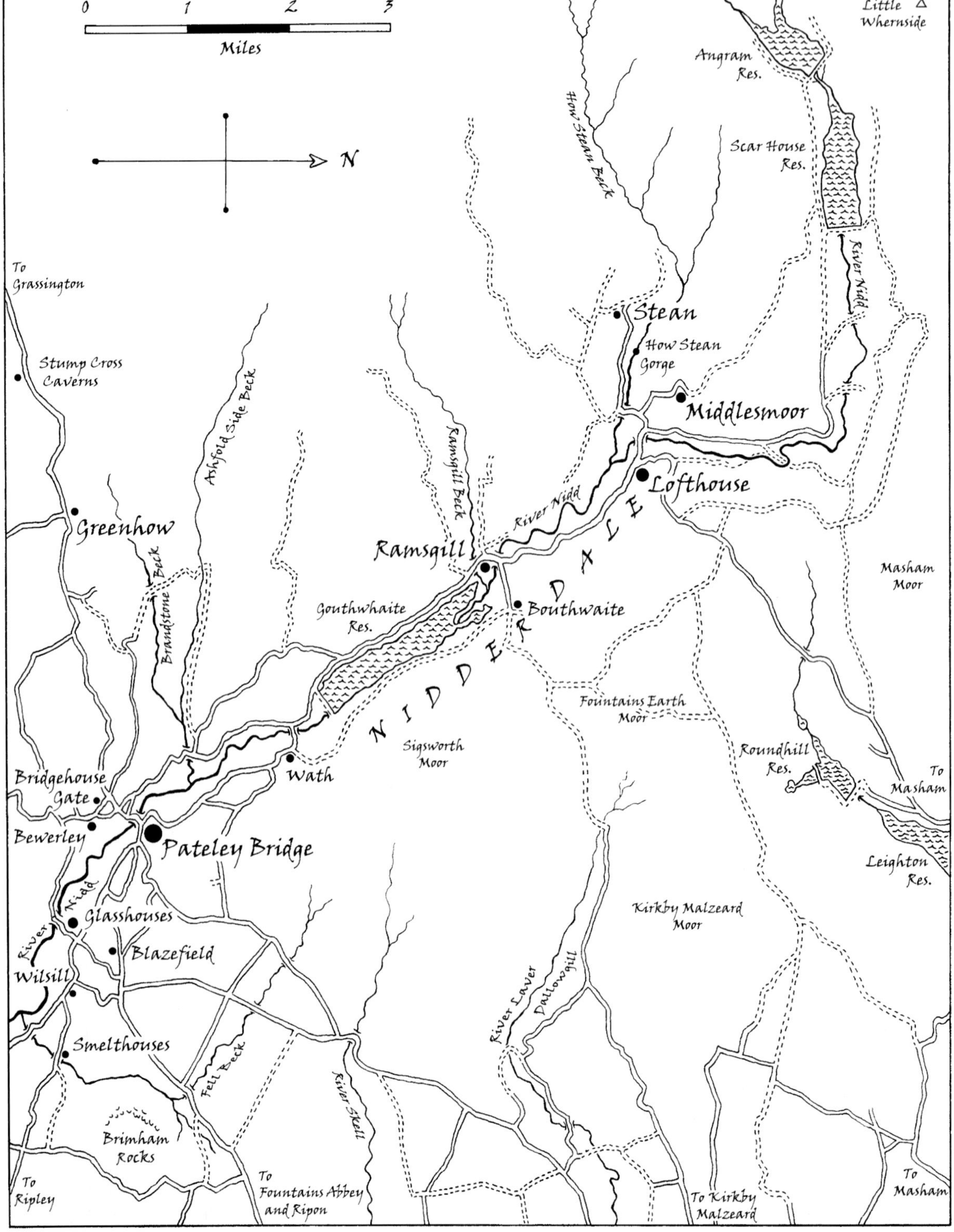
0 1 2 3
Miles
N
Little Whernside
Angram Res.
Scar House Res.
How Stean Beck
River Nidd
Stean
How Stean Gorge
Middlesmoor
Lofthouse
River Nidd
Ramsgill Beck
Ramsgill
Bouthwaite
NIDDERDALE
Masham Moor
Gouthwhaite Res.
Ashfold Side Beck
Brandstone Beck
Greenhow
To Grassington
Stump Cross Caverns
Fountains Earth Moor
Sigsworth Moor
Wath
Roundhill Res.
To Masham
Leighton Res.
Bridgehouse Gate
Bewerley
Pateley Bridge
River Nidd
Glasshouses
Blazefield
Wilsill
Smelthouses
Kirkby Malzeard Moor
River Laver
Dallowgill
Fell Beck
River Skell
Brimham Rocks
To Ripley
To Fountains Abbey and Ripon
To Kirkby Malzeard
To Masham

Nidderdale

Nidderdale

Great Whernside with its boulder-strewn summit forms a formidable barrier between Wharfedale and the head of Nidderdale and so naturally is a watershed of these two beautiful dales. Though more usually associated with Wharfedale and especially Kettlewell from where it is often climbed, this somewhat shapeless mountain prefers to issue most of its water eastwards as the source of the River Nidd. So much in fact that two great Victorian reservoirs 'Angram' and 'Scar House' were built at its foot to supply Bradford with fresh water. Curiously, also on this eastern side, the streams are commonly named 'sike' or 'dike', whereas on the western side they are predominately 'beck' or 'gill'. This upper part of the valley ringed by sweeping bleak moorlands has a wild grandeur and remoteness that, surprisingly, the stark reservoirs only seem to enhance.

Two miles south, perched high on the moorland's edge, is the aptly named village of Middlesmoor. The huddle of gritstone buildings and particularly the church, being so elevated from the valley floor, enjoy one of the best views in Yorkshire. Mapped out before us are Nidderdale's fertile green pastures, enchanting woodlands, half hidden barns and the church tower of Ramsgill. Far in the hazy distance Gouthwaite's shimmering water reflects the bright sky. This lovely scene could easily be one of those idyllic illustrations from a Rupert story.

"Far in the hazy distance Gouthwaite's shimmering water reflects the bright sky. This lovely scene could easily be one of those idyllic illustrations from a Rupert story"

The course of the Nidd from Scar House to Lofthouse tends to be intermittent because limestone fissures in the riverbed allow water to come and go underground. A narrow toll road alongside is made on the route of the old dam-construction railway. Lofthouse with its mix of working farms and clematis-clad cottages was the terminus of the Nidderdale Light Railway. It was, I believe, the first municipally owned passenger line in Britain, but alas, since 1927 no longer in existence. What a remarkable spectacle it would have been in the mid 19th century to see those billowing iron monsters rumbling their way through the valley: so modern and exciting to some, though to others perhaps — a blight on the surroundings.

'Little Switzerland' is a local name for the wondrous half-mile of How Stean Gorge near the tiny community of Stean. This deep limestone ravine, where water swirls beneath towering walls of rock, has been partly tamed by the introduction of walkways and bridges. The action of water has shaped and carved the rock into many exquisite and unexpected forms. The small admission charge is well spent — artists and photographers can have a field day here.

The Nidd now meanders through two beautiful and peaceful miles of lush meadowland before its precious waters are collected once again at Gouthwaite Reservoir. This is the earliest of the three large reservoirs in Nidderdale and although Gouthwaite village was demolished and flooded for its construction, it really has the look and characteristics of a natural lake. Mud beneath the shallow water is extremely rich in small organisms, which in turn attract a great number and variety of birds. At the reservoir's head, the quiet hamlet of Bouthwaite and the sleepy village of Ramsgill stand dreamily on opposite sides of the river. Ramsgill, whose church tower could be seen from Middlesmoor, is a picturesque village with a most attractive green. An ancient stony track starts from Bouthwaite, climbing endlessly to the expansive Fountains Earth Moor — once owned as the name suggests by Fountains Abbey.

Painting Moorland can be both amazingly simple and perplexingly difficult. No trees, no people, no buildings or anything complicated to worry about. Only land and sky. But that's the problem: how to give the vast openness a sense of scale and distance? The answer lies simply in observation and the application of 'aerial' or 'atmospheric perspective'. Colour, tone and contrast are stronger near-to and diminish in the distance. This is more obvious in the land but also applies to the sky, as it is not just a flat backdrop to the landscape, but an intrinsic part of it, going overhead like a many-layered ceiling.

"Painting Moorland can be both amazingly simple and perplexingly difficult. No trees, no people, no buildings or anything complicated to worry about. Only land and sky. But that's the problem: how to give the vast openness a sense of scale and distance?"

Past the tranquil village of Wath at the foot of Gouthwaite the scenery begins to change. As we travel down to Pateley Bridge the haunting beauty and relative narrowness of the upper valley gives way to a gentler broader span. The heathered gritstone moors flanking the dale are still very much in evidence, but their high curvy contours seem a little more removed.

Built on a hillside, Pateley Bridge acts as Upper Nidderdale's capital. It prospered and grew mainly through the quarrying and lead mining industries in the vicinity. Now, its steep and winding main street is dedicated mainly to the tourist trade, with a variety of interesting shops, cosy cafes and pubs. Greenhow, three miles to the west of here is the highest village in Yorkshire at 1260 ft above sea level. This rather wild settlement evolved almost entirely through the intense lead mining activities on Greenhow Hill in the 17th century. The oldest pig of lead in Britain, which dates from Roman times was discovered near here and is now an exhibit at Ripley Castle. Miners in this region accidentally stumbled upon and discovered Stump Cross Caverns when one of their workings broke into a cave passage. This magical subterranean showpiece, which is open to the public, has many impressive stalactites and stalagmites, now imaginatively and beautifully illuminated.

The area below Pateley Bridge is referred to

as Lower Nidderdale and although this is still a very green and pleasant land, the features we associate with Dales country have less presence. The Nidd wanders sedately through a grander, more cultivated landscape.

Away from the river, near the hamlet of Smelthouses (where the monks of Fountains smelted galena from Greenhow) can be found perhaps the most bizarre natural wonder in Britain. Quite densely spread over a 50-acre site are the astounding Brimham Rocks. These monumental gritstone rocks laid down 320 million years ago, have been continually hacked and honed by the elements. The resulting natural forms with their weird and wonderful shapes are astonishing, and in many cases appear so uncannily like animals that the 18th century antiquarian Hayman Rooke published a paper claiming them to be the work of Druids.

Whatever their origin, they certainly make fascinating subjects for the artist, and I have a hunch that they provided a large dose of inspiration for the famous Yorkshire sculptors Henry Moore and Barbara Hepworth. The price of their work might have gone through the roof but these natural sculptures are priceless. The National Trust manages the site.

Five miles to the east of Brimham sees another National Trust site of a very different nature: the majestic Fountains Abbey. Not strictly in the Dales, this Cistercian monastery held great tracts of land there, and had enormous influence on Dales life. Set in the valley of the Skell, it perhaps lacks some of the romance and loveliness of Bolton Priory, but the scale of the magnificent ruins and the magnitude of the site are awe-inspiring.

The River Nidd journeys onwards through much fertile countryside to Knaresborough and beyond, where it relinquishes its name and unites with the River Ouse near the Civil War battlefield at Marston Moor in the Vale of York.

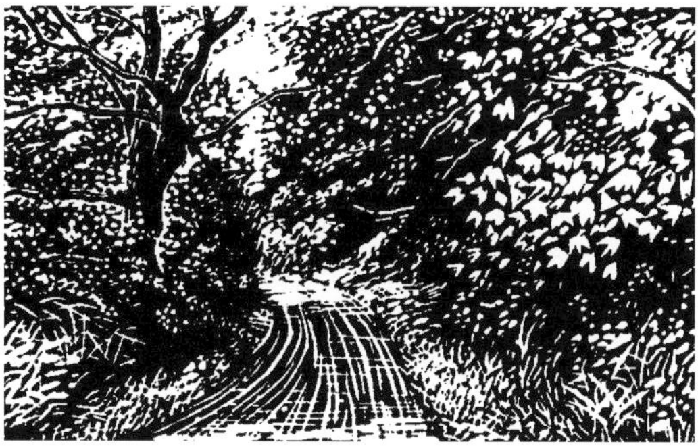

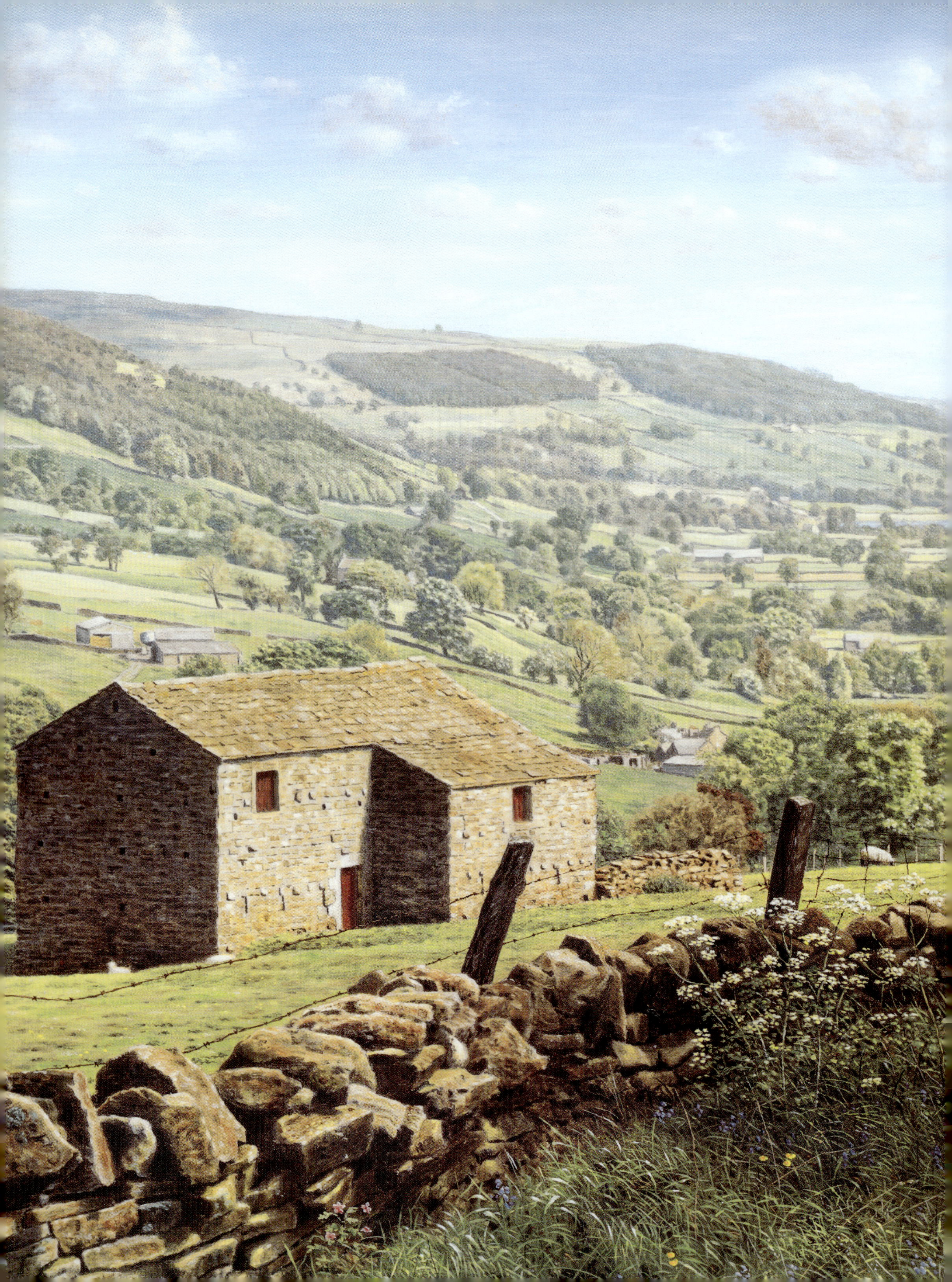

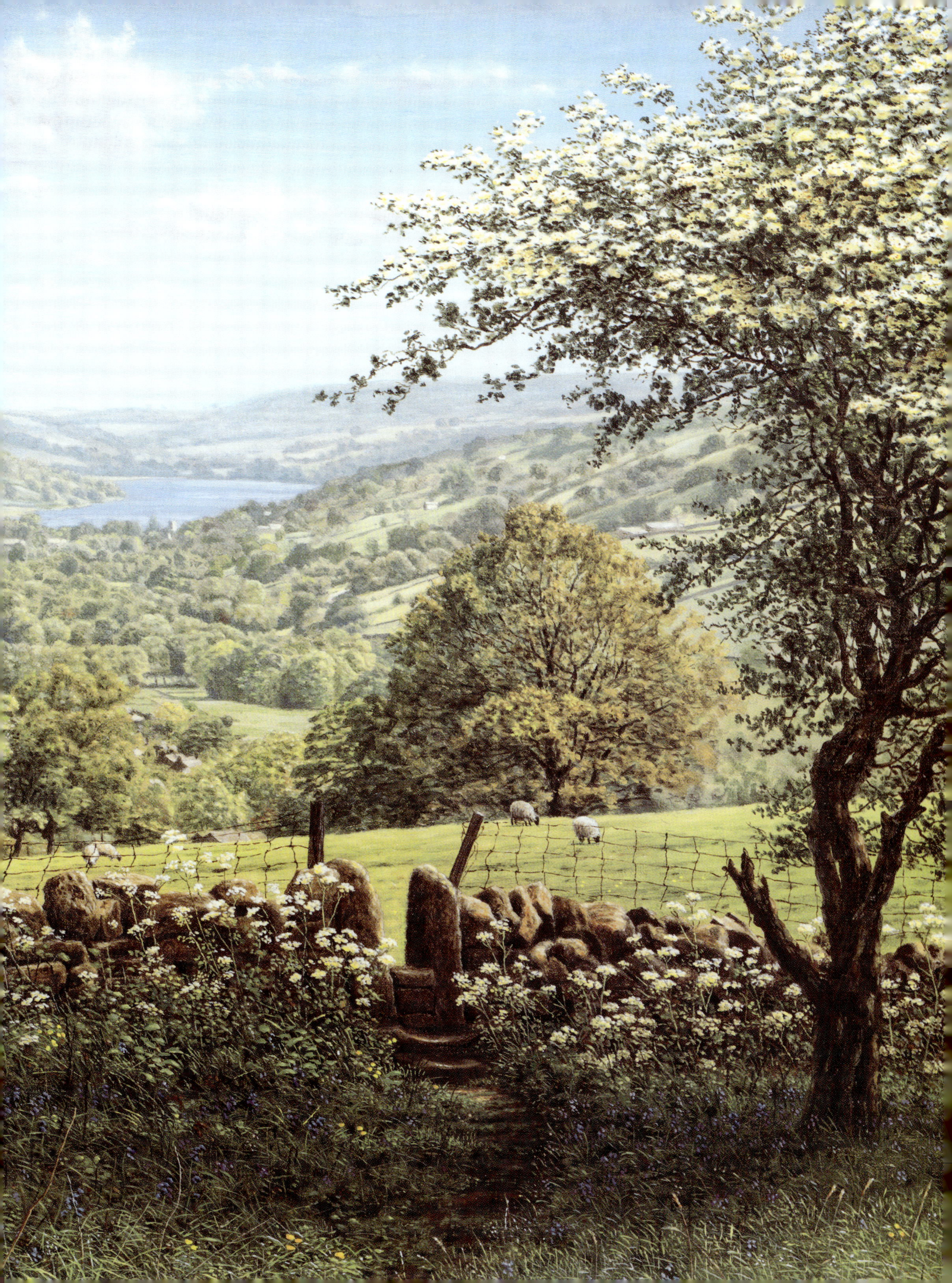

Nidderdale from near Middlesmoor

1997 Oil 18 x 26in

Many-a-walker has been stopped in their tracks, entranced by the wonderful view down-dale from Middlesmoor. I've been under its spell too and knew from the very first that I would paint it. A puzzling feature of the scene is the apparent profusion and density of trees in the valley. The trees are really there of course; by the river, lining the road and around the field edges, with the odd wooded patch dotted here and there, but from Middlesmoor and especially in summer, the dale appears more thickly wooded than it actually is.

The field-barn, so typical of those in this valley, makes a good subject to show clearly both the direction and intensity of the sun. After much pondering over the problematic foreground, consisting of a dreary uniform fence, I decided to shift a wall into the picture from a neighbouring field. The flowering hawthorn, quite common in the area, I must confess to painting from memory and imagination. A typical wall-stile offers a way for us to enter the picture and allow our gaze to zigzag over the trees and meadows to Gouthwaite Reservoir 3 miles away. Although the foreground elements have been reshuffled somewhat, the general view beyond the wall hasn't altered and hopefully the painting still gives a faithful impression of this beautiful dale.

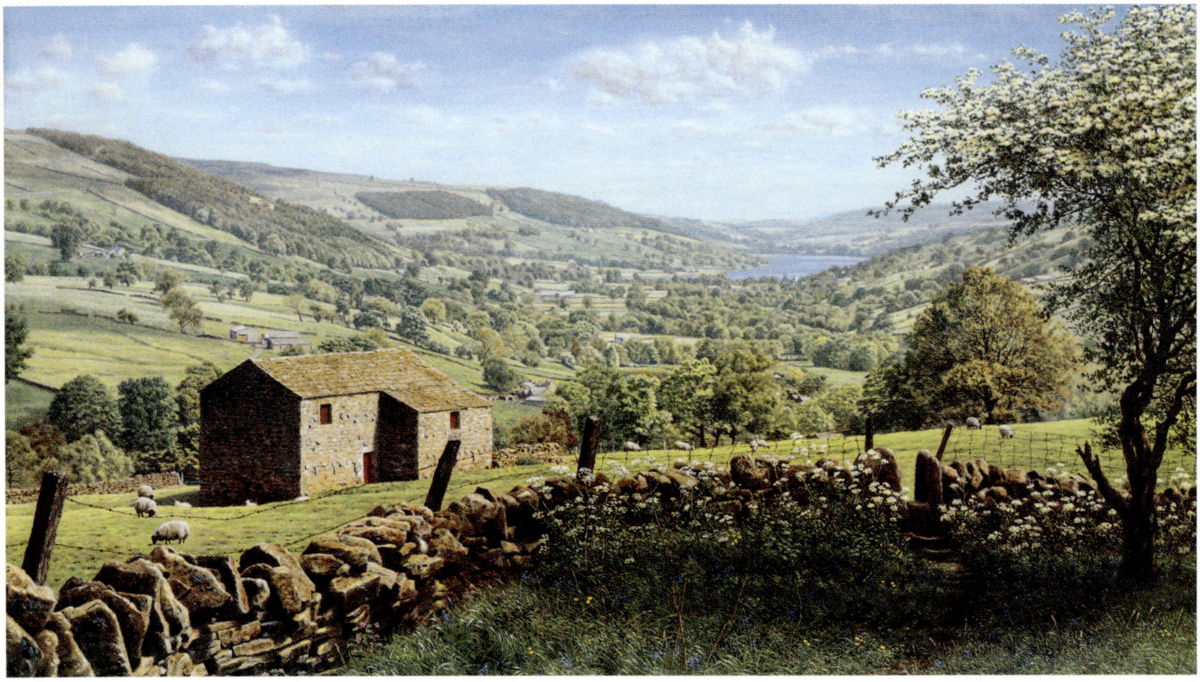

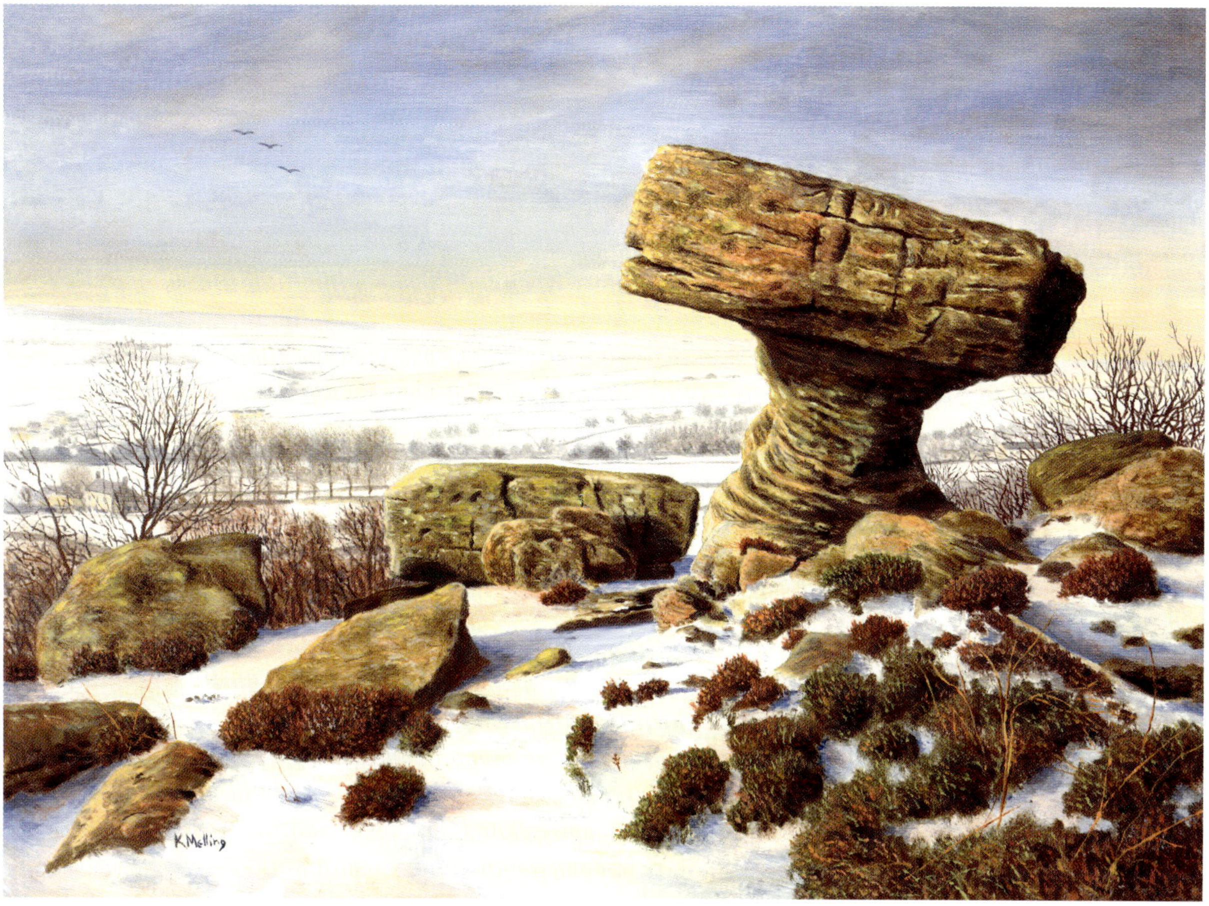

Brimham Rocks

1992 Oil 9.8 x 13.3in

Located on the Dales periphery, 4 miles east of Pateley Bridge, these bizarrely shaped gritstone rocks are a natural phenomenon. Whilst there are similarly eroded rocks dotted around the uplands of Britain, there isn't any other region that can boast so many on such a grand scale. Standing proud of a glacier during the Ice Age they were eroded by fierce winds picking up ice particles and blasting at the rock base, similar to sandblasting. The resulting forms are more undercut at the rock foot and often resemble animals or man-made objects. Many have been given names, for example — Idol Rock, Dancing Bear and Anvil. The distinctive rock in this painting is known as the Druids Writing Desk.

Though impressive in any season, I particularly like to see the site under a covering of snow, when the dark rock shapes appear even more individual, independent and animated.

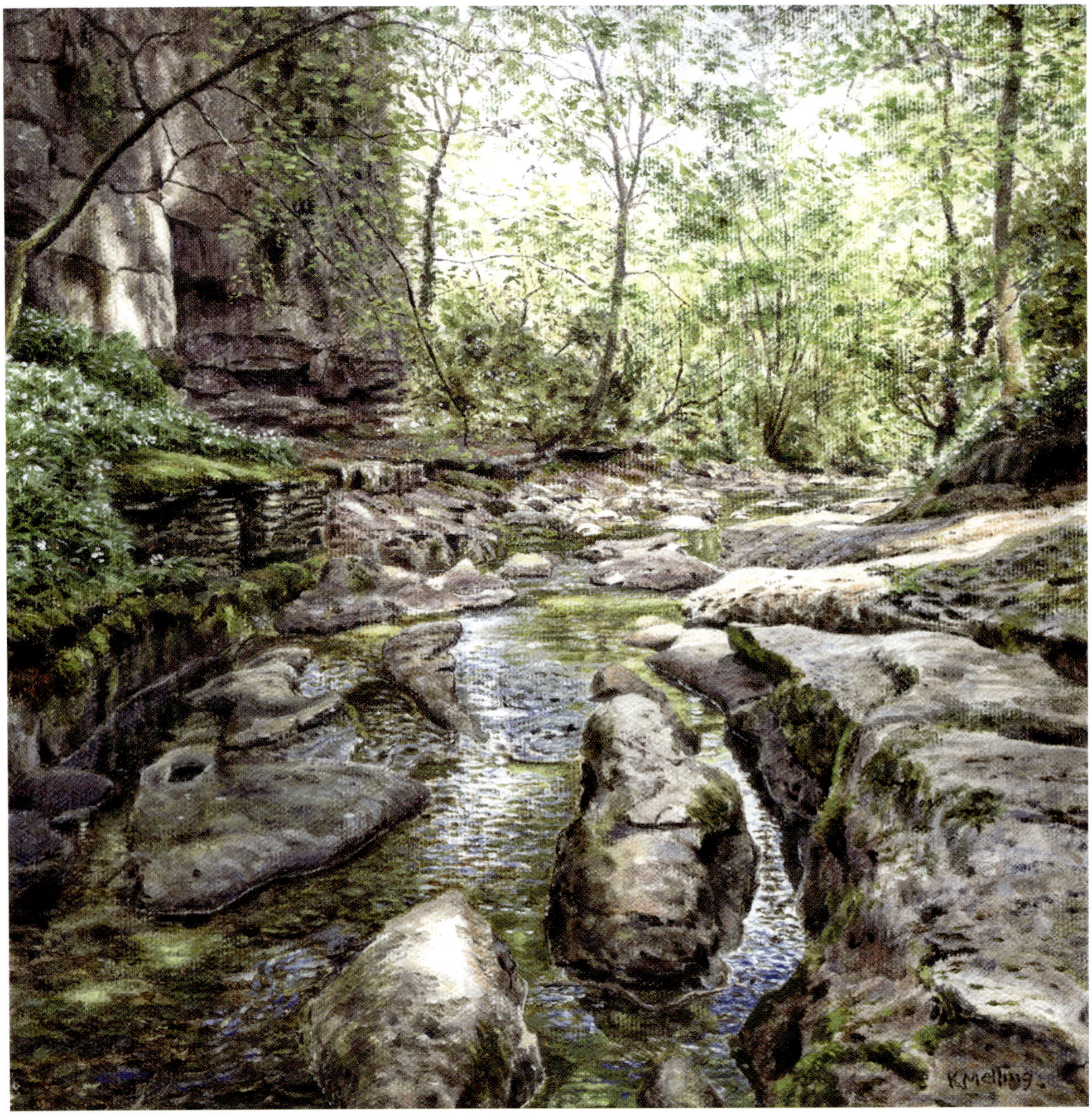

How Stean Gorge
2007 Acrylic 10 x 10in

The Yorkshire Dales has more than its fair share of limestone gorges, and they come in all manner of shapes and sizes: some are blatantly awesome, think of Gordale Scar, some, as Trollers Gill are more like miniature canyons, others, as at Ling Gill can be bewitchingly beautiful. How Stean manages a harmonious mixture of all these attributes, making a single gorge of superb sublimity.

Known to the Victorians as 'Little Switzerland', this dynamic half-mile has long been a popular visitor attraction. Privately owned, the only way to experience its hidden wonders is to pay the admission fee and follow the way-marked route by the tastefully constructed walkways and bridges. There is much to see. Sheltered by a canopy of trees consisting mainly of oak, ash and hazel, the spectacular gorge, 80 ft deep in places remains relatively cool in summer, and not surprisingly even cooler in winter when the exhibition of icicles outlasts the freezing temperatures. The mood of the gorge literally changes like the weather, for How Stean Beck, gurgling to life on the watershed of Great Whernside, can be either a terrifying torrent or tame trickle.

Consistent with such places there are caves here: Tom Taylor's Cave, named after a legendary highwayman who used it as his secret hideout, can be carefully explored (with the help of torch and helmet hired from the cafe). The cave, which starts in the gorge and emerges at Cat Hole, is 530 ft long. In 1868 two local lads found a hoard of Roman coins lying on a ledge some way inside — now displayed in York Museum.

For my painting I've chosen the quieter and gentler downriver section of the gorge, which, on certain days, when sunlight flickers through the swaying trees, has an indescribable subtle serenity about it.

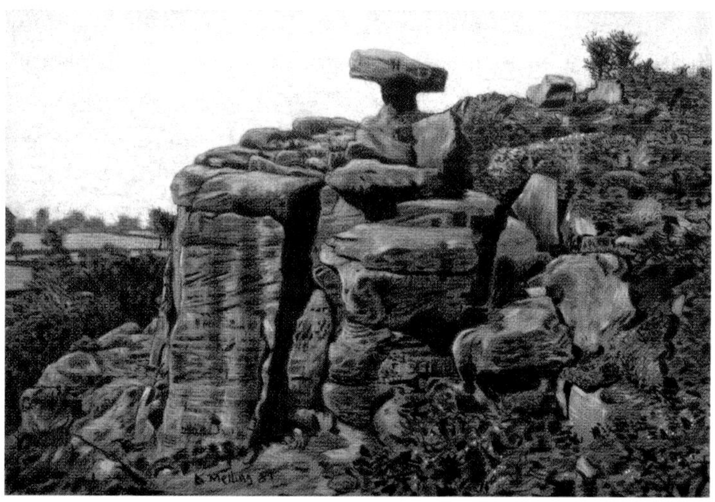

Brimham Rocks

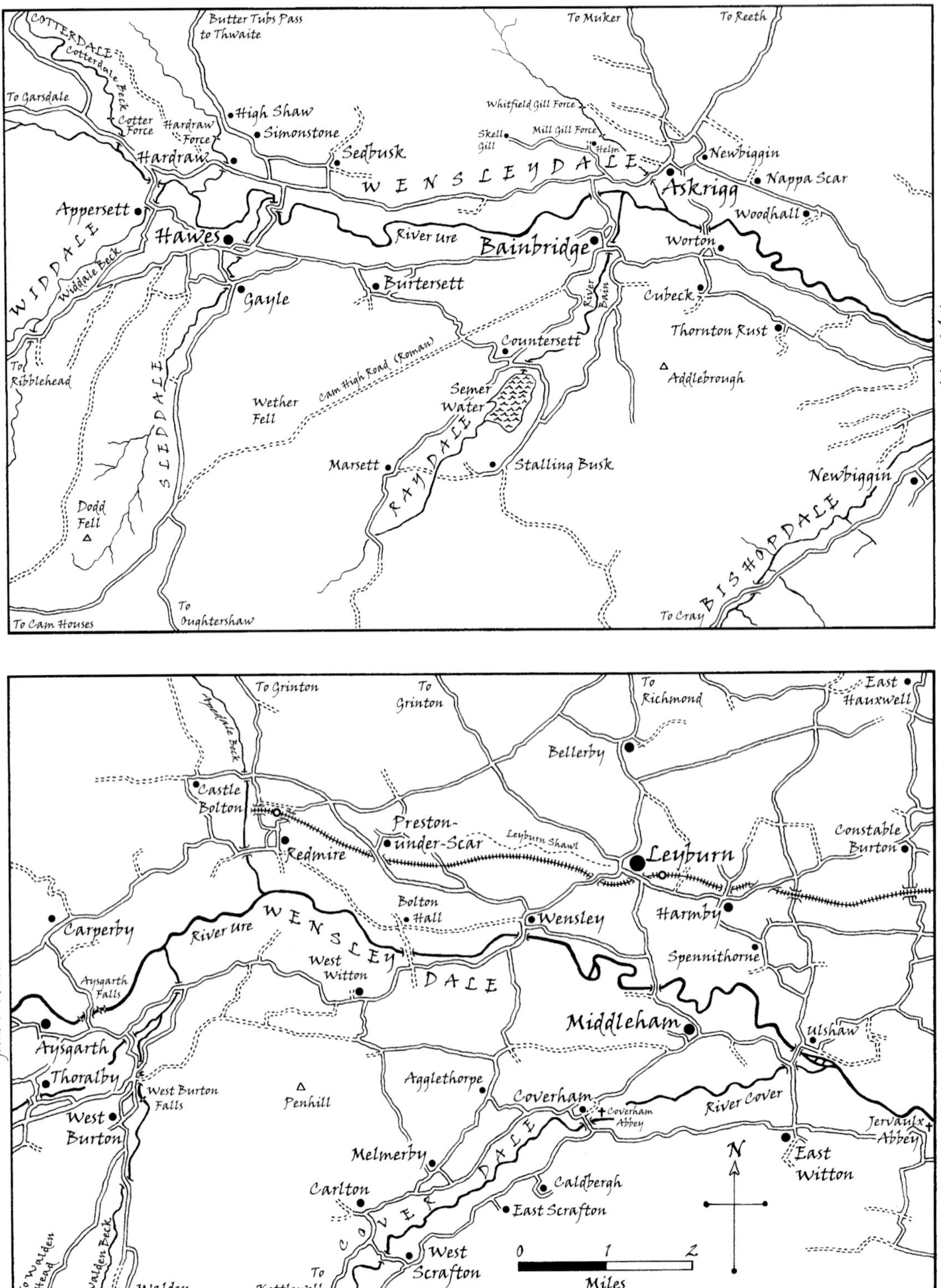

Wensleydale and tributary dales

Wensleydale

This beautiful broad valley must be the daddy of all dales. It is the longest, grandest, greenest and agriculturally the richest of them all. Often described as a family of dales, some of the numerous side valleys are really fully independent dales themselves. Of these, the narrow and knobbly Coverdale, beloved by James Herriot, and Bishopdale with various isolated farmsteads are the largest. Also the wonderlands of Walden, Widdale, Raydale, Sleddale, Colsterdale and several even smaller dales make up the family. The main valley runs west to east, dividing the Pennines with a yawning green gap, the western end narrows and gradually merges into the remote Garsdale.

Wensleydale has so many guises and parts that after many visits I feel to have hardly touched upon it. Indeed, many paintings would be necessary to do justice and represent it properly. When I first started to search for subjects here, I was ideally looking for a panoramic view over a village perhaps, which also showed the river and valley fields backed by dappled fells. The vision in my head was going to be my masterpiece. Page after page of wall details, barns, stiles, moody skies and the like, accumulated in my little sketchpads, and snapshots were taken of sheep, walkers and other awkward models that might be included, but the epic blockbuster composition that was going to epitomise Wensleydale was never glimpsed. It dawned on me that what worked in Wharfedale or Ribblesdale would not be possible in this wide valley, I had to look with fresh eyes and forget my previous work.

Once called Yoredale after its magnificent River Ure (or Yore), the dale was later renamed after the village of Wensley, which in ancient times was the only market town serving the area. After the plague of 1563 Wensley dwindled into insignificance and never recovered, the market was transferred to Askrigg.

The River Ure groggily emerges in a boggy patch high on Lunds Fell, gathers itself together and splashes and dances to the valley floor where it is boosted by the Cotter and Widdale Beck. At Appersett the characteristics of a voluminous mature river is already apparent. The high fells respectfully look on from a distance, even in these upper parts of the valley they do not crowd in.

Hawes, the capital of the upper dale is a small town with a big reputation. The world-famous Wensleydale cheese is made here in a creamery where visitors can watch the process. The haphazard placing of buildings and alleyways of Hawes give the impression of a very old place though many buildings date only from the 18th and 19th centuries. As interesting as Hawes is, the neighbouring village of Gayle always seems a more satisfying spot for the painter, mainly due to the glittering waters of Gayle Beck, which tumble through the village over several limestone slabs. Across the Ure at Hardraw, a spectacular 100 ft waterfall, is set in a rocky cove at the end of a small ravine (access to Hardraw Force through the Green Dragon pub). Turner painted this famous spectacle in typical Turneresque fashion, dramatically exaggerating the effect. A pleasant stroll from Hardraw to Sedbusk passes through some of the greenest fields I've ever seen; pure emerald, Van Gogh would have loved this. Shutt Lane rises steeply above Sedbusk and seemingly heads for the middle of nowhere on the high moors. A vista opens over the village rooftops to the valley with hazy Widdale Fell in the background.

The River Ure meanders leisurely through verdant pastures, blissfully unaware of its turbulent future at Aysgarth. Field-barns punctuate the meadows; especially plentiful around Burtersett on the south side of the valley. Two roads, one either side of the Ure serves Wensleydale's long length, and once there was a railway. Plans are afoot to re-establish this service, which at the present time goes as far as Redmire from Leeming Bar. Hopefully this project will succeed.

"A pleasant stroll from Hardraw to Sedbusk passes through some of the greenest fields I've ever seen; pure emerald, Van Gogh would have loved this"

Cradled into the arms of Raydale, Semerwater is one of only two natural lakes in the Dales (Malham Tarn is the other). It is an intriguing place with a mysterious atmosphere, though not easily put into a picture. Literature may be more Semerwater's forte, as myths and legends are woven fast into its history and each of the small hamlets around its shores, Stalling Busk, Countersett and Marsett have fascinating tales to tell both of fact and fiction.

At Bainbridge, the site of a Roman fort on Brough Hill overlooks the tidy spacious village and large sloping green. A Roman road nearby, now a walled green lane, runs ruler-straight, up and over Wether Fell — bound (once) for Kirkby Lonsdale. The River Bain, flowing the two and half miles from Semerwater to meet the Ure, is the shortest named river in England, and as it gathers pace to enter Bainbridge is very attractive.

Askrigg, lying downriver across the Ure from Bainbridge, is close enough to be its twin, but never identical. The two villages barely a mile apart are similar in size only, their characters are very different. Whereas Bainbridge is spread out and interspersed with much greenery, Askrigg, though not lacking trees is gathered together more like a small town. The scene from the moor road towards Addlebrough is one of the classic Dales views and compels you to look; the village huddled tightly appears a little incongruous yet lovely when cloud shadows roll over the stone roofs. The many tiny communities either side of the river between Askrigg and Aysgarth are deserving of exploration. Each exudes tranquility in its own way. Worton and Woodhall hug the Ure while Newbiggin, Nappa Scar, Cubeck and Thornton Rust back up to the fells and blend into the ample landscape harmoniously.

Aysgarth, well known for its breathtaking waterfalls is without doubt Wensleydale's highlight. Here the unsuspecting murmuring river is thrown into tumultuous confusion as it thunders over a series of wide rocky steps, picturesquely framed by leafy trees. Thoralby and Newbiggin at Bishopdale's foot, and pretty West Burton in the Walden Valley are closely linked to Aysgarth. Carperby across the Ure makes up the cluster, and has an impressive seven-stepped market cross.

The majestic castle at Castle Bolton appears a formidable structure with towering walls nine ft thick. Mary Queen of Scots was imprisoned here, and during the civil war it was besieged by Cromwell's troops. The surrounding countryside is a joy to behold, I wonder if people in those far off days appreciated it? Near here at the foot of Apedale, the old lead mining village of Redmire is just outside the arbitrary National Park boundary. What a difficult task it must have been to decide where the boundary line should be.

One of the most exhilarating views in the Dales

is from Scarth Nick above Preston-under-Scar. Wensleydale can be seen from tip to toe on a clear day, and the scoop of Bishopdale directly opposite attracts the eye along its narrowing trough. I was once motoring on the narrow road above here when I came head to head with an army tank coming in the opposite direction; guess who had to give way? A very expansive area of wild moorland between Leyburn and Richmond is used by the military.

There is much archaeological evidence of ancient occupation throughout Wensleydale, with especially good examples of lynchets (Celtic field cultivation strips) near Preston-under Scar. The distinctive long ridge of Penhill to the south is probably the best known fell in the area and is visible from afar, not surprisingly it was used as a beacon hill. Tucked below its northeastern flank at West Witton, a curious ritual takes place on the Saturday nearest St. Bartholomew's Day (August 24th). This is the tradition of burning Old Bartle. Various tales exist of who Old Bartle was, but most believe him to be a thief who stole pigs from the monks of Jervaulx Abbey. The market town of Leyburn is the largest settlement in the dale and possesses a sizeable market square with some fine old buildings around it. Nearby, a mile long natural terrace was named 'The Shawl', because Mary Queen of Scots supposedly lost her shawl here. The terrace now shaded in places by old oak and ash still affords outstanding views over the lower dale.

Widening now, the valley begins to lose its intimate Dales character. At Middleham, renowned for the rearing of racehorses, there is yet another fine castle. This impressive Norman structure was sited here to guard the entrance of Coverdale and watch over the Skipton to Richmond route. For the painter, these romantic castles make good subjects, especially in the golden glow of evening when the crumbling walls are bathed in yellow light and lengthening purple shadows add depth and mystery.

Two roads along upper Wensleydale's length meet at Wensley and perhaps make this pleasant settlement busier than its inhabitants would like. Wensley, situated close to a serene stretch of the Ure not only gave its name to the dale but also to a cheese and a breed of sheep. The lovely old church is reputedly the most interesting in the Dales and the elegant four-arched bridge the most beautiful. Strangely, some arches of this bridge are pointed on one side and rounded on the other.

Veering southeastwards, the dale after East Witton opens out completely. Much natural beauty and interest can be found along the riverbanks, though the real Wensleydale has been left behind.

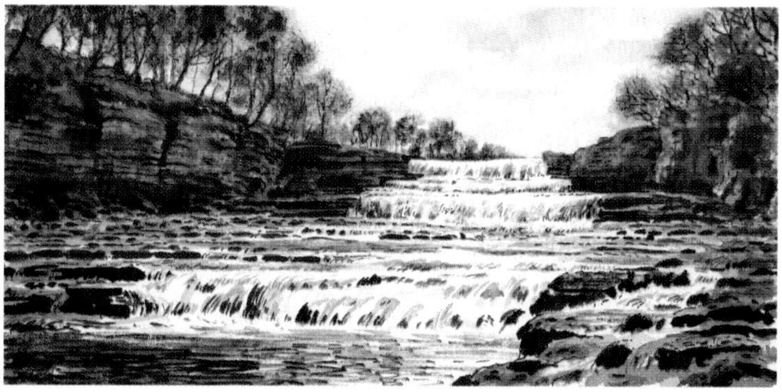

Aysgarth Lower falls

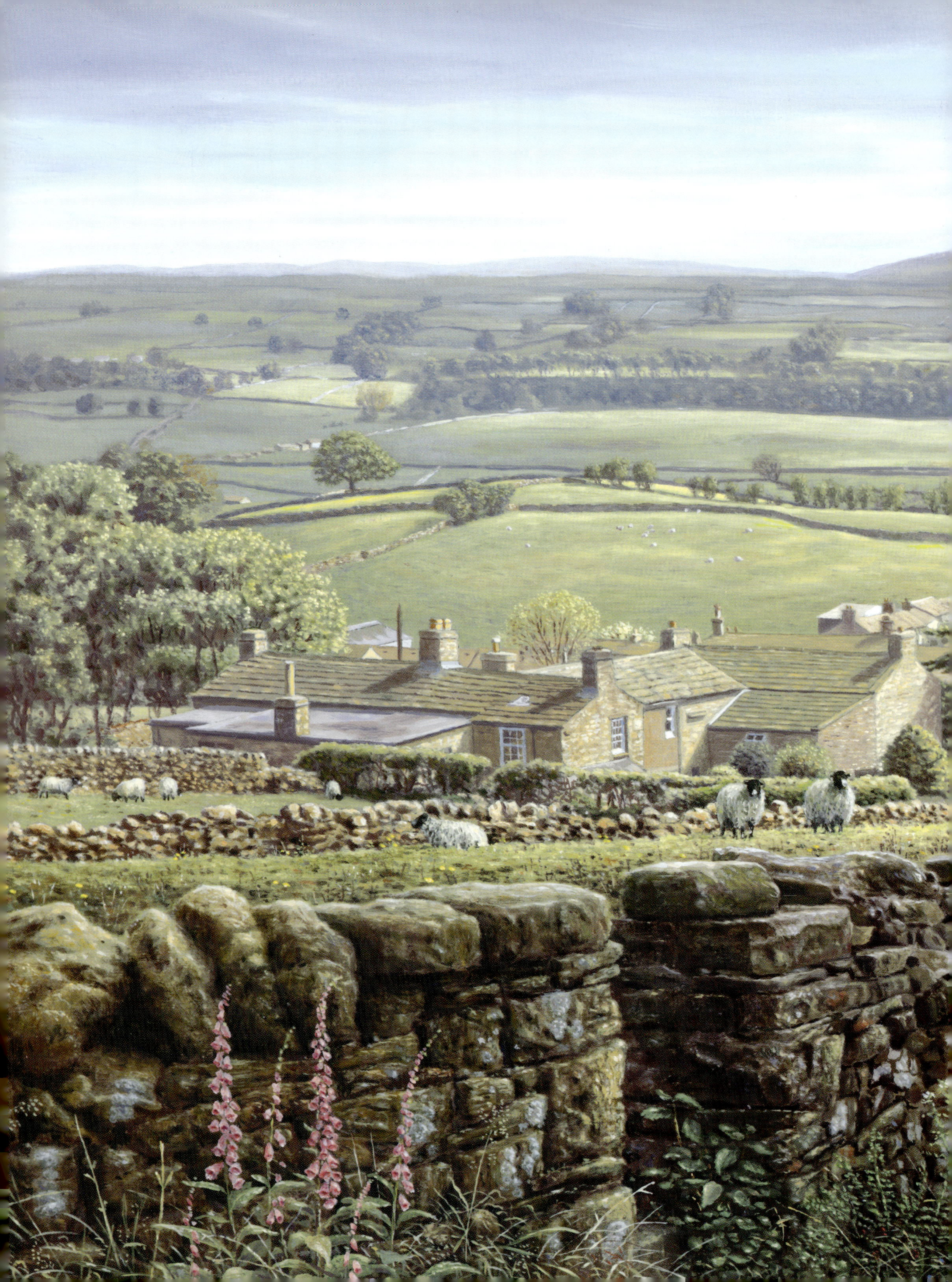

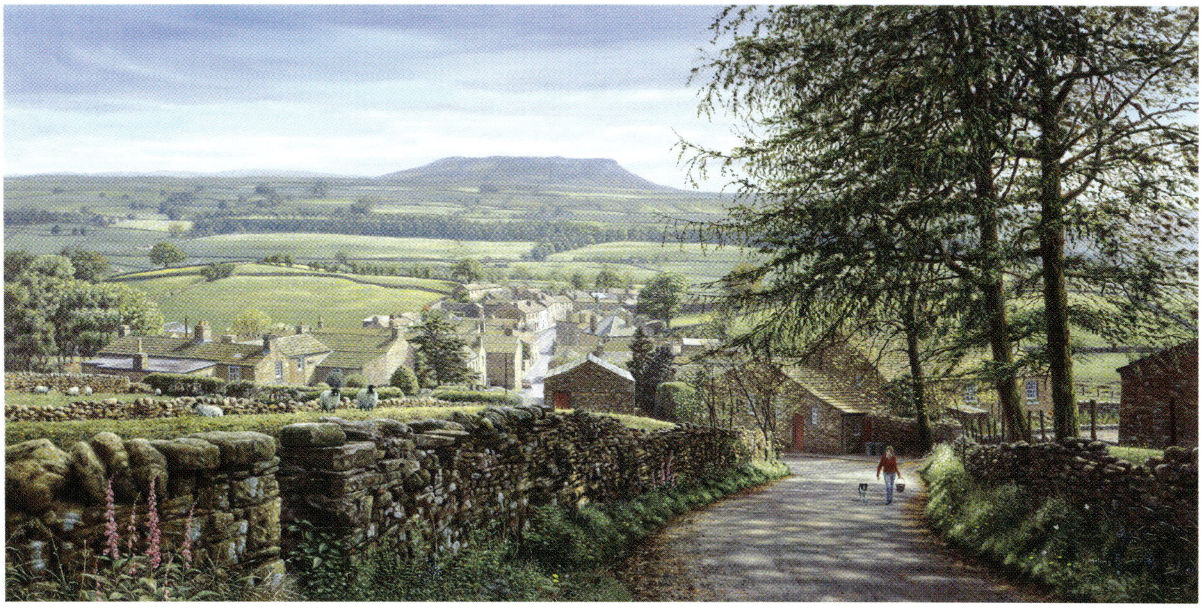

Askrigg from the Moor Road
1999 Oil 26 x 14in

The marvellous aspect from the moor road over the rooftops of Askrigg is quite a well-known view. Even so, although familiar with it, I spent ages wandering up and down the lane trying to pick my spot, and then refining it by moving a little this way and shifting a little that way until I was satisfied. After drawing for a couple of hours, the sun had moved to exactly the right place to shine through the tall larches and cast deep flickering shadows across the lane. Just then, a chap appeared next to me with rather a posh looking camera. 'Is this the quintessential view of Askrigg?' he said cheerily, setting up his tripod and explaining that he was taking photos for a calendar. He quickly took a couple of shots then left. Was he lucky or smart? I think spending time drawing directly from the subject is essential for a painter, heightening awareness of whatever is before the eyes; the intimacy joins one to the landscape in a kind of magical communion, you absorb and become part of it. Of course photography is very useful and I also make good use of it, it is especially wonderful not only for recording details but for conveniently capturing the moment. Yet I think it is always obviously apparent somehow when a painter has solely worked from photographs and not spent time working in front of the subject.

I actually painted most of the picture from just the other side of the stile, so the composition is really a combination of two viewpoints.... oh and I also nudged the stile a stride or two downhill. The drystone wall was a joy to paint though a marathon task; I felt to be personally building it stone by stone.

The village, renowned for clock making in the 18th and 19th centuries, now feels literally timeless. It is no surprise that it was chosen as the fictitious 'Darrowby' in the television series 'All Creatures Great and Small'. Many people have asked me what the distinctive flat-topped hill in the background is which has a look of Penyghent or Ingleborough. It is Addlebrough, named so we are told, after an ancient British Chief, Authulf. The remains of Iron Age settlements have been found on the southern slopes.

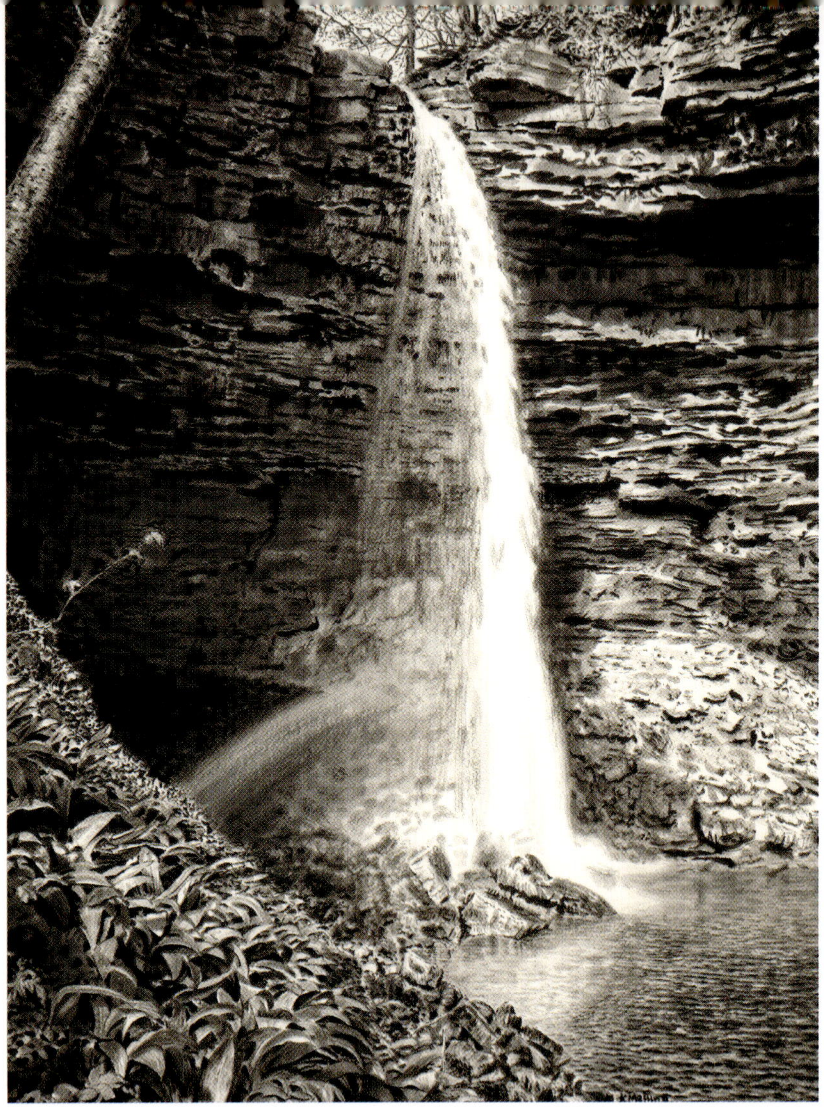

Hardraw Force

2005 Ink 16 x 11.5in

The Green Dragon Inn at Hardraw is no ordinary pub; for not only does it quench the thirst of bearded folk singers and lubricate the lungs of uniformed brass bandsmen who perform in the natural outdoor amphitheatre on festival days, but it possesses at the end of its own miniature canyon, probably the best water feature of any pub back garden in the world.

This spectacular 100 ft waterfall is reputed to be the highest single drop fall above ground in England, and partly due to this statistic, has been a popular visitor attraction since the 18th century. William Wordsworth and his sister Dorothy visited here in 1799.

A devastating flash flood in 1899 caused much destruction in the surrounding area and also destroyed the fall's overhanging lip, which greatly changed its character. The landowner at the time, Earl Wharncliffe, arranged the repair and restoration of the stone ledge, which was held in place by iron pins. So what we see today is actually partially artificial; not many people know that.

In spate after heavy rain the roaring water is awesome, though to my mind is most attractive in slightly quieter mood when a thinner column of white water rushes over the overhanging ledge as if poured from a jug. If it happens to be breezy then wispy veils of hanging spray flutter by its side, and if it is sunny you may be lucky enough to see a rainbow, as I have shown in the illustration.

Aysgarth Falls

2006 Ink 11.5 x 15.8in

The Ure's peaceful wanderings through Wensleydale's verdant pasture and meadowland is relatively pedestrian and uneventful, until that is, the vicinity of Yore Bridge is reached. Here the river is rudely awakened from its sublime slumbers by the singing surging waters of Aysgarth's upper falls. This is High Force, the first in a series of three dramatic waterfalls and arguably the finest. An excellent prospect of the cascades can be viewed from the road bridge, but, like the man in the picture, an exploration on foot is essential if more of its watery secrets are to be revealed.

Because these falls are very extensive and the river wide, I decided to home-in on one particular bit for my composition, even excluding the sky. There is no focal point, the eye scans the picture surface without coming to rest anywhere, then the figure is spotted, giving scale to the scene and somehow stabilising the whole. Of course this is psychological, if the figure was a rock, the eye would continue to search — try covering it with your thumb.

I often like to experiment and try different art mediums and materials; this illustration was made with an American ink called Higgins Black Magic.

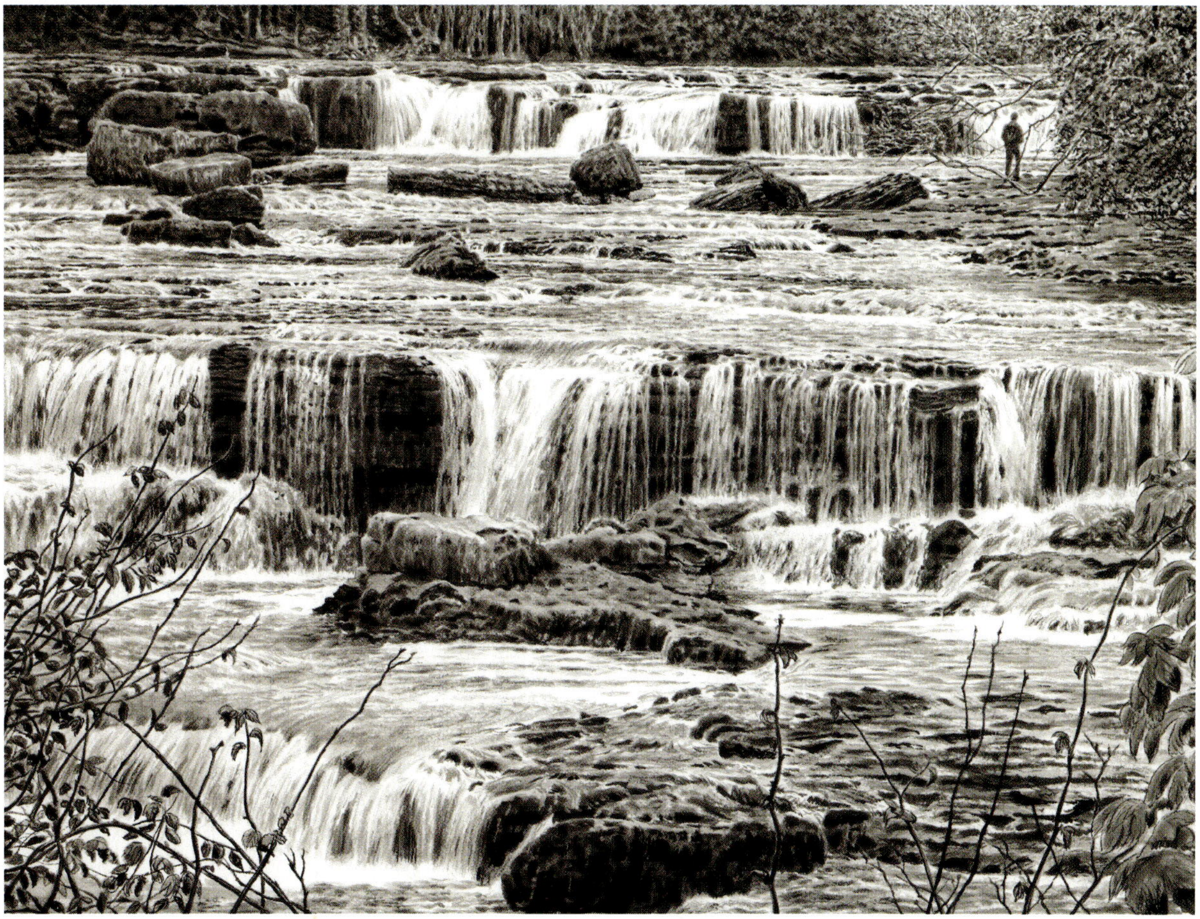

Semerwater

2004 Ink 11.8 x 11.8in

Raydale holds a rare treasure amidst its magic ring of encircling fells — one of only two natural lakes in the Dales domain. This silver saucer of shining water both attracts and repels, there is something a little eerie about it. Even when windsurfers skip the white-horse waves and young children paddle on sunnier days, there is still a strangeness woven fast into the atmosphere. There is an old tale that long ago a village stood here, visited one day by an angel dressed as a beggar. He went from door to door asking for food and shelter, but none gave it, until finally at the last cottage, a poor couple welcomed him in. They shared with him their meagre food and drink and made him a bed by the fire. The following morning the beggar turned to the village and cursed it, saying:

Semerwater rise, Semerwater sink,
And swallow all save this little house
That gave me meat and drink.

Suddenly a raging storm ensued and floodwater rose to cover the inhospitable village, yet left the poor couple's cottage untouched. Incredibly there could be a grain of truth in this story as the remains of Iron Age lake dwellings have been discovered off shore.

My illustration is from the foot of the lake and shows two large limestone boulders known as the Mermaid stones. There were no mermaids about on this day, but the stones which were deposited by glacial action during the Ice Age, conveniently made a strong foreground subject.

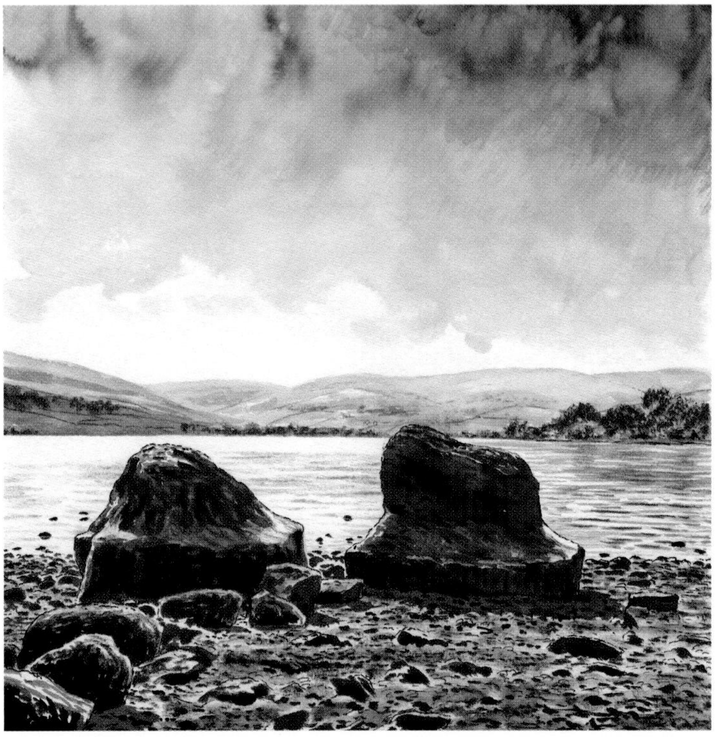

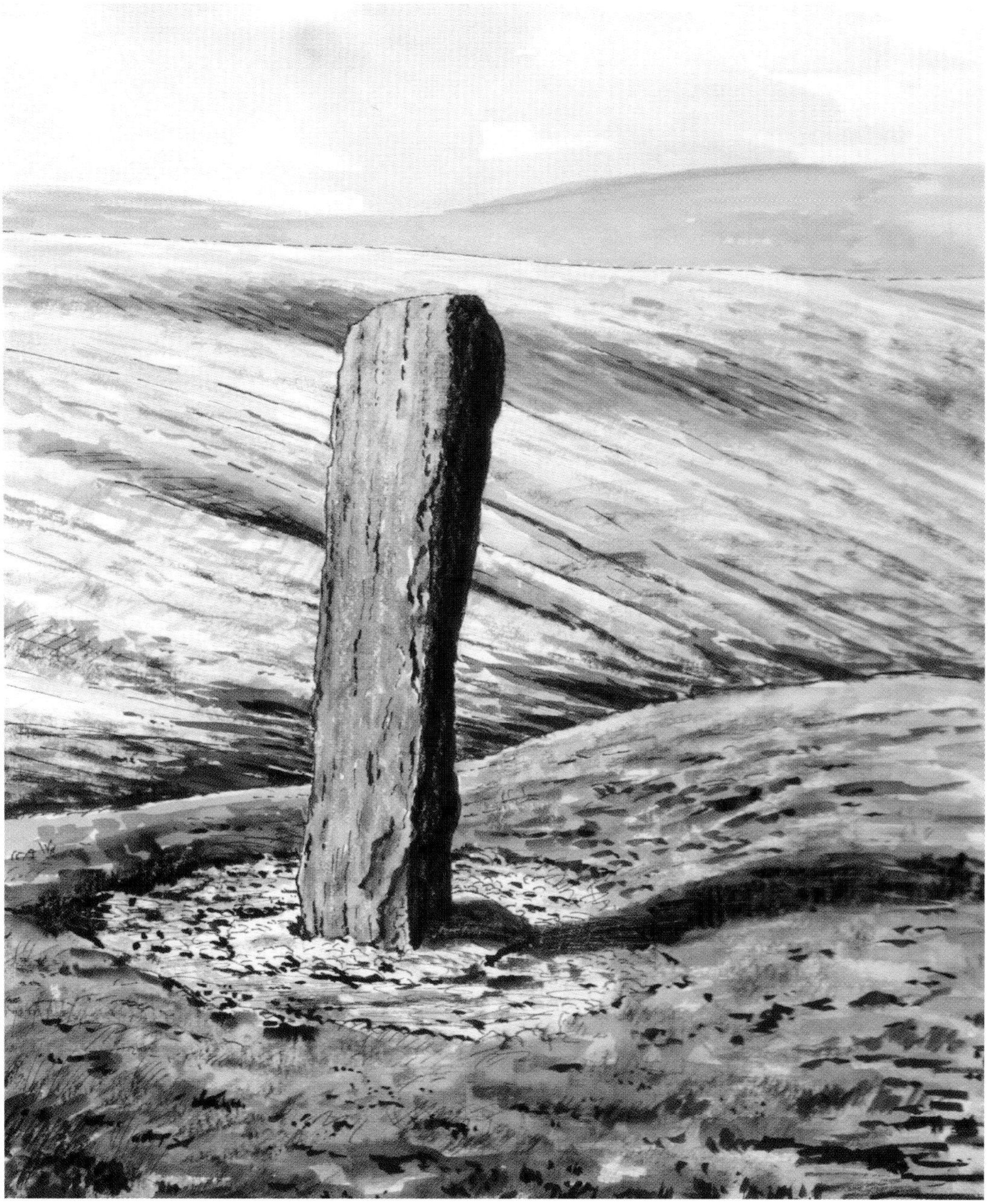

Hunter's Stone

2004 Ink 11.8 x 11.8in

This boundary stone of the hunting forests was later used as a monastic way marker. Standing in bleak solitude near the head of Coverdale, it guided travellers on the switchback route between Coverham Abbey and Kettlewell. The once rough track, now a metalled road can still be rather demanding as it twists, turns, rises and falls for a good length of the upper dale. A curious old folk tale tells of the stone turning round when the clock in Hunter's Hall strikes midnight. One face of the sturdy shaft displays a lightly engraved small cross.

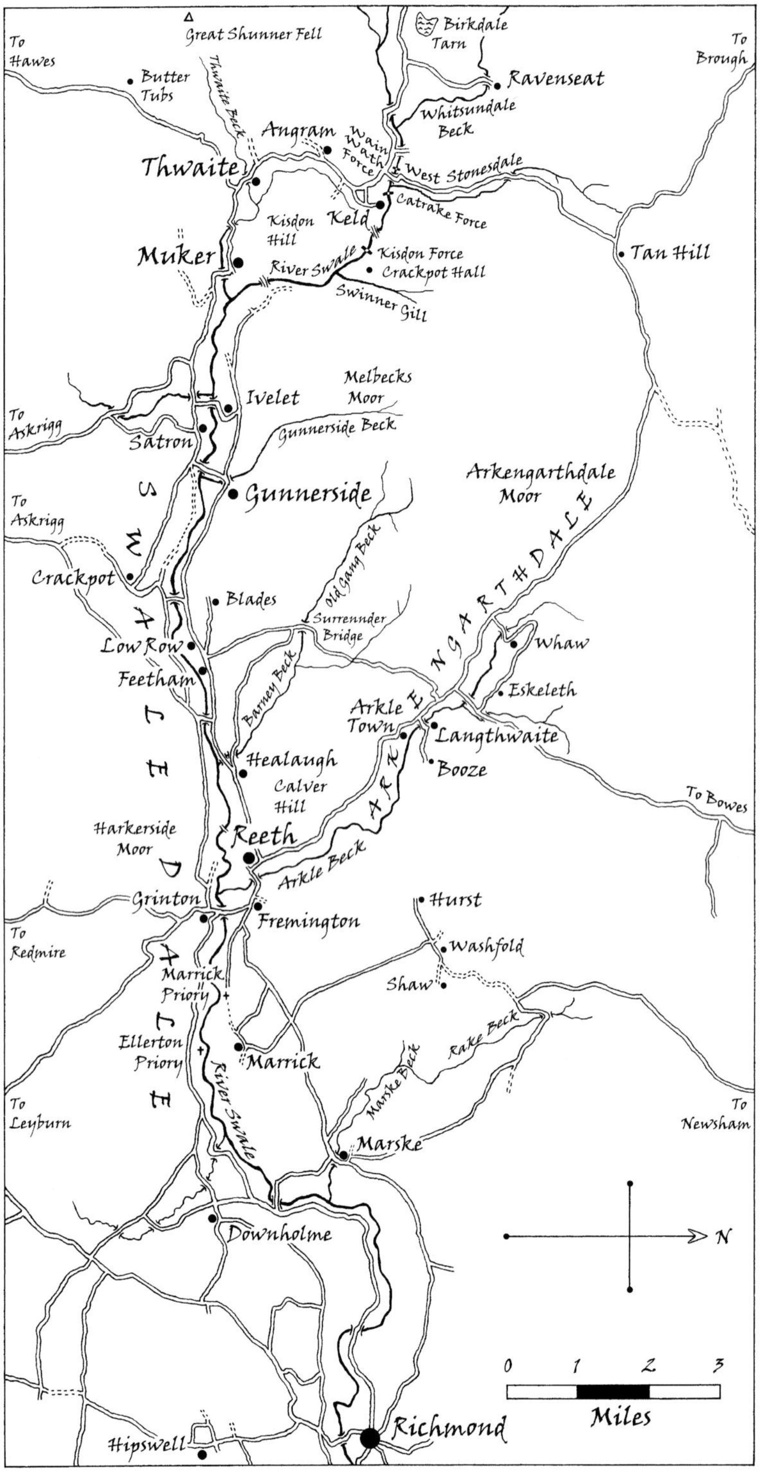

Swaledale and Arkengarthdale

Swaledale

This dynamic Yorkshire dale is thought by many to be the most beautiful, and if beauty lies in the eye of the beholder, then their opinion must be right. The dale runs across country west to east as Wensleydale does, but unlike that fair dale it cannot hold the high fells back, and the long unbroken hillsides squeeze close to the valley fields for almost 20 sublime miles.

Of the various scenic ways to enter Swaledale, the approach from Hawes over Buttertubs Pass holds the most drama, and is my favourite. We descend into the dale on a precipitous mountain road as if from the air. Set out before us, the jigsaw field patterns dotted with barns and sprinkled with tiny sheep stretch down-dale into a translucent blue-green distance. Whilst the utmost care by drivers is necessary, it is a wonder, with such a magnetic distraction, that there is not a pile of rusting cars in Cliff Beck below. Luckily there are places to stop to enjoy the view, and one of these is at the site of the remarkable Buttertubs themselves. These deep potholes were supposedly used to keep butter cool while farmers rested on their way to Hawes market. Their design, some say, does resemble the old style butter tubs, but I think you need a large dose of imagination to see that.

"We descend into the dale on a precipitous mountain road as if from the air. Set out before us, the jigsaw field patterns dotted with barns and sprinkled with tiny sheep stretch down-dale into a translucent blue-green distance"

The pass alights safely in Swaledale near the orderly village of Thwaite. In summer the hay meadows around here are ablaze with a great assortment of wild flowers. The flowers attract many butterflies and other insects, which in turn attract a variety of birds. This is a nature lover's paradise. A typical squat humpbacked bridge spans the babbling waters of Thwaite Beck, which, could be mistaken for the young Swale. Actually the Swale is nowhere to be seen on this western side of Kisdon Hill, as it defected to the east far back in its history. The colourful hump of Kisdon stands proudly isolated from the neighbouring fells, and in fact used to be an island when in ages past, the river encircled it completely.

The Swale, said to be the fastest flowing river in England, begins its boisterous life as a mere trickle high on the wild moorlands near the old Westmorland Yorkshire border. Chuckling its way through Birkdale under the guise of Birkdale Beck, the river reveals its true identity after meeting Great Sleddale Beck, thereafter it is known as the Swale. Whitsundale Beck joins the fun, and the waters merrily dance and tumble over Wain Wath Falls near the Norse named settlement of Keld. This quaint hotchpotch of buildings is the first (or last) proper village encountered in Swaledale. Frustratingly for the artist, some interesting old cottages here appear to defy the laws of perspective, and even when sketched accurately, still seem badly drawn. Many place names in the upper valley are derived from the language of the Viking settlers; among others there are Thwaite, Muker, Gunnerside and Feetham. It is said that the broad dialect of these parts (alas being replaced by a more sanitised English) can be well understood in Iceland and Norway.

Not to be outdone by Wensleydale, Swaledale also gave its name to a sheep and a cheese; the cheese may not be as well known as its neighbours, but the sheep is famous. It is a particularly hardy animal suited to the fells, and so familiar in the Dales that the National Park has used its distinctive black face as its emblem.

A narrow road from Keld climbs solemnly through West Stonesdale to arrive with much relief at the highest pub in England, the Tan Hill Inn. This famous watering hole seems lost in an unrelenting dark sea of moorland. The ever-changing vapour laden sky and vast horizons, together with refreshments available, would keep watercolourists happy for hours. It is almost 5 long miles to Keld, the nearest village, but the little hamlet of Ravenseat hidden in lonely Whitsundale is nearer, albeit, as the crow flies over the moors. It is doubtful however, that reluctant leavers of this cosy public house would walk so straight!

"This famous watering hole seems lost in an unrelenting dark sea of moorland. The ever-changing vapour laden sky and vast horizons, together with refreshments available, would keep watercolourists happy for hours"

The River Swale is no capering cygnet now, but a swan; mature, proud and beautiful, and, at times if approached too closely, aggressive; for the great tracts of surrounding high ground can swell its waters dramatically and rapidly after rain, which is rarely in short supply. It is difficult to imagine the dale without the river. It is its life force, its spirit, its heartbeat and its blood. It can look like blood too after a storm when the peaty fell water dyes it a warm rich brown. As the Swale cuts a magnificent course around Kisdon Hill, it enters arguably its finest section, and therefore the dale's finest section. The sweeping river rolls over Catrake Force into a deep swirling pool and races through a gorge where Kisdon Force angrily thunders and foams under a canopy of admiring trees. Crackpot Hall surveys the wooded valley from a commanding position higher on the opposite bank, but is in a ruinous state, apparently from subsidence caused by mining at nearby Swinner Gill. The ugly scars in the gills and barren wastelands on the open fells are a sad reminder that lead mining was a major industry in Swaledale, providing employment for thousands.

South of Kisdon Hill and raised above its own beck a little way from the main river, Muker (pronounced Mooker) could not have a more pleasant aspect. The cottages here, dwarfed on all sides by the giant hills, blend perfectly into the landscape. On closer inspection, the surprising Literary Institute stands out for its fanciful facade and bright paintwork, but still does not seem incongruous. Around Muker, small field-barns are very numerous, with more than a hundred within a square mile.

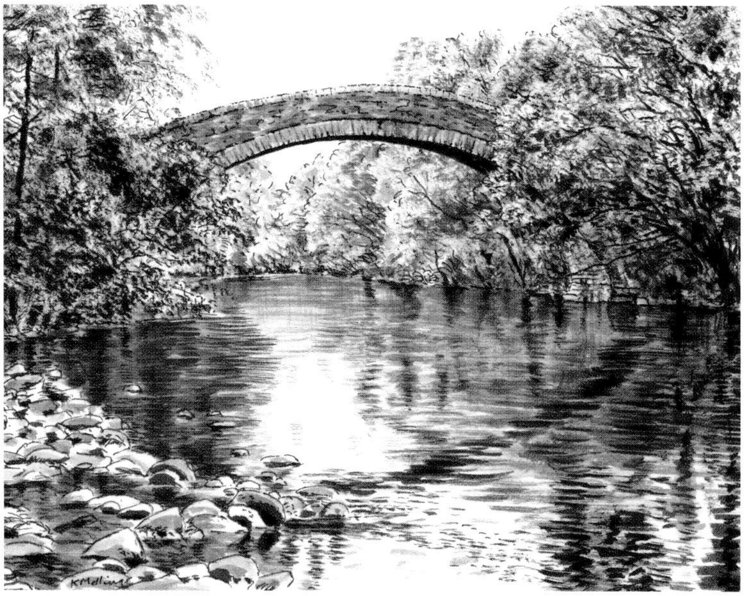

Ivelet Bridge

An old packhorse bridge spanning the Swale at the pretty hamlet of Ivelet rises beautifully in a slender rainbow arch. Opposite, two steep and twisty moor-roads ascend Oxnop Gill, merging above Oxnop Scar on the way 'owertops' to Askrigg. From the clustering village of Gunnerside, the richly wooded Gunnerside Gill gives way to a more austere landscape as Melbecks Moor is approached. Extensive lead mining has taken its toll here, and left desolation in its wake. The ruins, remnants and spoil heaps exude a sombre melancholy air, making this a spooky otherworldly place. A painter would only need the earth colours here; raw and burnt umber, raw and burnt sienna, yellow ochre and neutral tint. These colours are in complete contrast to those needed for the summer fields around Gunnerside where the waves of buttercups rippling in the breeze would demand the brightest of hues.

Along the Swale between Ivelet and Healaugh, small hamlets and farmhouses are strung out like knots on string, others look down aloofly from their high fellside perches. Many have intriguing names such as Satron, Smarber, Blades, Turnip House, Crackpot, Hatters Roof and Dagger Stones. Low Row must have been at the back of the queue when names were given out, for the title seems too banal for this dale. The straggling little village doesn't mind though, it knows its location on the Swale is enviable, enjoying exquisite views to the hills of Calver, Blea Barf, Harkerside and High Carl. A steep little road takes a direct route from Feetham over to Langthwaite and passes Old Gang Beck at Surrender Bridge. Many a miner has trodden this course on his way to and from work and must have felt a great freedom in the exposed vastness, a soothing antidote to the grimness and gloom underground, except of course in severe winter conditions.

At Scabba Wath Bridge another winding lane climbs Whitaside Moor on its lofty trek to Wensleydale. The exhilarating aspect over the deep valley is quite astonishing. The jumble of irregular fields stacked up the fellsides are uncountable, their delicate differing shades sliced through with dark scratchy walls. The higher fields, blotched with bracken and reeds, blend imperceptibly with the blue-brown moors, and when shrouded in thin veils of mist have a mystical appearance.

The huddle of houses at Healaugh has a look of expectancy, but for what I'm not sure. Maybe they're waiting for former days to return when there was a renowned hunting manor here, and wild boar, wolves and deer ran freely in the forest. It is a sleepy place now, though there is a reminder still of the great tracts of forest in the nearby woods along Barney Beck. On the lower slopes of Harkerside the earthworks of a rather large Iron Age hill-fort, Maiden Castle, surveys the valley from its excellent vantage point. Evidence in Swaledale of very early times is a little scanty but around this area there are several good examples of defensive ditches and dykes.

Grinton is well known for its grand old church, which is often called the 'Cathedral of the Dales'. In medieval times this was the only church for many a mile, with a parish stretching as far as the Westmorland border. Inhabitants of the upper valley had a long and arduous journey to reach it. They carried their dead here along the legendary Corpse Way, a two-day slow procession over the hills from Keld.

The village of Reeth, the capital of the upper dale, is situated on a sloping shoulder of Calver Hill where Arkengarthdale meets Swaledale. During the lead mining years it was equally important to both of these dales as its relatively large size reflects. An assortment of Georgian houses, old cottages, pubs, craft shops and cafes surround an exceedingly spacious green, behind which there is much interest for the artist in the hidden corners and alleyways. With the limestone etched Fremmington Edge as an impressive backdrop and views to the verdant valley, Reeth's location is second to none.

"A painter would only need the earth colours here; raw and burnt umber, raw and burnt sienna, yellow ochre and neutral tint"

In the folds of Arkengarthdale which is Swaledale's major side-valley, Langthwaite nonchalantly straddles Arkle Beck and seems locked in a time warp. Fans of James Herriot may recognise the scene. The little humpbacked bridge here appeared in the TV series 'All Creatures Great and Small'. This long and lonely dale is sparsely populated, with just a handful of additional scattered hamlets, amongst them - Arkle Town, Booze, Eskeleth and Whaw. As the road winds higher, the landscape becomes bleaker, treeless and wild, curlews have the freedom of the huge sky and grouse hidden in the heather call 'go back, go back'. At last we arrive once again at Tan Hill where coal was mined and carted to the smelting mills in the lower valley.

Midway along Swaledale's serpentine length, Fremmington marks the beginning of change. The dale softens, trees become conspicuously more abundant and buildings don't only do battle against the elements but make their peace and try for a little elegance. Downstream, the ruins of Marrick and Ellerton Priories cast calming spells over the rich luxuriance of a country brimming with tales of yore. The shady Steps Wood rises steeply behind Marrick Priory, and is divided by an ancient flagged pathway of 375 worn steps known as the 'Nuns Causey'. When evening sunbeams flicker through creaking branches and the lonesome tawny owl begins to hoot, it's not difficult to imagine the ghosts of Benedictine Nuns lightly descending the leafy path — thinking 'heaven couldn't be better than this' and all loath to leave their beloved vale. Though sadly, in 1539 when a commissioner of King Henry VIII, with heavy heart, knocked solemnly on the Prioress's door, leave they must.

The way leads eventually to the hillside village of Marrick. A feeling of airy openness pervades this loosely gathered community. Its high elevation ensures glorious vistas up and down dale and a map-like perusal of the facing arc of Ellerton Moor. Far below, the Swale's banks are swaddled in a sinuous blanket of green, as mature trees form a guard of honour almost every step of the way to Richmond. Behind the charming village of Marske, the wooded valley of Marske Beck encapsulates in miniature all the attributes of Swaledale, as if the divine parent dale had fashioned it in its own image. Here, the painter of landscapes would be inclined to linger, for every turn of the head reveals something worthy of sketching. Clints Scar is especially pleasing as it stretches out like a crumpled banner above Limekiln Wood, the play of light on its craggy face forever changing.

Across the Swale, a road destined for Bellerby and Leyburn passes the quiet village of Downholme before circumnavigating a huge area of moorland allocated to the MOD. The River Swale, beautiful as ever, negotiates a particularly lovely stretch of the dale, chinking and chattering between rising fields and wooded slopes topped with shattered escarpments of limestone. During the summer months the deciduous woodlands here are especially floriferous and varied; the lovely tracks and paths through them are a delight to tread and ought to lift anyone's spirits.

The market town of Richmond, which evolved around the imposing castle, is strategically placed on a rocky hill near the mouth of Swaledale. It is probably more famous in song and verse than in painting, although it has been portrayed many times by numerous artists, including Turner (all perhaps hoping for that 'sweet lass' to pass by). There are countless vantage points; a popular one being the splendid view from Bargate Green where, the massive castle-keep towers above the more humble two and three storey cottages. Another and perhaps best aspect, is from across the river with the handsome stone bridge in the foreground. This was Turner's choice; always attracted to the ephemeral, he not only included the sparkling waters, but also bathed his subject in a magical golden light.

Beyond Richmond the Swale flows serenely past the romantic pale walls of Easby Abbey and takes leave of Dales country. Ahead, the Vale of York beckons. The river will unite and exchange tales with the Ure, and together their now placid waters will join the Ouse on a slow passage to the Humber and North Sea.

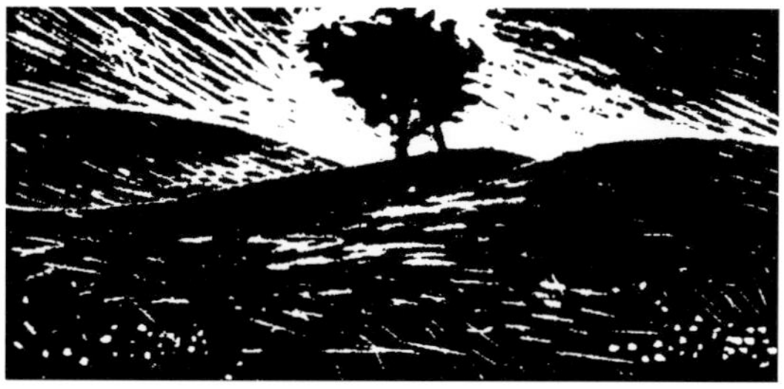

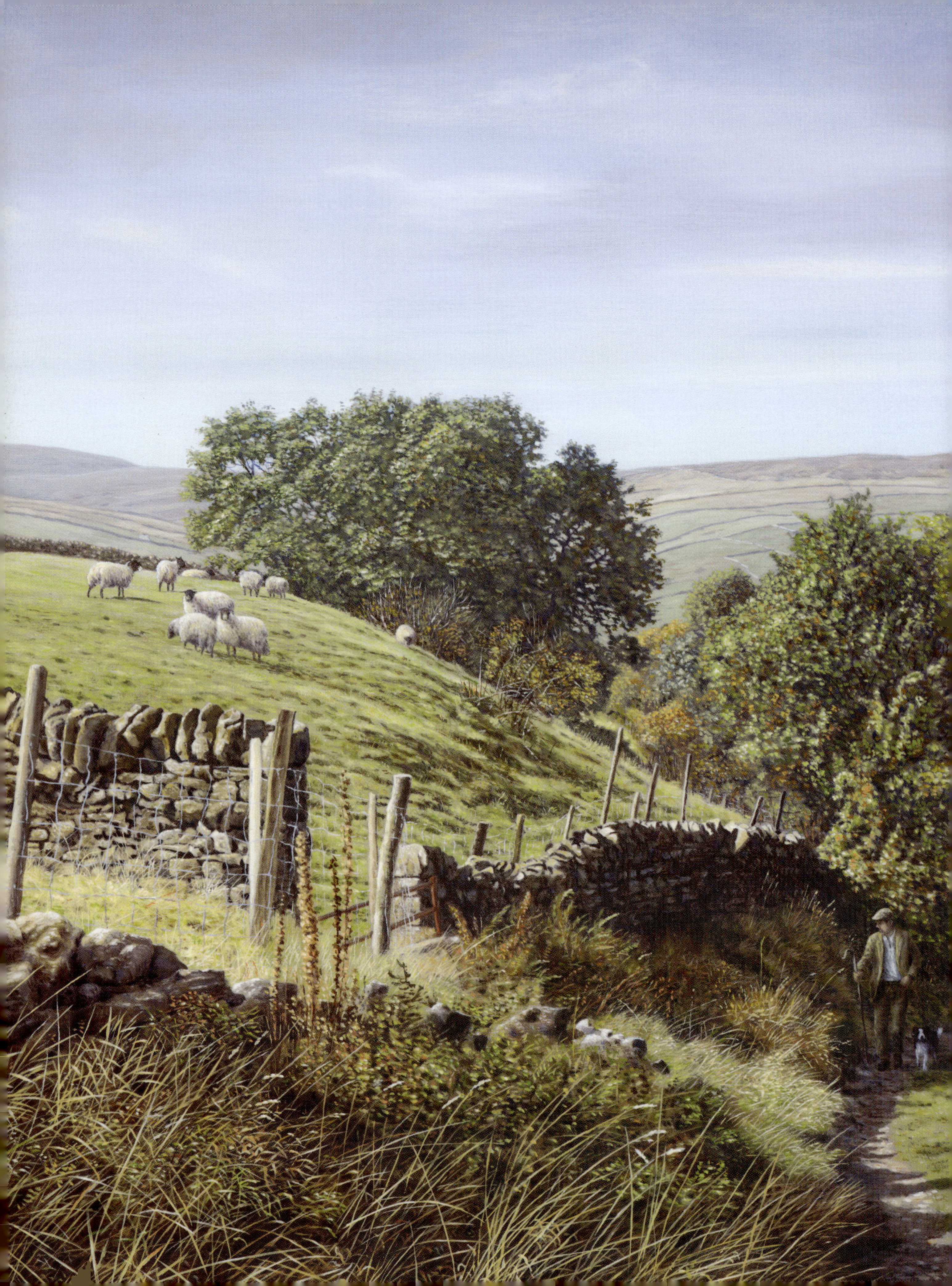

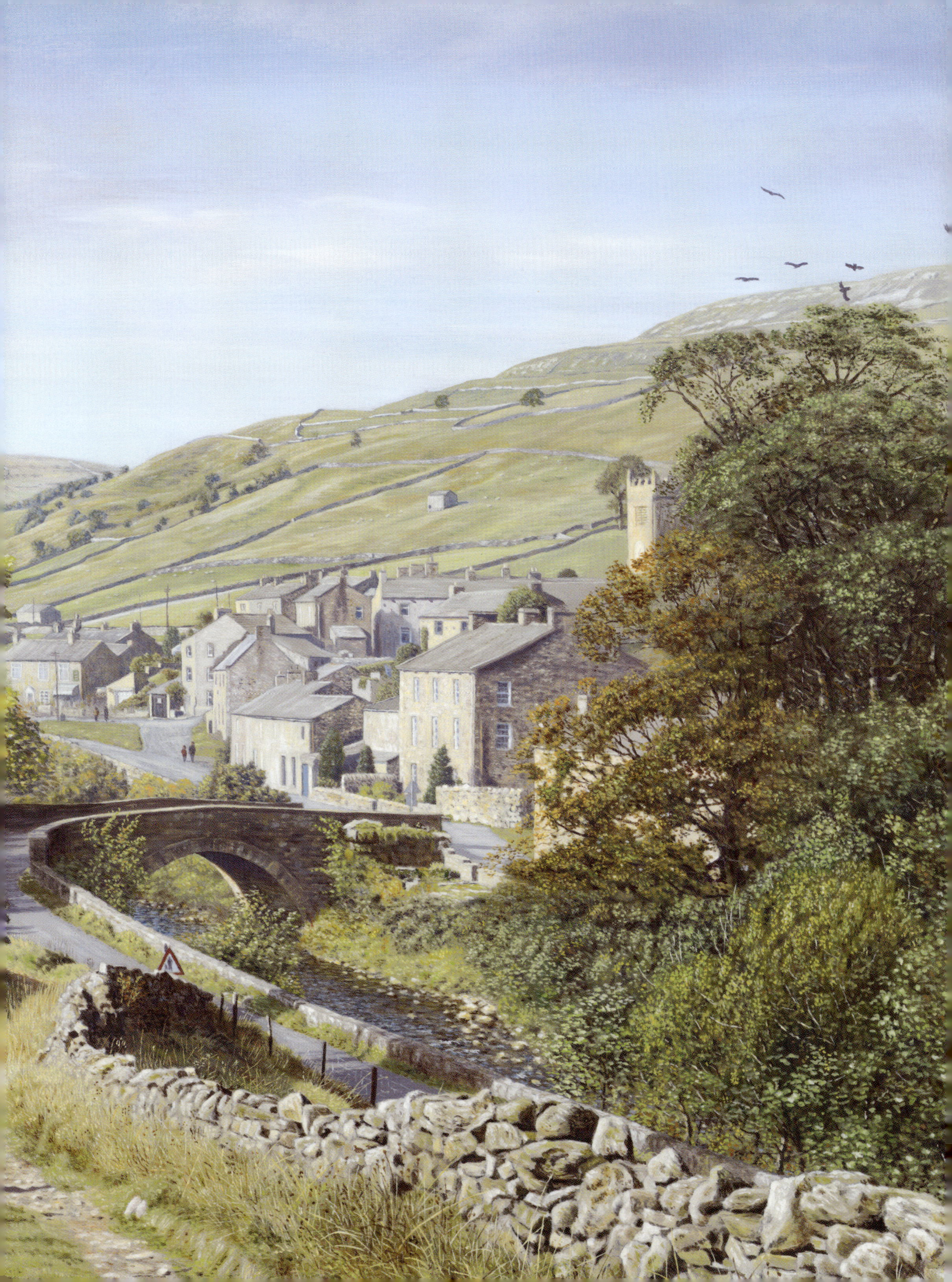

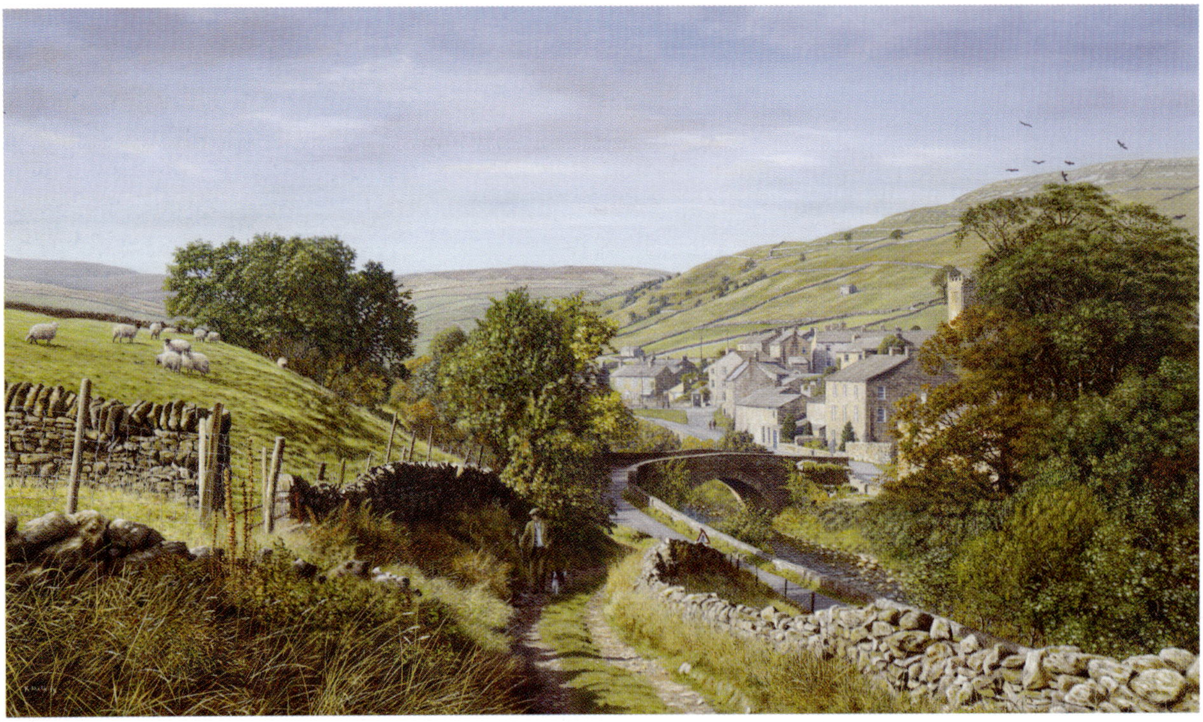

Up to the Fells, Muker

1995 Oil 14 x 24in

Content at the foot of Kisdon Hill near the confluence of Straw Beck and the fast flowing Swale, Muker is a delightful village with a hint of independence and self-sufficiency. Once here, I found a viewpoint very quickly and thought it perfect. I just sat on the wall transfixed by the scene before me, drawing in my mind's eye, going around the shapes and forms in a linear way, taking an imaginary line for a walk. The various parts and details seemed to combine together unbelievably well; this was a subject crying out to be painted. It's not the details however which are important in a painting, but the overall composition, and I puzzled over this for some time. In fact a couple of hikers who had passed me earlier, came down the track after their walk and were a little concerned that I was still in the same spot.

This picture was a first for me in that it was painted entirely with oil paint made by myself. Why bother to make paint when good paint is available commercially? Well, making paint as the old masters used to do, gives a better understanding of the medium you are working with, and besides, it's possible to produce paint with a richer pigment content and know that it contains no extenders or binders. This, and the way I prepare a surface for painting, which is a repetitious process of coating, scraping and sanding, may be time consuming but is well worth the effort. I can't imagine, though, that this procedure will catch on and become popular.

The trees are beginning to change to their autumnal attire, which always helps to break the monopoly of green. Rooks and jackdaws are very common birds in the Dales and can nearly always be heard or seen. Including a few here adds a bit of interest and draws the eye to the soaring Kisdon Hill. It seemed only right also to include Swaledale sheep in a picture of the dale they were named after.

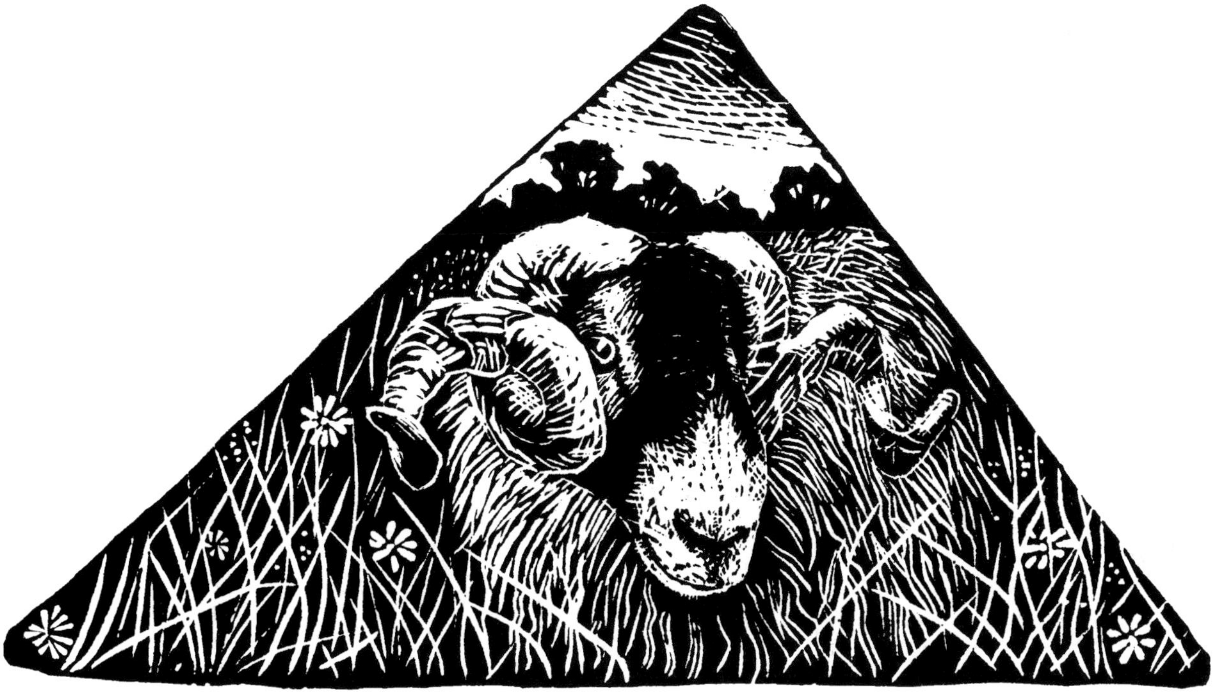

A Swaledale Tup
1994 Wood engraving 3 x 5.5in

This hardy breed of sheep is a familiar sight in the Yorkshire Dales and may well be seen in many other regions. Especially suited to exposed situations on the high fells, the ewes are excellent lamb rearers, proving to be good mothers even in the most atrocious conditions. The breed originated around the Tan Hill area from the same genetic group that also produced the Blackface and Rough Fell. 'Tup' is a local word for 'ram'.

This little wood engraving, one of my first efforts in this craft, was engraved on a lemon-wood off-cut which explains the odd triangular shape. Off-cuts were sold as practice pieces by most printmaking suppliers.

If you watch Emmerdale on TV you may see a framed copy in the Woolpack, its shape makes it easy to spot.

Swaledale from above Crackpot

1996. Oil 15.5 x 24in

An alternative title for this painting might have been the clichéd 'September Sunlight' or perhaps 'Location Location Location' — for what property could have a better one. Birks End farmhouse, which has braved much extreme weather over many severe winters, is more than compensated when it enjoys such days as these. The valley holds the light as if in a bowl and rolls it slowly around its steep sides. To the landscape painter, a sky with a smattering of clouds is more appealing than one that is completely cloudless; the scudding patches of shadow caress the fells and give them shape and form.

The viewpoint here is beside the narrow High Lane above Crackpot, looking updale towards Gunnerside and Black Hill. Rowleth Wood, which rises steeply from the river, displays an incredible range of wildflowers in the spring and is a great haven for wildlife.

Normally I paint on a neutral grey-brown ground, but occasionally, as for this picture I use a bright white as the Pre-Raphaelites did to retain the luminosity and freshness of nature.

After completing this picture I noticed that by pure chance I had painted what appeared to be a man's head in the wall (just left of the tree). Of course with a little imagination it's possible to see faces in all sorts of things, we seem to be programmed to recognise them. Nevertheless, this kind of phenomenon can be frustrating for the artist (unless you're Salvador Dali) — how to prevent weird woolly creatures from forming in the clouds and suchlike.

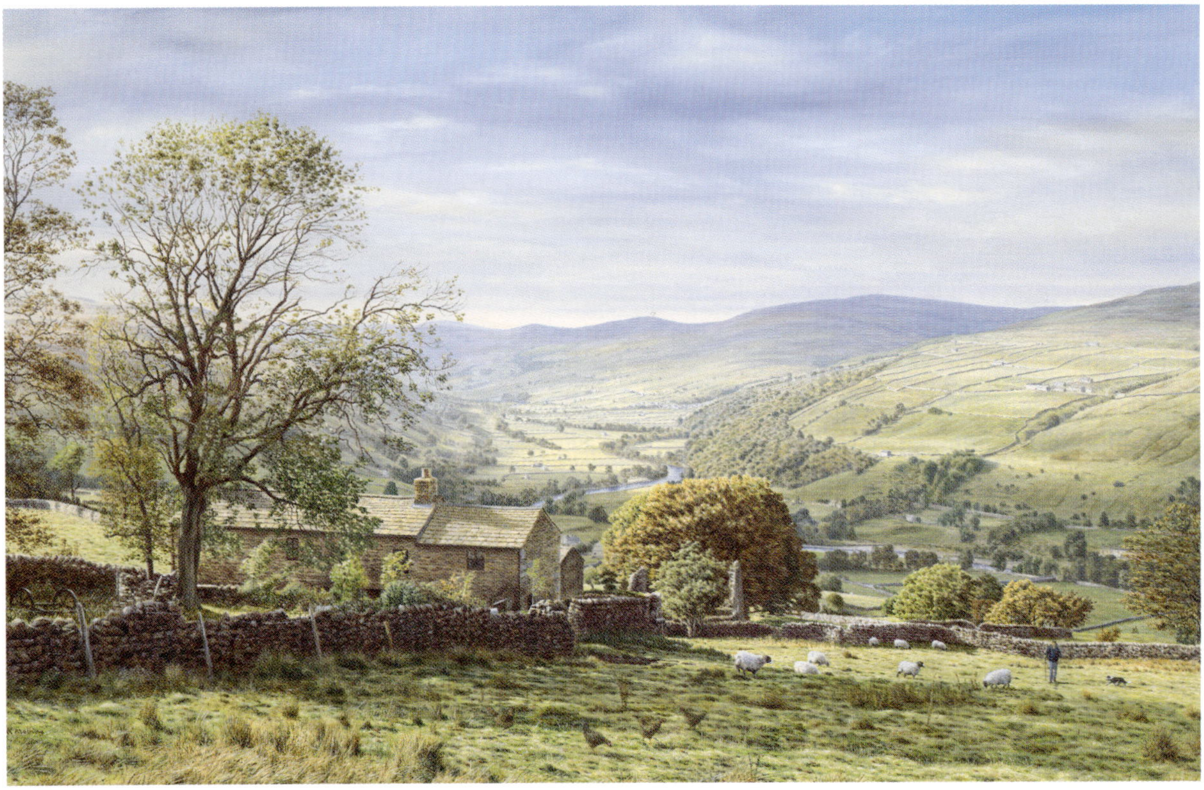

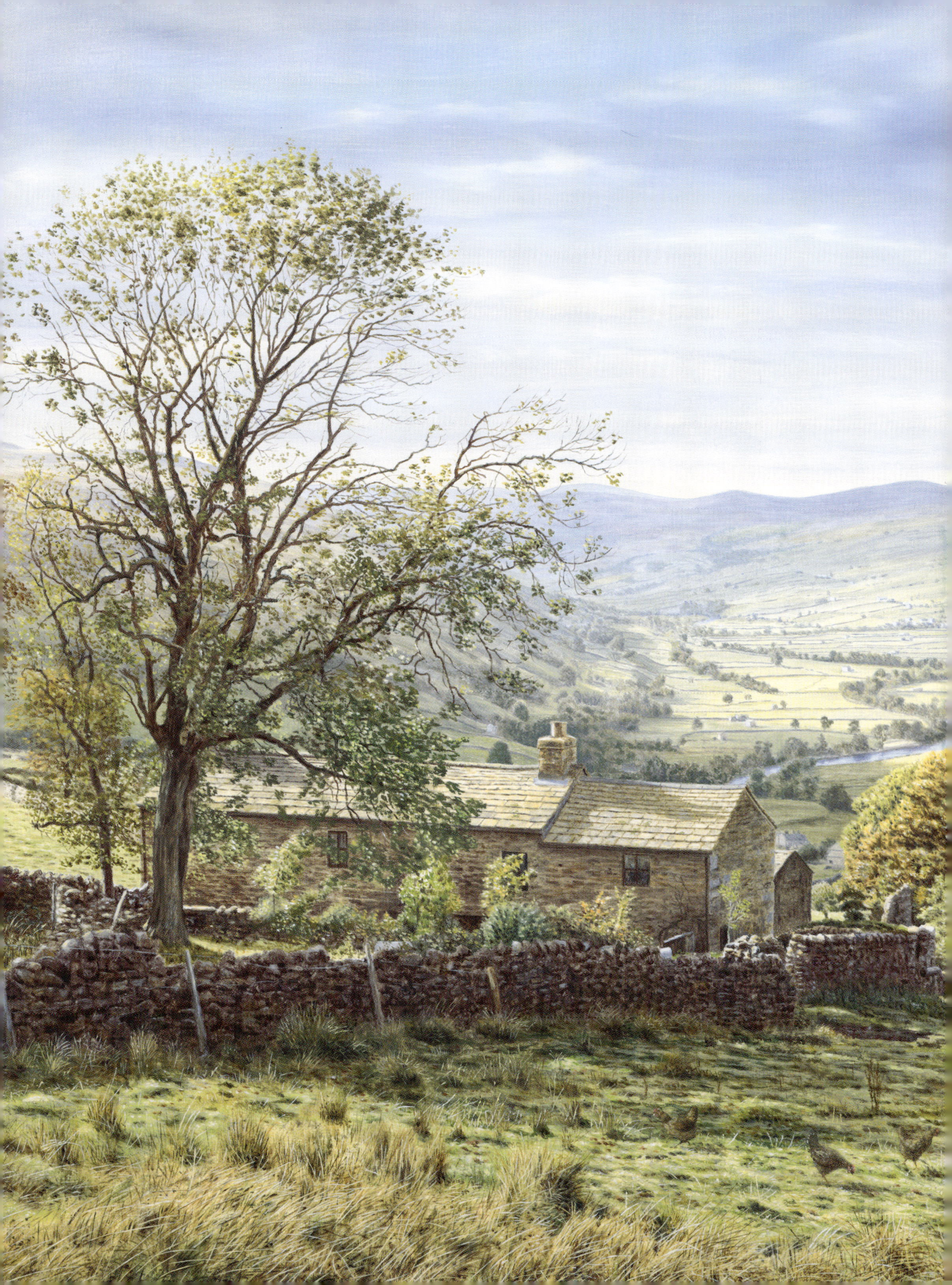

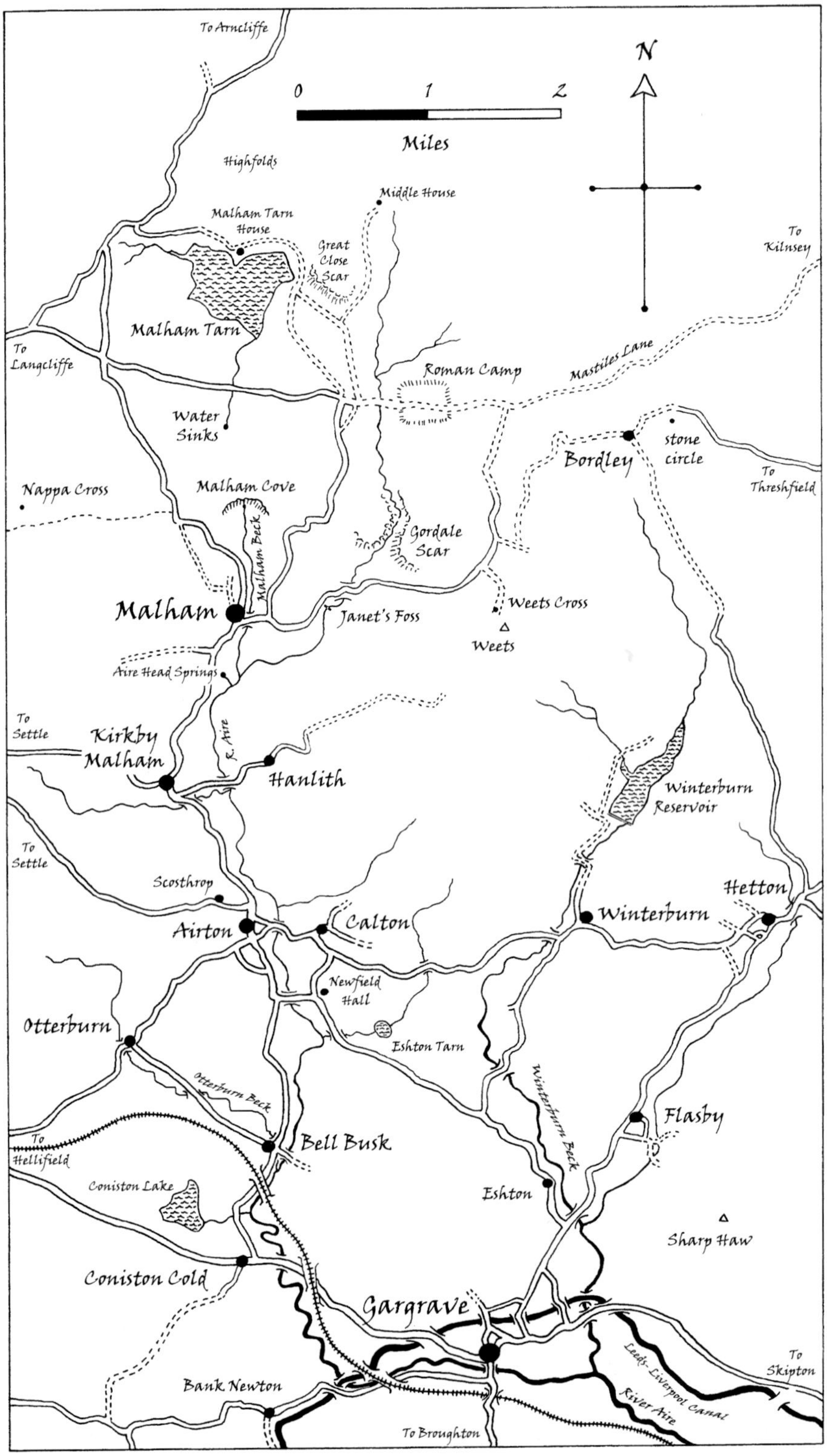
To Arncliffe
0
1
2
Miles
N
Highfolds
Middle House
Malham Tarn House
Great Close Scar
To Kilnsey
Malham Tarn
To Langcliffe
Mastiles Lane
Roman Camp
Water Sinks
Bordley
stone circle
To Threshfield
Nappa Cross
Malham Cove
Malham Beck
Gordale Scar
Malham
Janet's Foss
Weets Cross
Weets
Aire Head Springs
To Settle
Kirkby Malham
R. Aire
Hanlith
Winterburn Reservoir
To Settle
Scosthrop
Hetton
Airton
Calton
Winterburn
Newfield Hall
Otterburn
Eshton Tarn
Winterburn Beck
Otterburn Beck
Flasby
To Hellifield
Bell Busk
Coniston Lake
Eshton
Sharp Haw
Coniston Cold
Gargrave
To Skipton
Leeds-Liverpool Canal
River Aire
Bank Newton
To Broughton

Malhamdale

Malhamdale

The most spectacular and best-known limestone scenery in Yorkshire, and therefore possibly in the whole of England, lies at the head of this lovely green valley. Watered by the Aire, Malhamdale is really the upper section of Airedale, stretching barely 7 short miles from Malham to Gargrave.

A short distance from the village of Malham, the immense naked cliff of the Cove and the deep towering gash of Gordale Scar compete for wows. Malham Cove is a colossal concave crag whose broad face glows white in the sun; perceptible from Lancashire 10 miles away, its apparent visibility has even helped to sell houses there. In contrast, Gordale Scar keeps its gnarled face well hidden and despises its neighbour's flagrant forwardness. On turning the last corner of Gordale Beck, early tourists supposedly shuddered at the sight that confronted them. Lofty vice-like jaws of overhanging rock, rising giddily to the clouds, engulf daylight and all else that dare enter. A Roaring waterfall set like a sparkling jewel in a shadowy crown, somersaults clumsily down from a natural eyehole of rock far above. If you were here alone you would think it eerie and grotesque. But you are not likely to be alone. The famous features of Gordale Scar and Malham Cove have been responsible for making Malham at times rather busy; yet who could resist such awesome wonders? People have been sightseeing here for centuries. The writers — Thomas Gray, Wordsworth, Ruskin and Charles Kingsley were inspired here. The artists — James Ward, Turner, John Piper and a multitude of other painters have given us their visual interpretations, all so different. This is an artist's paradise, although, according to Alfred J. Brown — all have failed. He thought this place impossible to describe either in words or pictures, it needed to be seen and experienced. The majority of visitors come to do just that, usually combining their visit with some kind of walk, be it either a gentle stroll or a more arduous hike around the fell tops, for this is exquisite rambling country.

Near the dalehead quite unexpectedly rests another strange phenomenon — Malham Tarn. Lakes are a rarity in limestone areas because of the permeability of the underlying rock, but this glacial sheet of water lying 1229 ft above sea level sits on a bed of older slate. The elegant Malham Tarn House, extended from a former shooting lodge, is seemingly out of place here and is now a field study centre. The Tarn, managed by the National Trust is a wildlife conservation area, habitat for a variety of waterfowl and fish. There is an excellent bird hide placed unobtrusively near the waters edge. Whilst sheltering there once, I spotted a kingfisher perched in classic pose on a nearby overhanging branch. Of course I thought sketching it pointless, as it would surely fly away any second, so I grappled with trying to draw the grebes and coots. The grebes kept on diving and the coots swam around too much, but for a good ten minutes the kingfisher sat motionless, the perfect model. Immediately I started to sketch it, the blighter flew off — Shucks!

Various old track-ways criss-cross the surrounding hillsides, including the magnificent Mastiles Lane to Kilnsey, the mysterious Monk's Road to Littondale and the rugged Stockdale Lane to Settle. Along these splendid routes the medieval monks placed their monastic crosses as way markers, few of which survive complete. Probably the best example is sighted on the track near Weets Top summit, this has base and shaft intact.

Other cross bases have been built into the later drystone walls.

The area is steeped in ancient history: stone circles and field systems from Bronze and Iron Age are in evidence on the surrounding hillsides. The neat rectangular lines of a Roman marching camp evokes wonderment as we imagine those soldiers from afar camped here in their heavy hide tents, keeping watch for the resisting Brigantes. Remains of medieval sheep enclosures exist in profusion, many taking advantage of the limestone scars. I came across a curious wall at Back Pasture, where large upright slabs had been built up further by a single thickness of smaller stones.

Of the dale's villages, Malham is the most visited and although touristy, still retains much character and olde-worlde charm, with babbling brook, bonny bridges and sloping green at its heart. A sprinkling of good pubs and cafes cater for the hungry and thirsty and the obligatory outdoor and gift shop for those with a bit o' spare brass. An excellent National Park Centre is usefully situated near the car park.

Gordale Beck, after leaving the Scar tumbles gracefully over the pretty waterfall of Janet's Foss to meet Malham Beck south of the village. Water from the tarn which disappeared underground two miles away at Water Sinks emerges near here at Aire Head Springs to also join the flow. From now on the river is called the 'Aire'. A canal-like structure diverts water from the river near here to Scalegill, which has been the site of a mill since the 11th century.

Kirkby Malham is the next village downstream, and as the name implies (Church-by-Malham), a rather imposing church is sited here. In fact like Grinton church in Swaledale, the somewhat grandiose title 'Cathedral of the Dales' is claimed. Both interior and exterior hold some fascinating details, but the mysterious Celtic stone heads carved on the external walls are my favourite.

Across the Aire, the tiny hamlet of Hanlith clings stoically to the lower slopes of Haw Hill. A pleasant mile to Airton is marked by an abundance of mature trees that grace the flatter pasturelands with spreading canopies of shady leaves. The river, which left its youthful mischievousness behind at Malham, winds peacefully southwards to Airton bridge, where, it was made to grow up quickly in bygone days by working the waterwheel of a linen mill. The converted mill buildings are now comfortable apartments with an enviable position overlooking the Aire. Airton's cottages are gathered loosely around a triangular green, where one abode, known as the squatter's house has actually been built upon it (before the days of planning permission). Not many people notice this as they motor past on their way to Malham.

Beyond Airton the landscape becomes progressively softer, tamer and less shut in by hills; to my mind not true dales country. The river meanders through beautiful countryside near Bell Busk before passing discreetly under the busy A65 at Coniston Cold. At Bank Newton, a tangle of bridges carries road, railway, river and canal over each other — a kind of rural Spaghetti Junction. The Aire continues to Gargrave, onwards towards Skipton and through the Aire Gap where it once served some of Yorkshire's oldest mill towns.

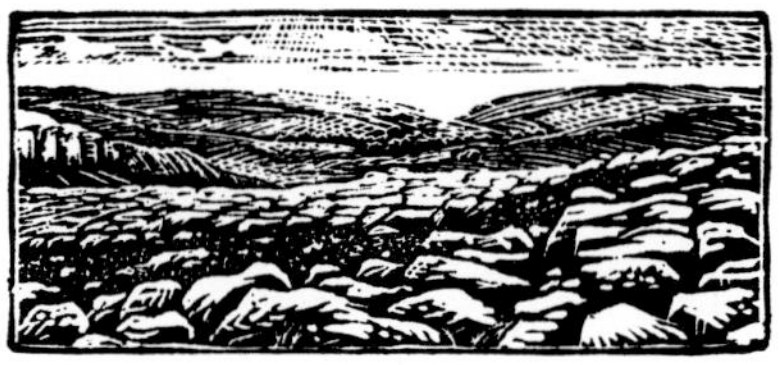

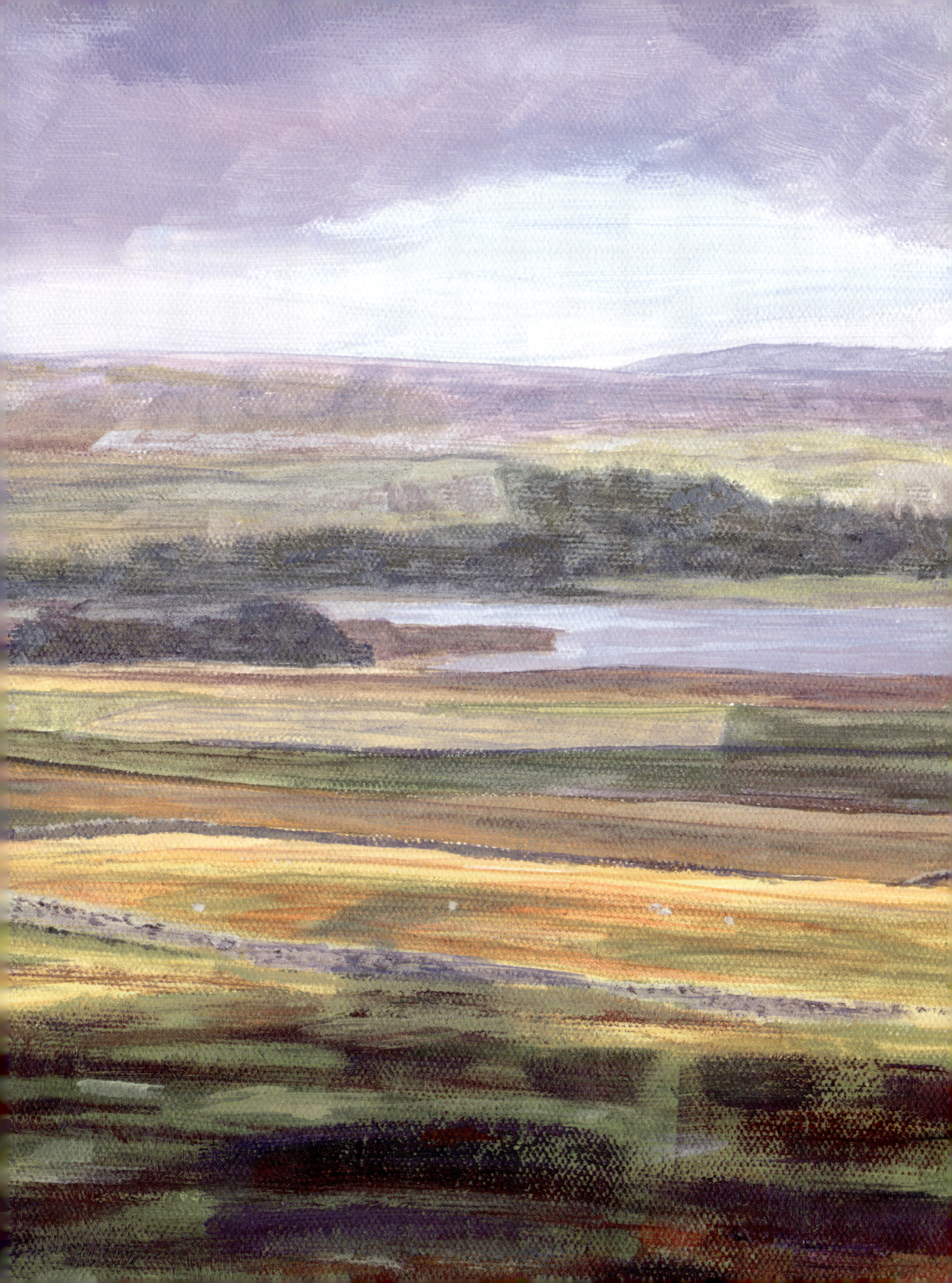

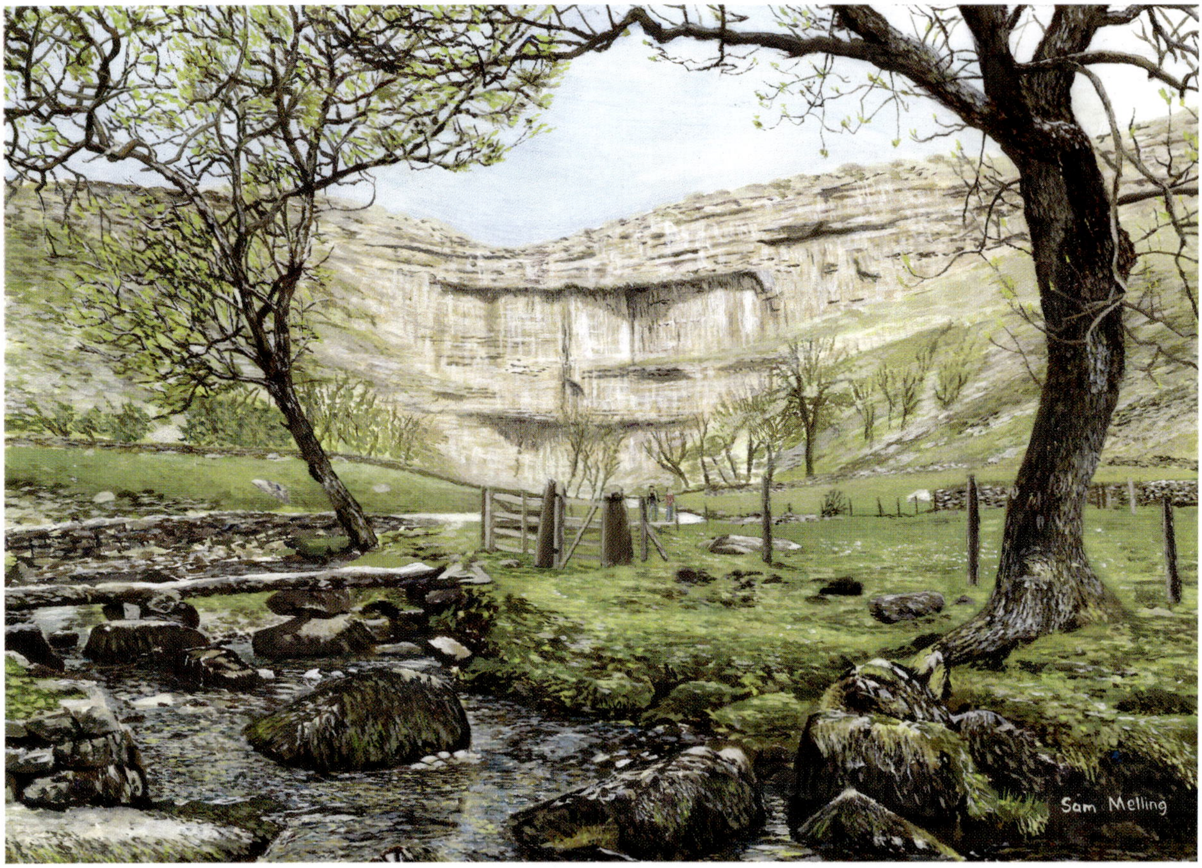

Malham Cove

1998 Acrylic 8 x 10.5in

This picture was painted not by myself but by my son Sam. His style is different from mine, as it is bound to be. Every artist's brush technique is unique, as his or her handwriting is. That is why when we look at the work of other artists; their pictures are often preferable to our own. Our own always appear ordinary. Well of course they will look ordinary, it's because we produced them, just as our own handwriting always seems uninteresting to us. I like the style of this painting; it has certain vigour in the brushstrokes and yet is still quite detailed, describing the approach to the Cove very well.

Malham Beck, which oozes from a narrow slit at the base of the Cove, was once thought to have its beginnings at the tarn above. Indeed you can understand the logic. A stream flows from the tarn in the direction of the Cove, subsequently disappearing underground in a nondescript area of stony ground known as Watersinks. The resurgence is not at the base of the 300-ft cliff as expected, but amazingly south of Malham at Aire Head Springs. The water issuing directly from beneath the Cove is that of a stream which vanished on moorland near the smelt mill chimney about a mile away. There's nowt as queer as limestone.

Malham Tarn from Nappa Cross

Triptych 2006, Acrylic, each 10x10in

I've visited the shore of this tarn many times with the idea in mind (perhaps corny) of catching a blazing sunset reflected in mirror still waters. It must happen sometime, but so far, all I've witnessed is — waves choppy enough to rock the Titanic and angry clouds doing their utmost to completely obliterate all sunlight. Sometimes I think a better idea is to just let subjects suggest themselves naturally rather than having a preconceived notion of them. This composition was one I chanced upon whilst walking from Settle along Stockdale Lane to see Nappa Cross. I was pleasantly struck by the sudden vista that opened out over the brow of Grizedales. Malham Tarn is seen map-like in its entirety, nestling in a slight hollow with the limestone crags of Highfolds and Great Close Scar clearly visible.

The panorama was painted across three square canvases in a fairly broad swift style. Why three canvases you might ask, is there a special reason? Yes because I had a box full of them and they needed to be used.

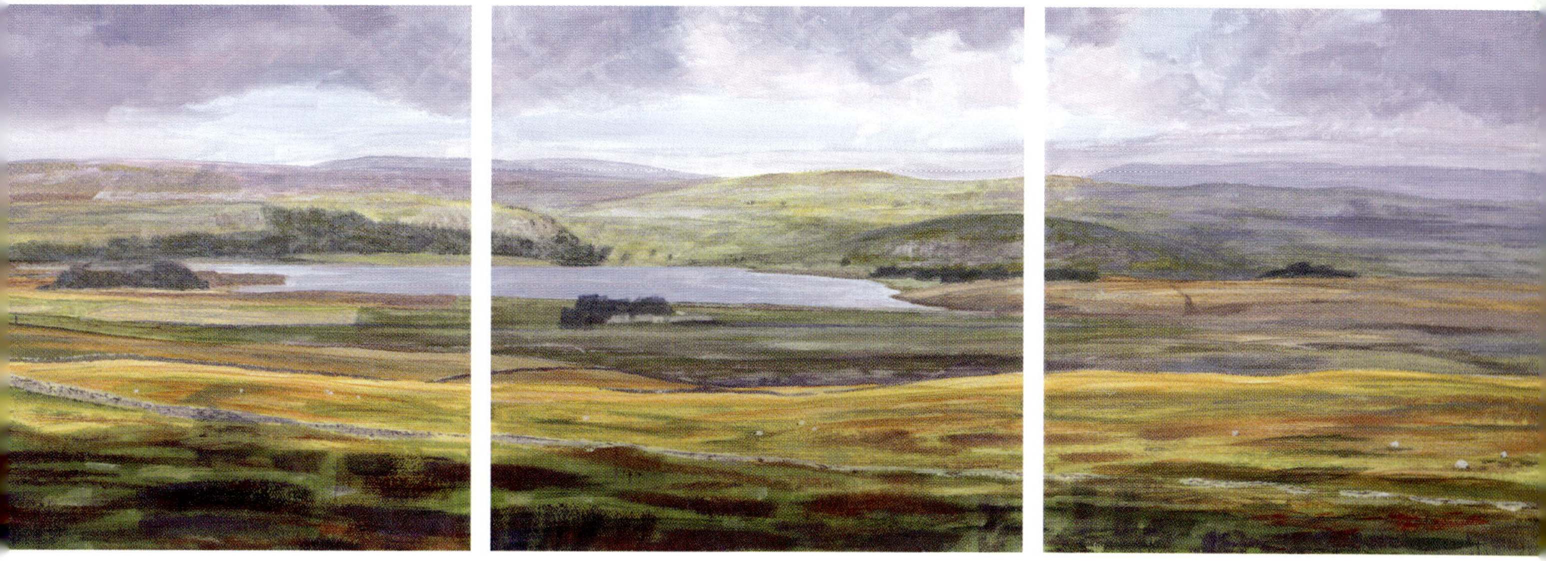

PS. After persisting in my quest, I eventually did experience a sunset at Malham Tarn and very beautiful it was too, see next two pages.

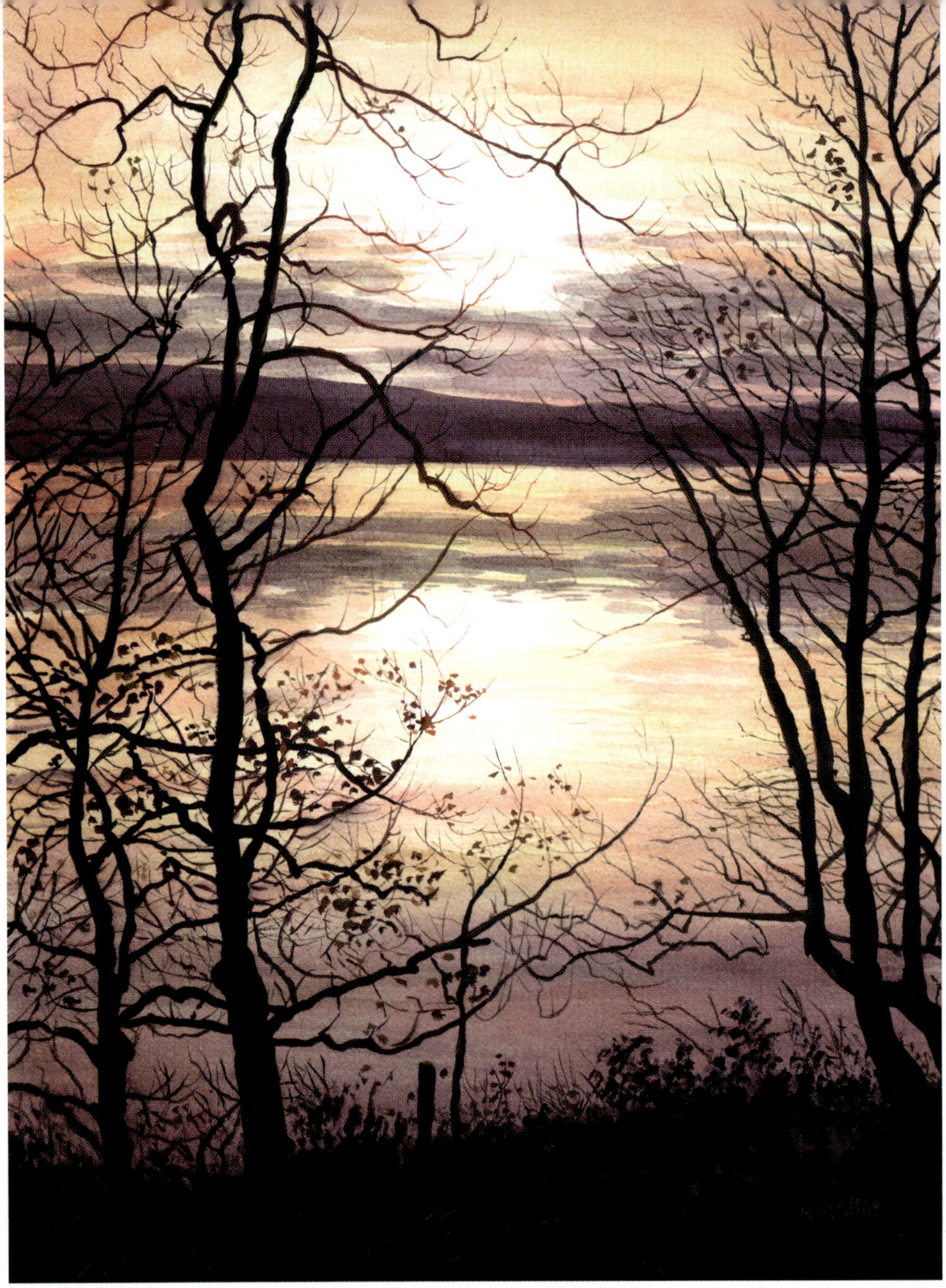

Malham Tarn at Sunset

2007 Watercolour 16 x 11.8in

After many visits in search of that elusive Malham Tarn sunset, I finally struck lucky. One still evening when hardly a ripple disturbed the lake's mirror surface, the sun obliged in displaying his finest headdress like a Red-Indian chief. Feather-rays of crimson, yellow and the brightest molten white combined to suffuse all heaven with a luxurious golden glow. The delicate tracery of tree branches and twigs at the waters edge were thrown into stark silhouette and perfectly accentuated the intensity of light.

Of course these lighting effects are very fleeting and in a matter of minutes the show would be over. So, quickly taking snapshots and scribbling thumbnail sketches and colour notes, I hoped to swallow enough information to later regurgitate the scene in the studio. The painting process was not an elaborate affair, executed freely with watercolour washes, it was more important to capture the general impression. The trees also were painted directly without any preliminary drawing and the whole was completed in one session.

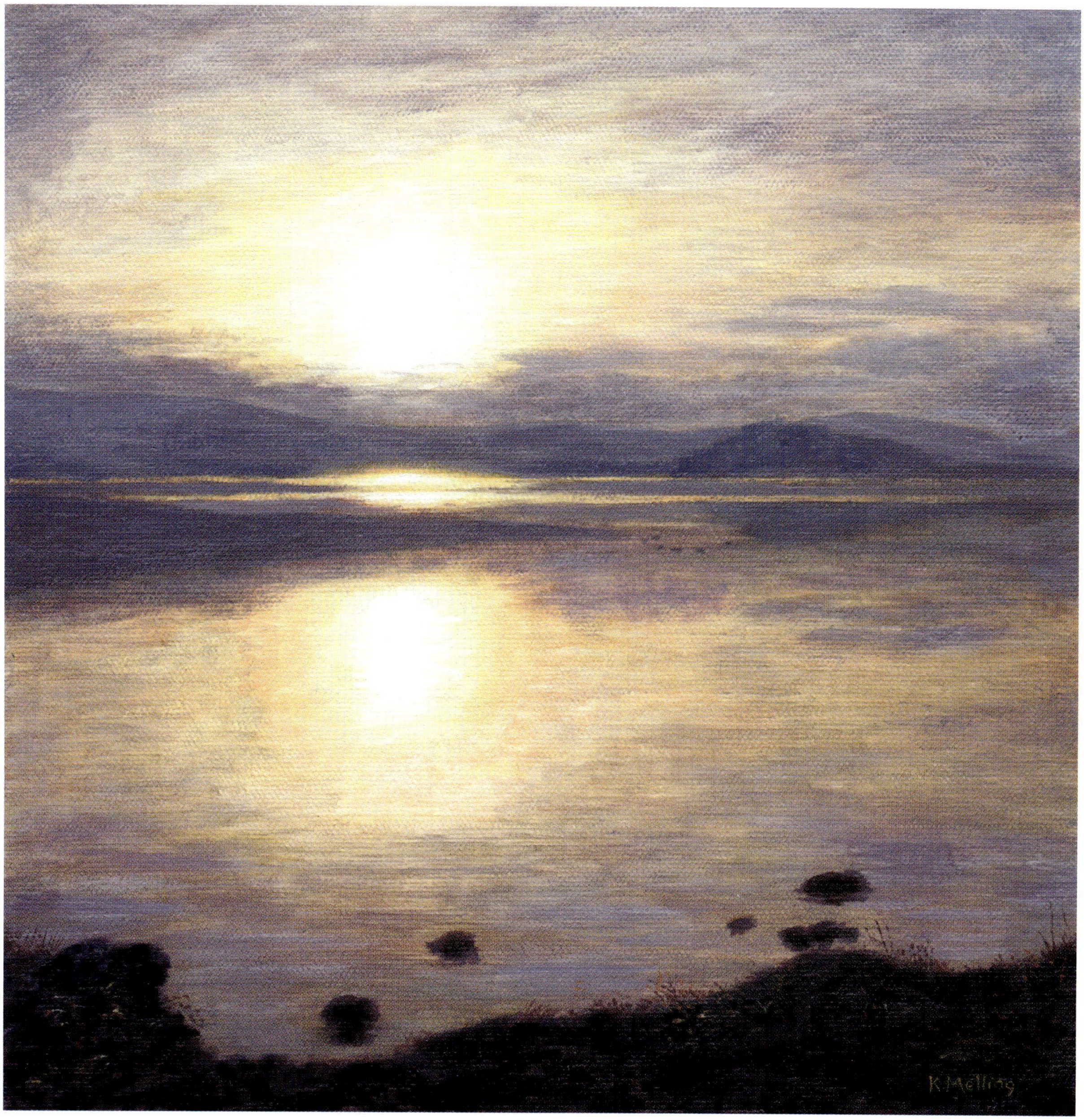

Malham Tarn at Sunset II

2007 Acylic 10 x 10in

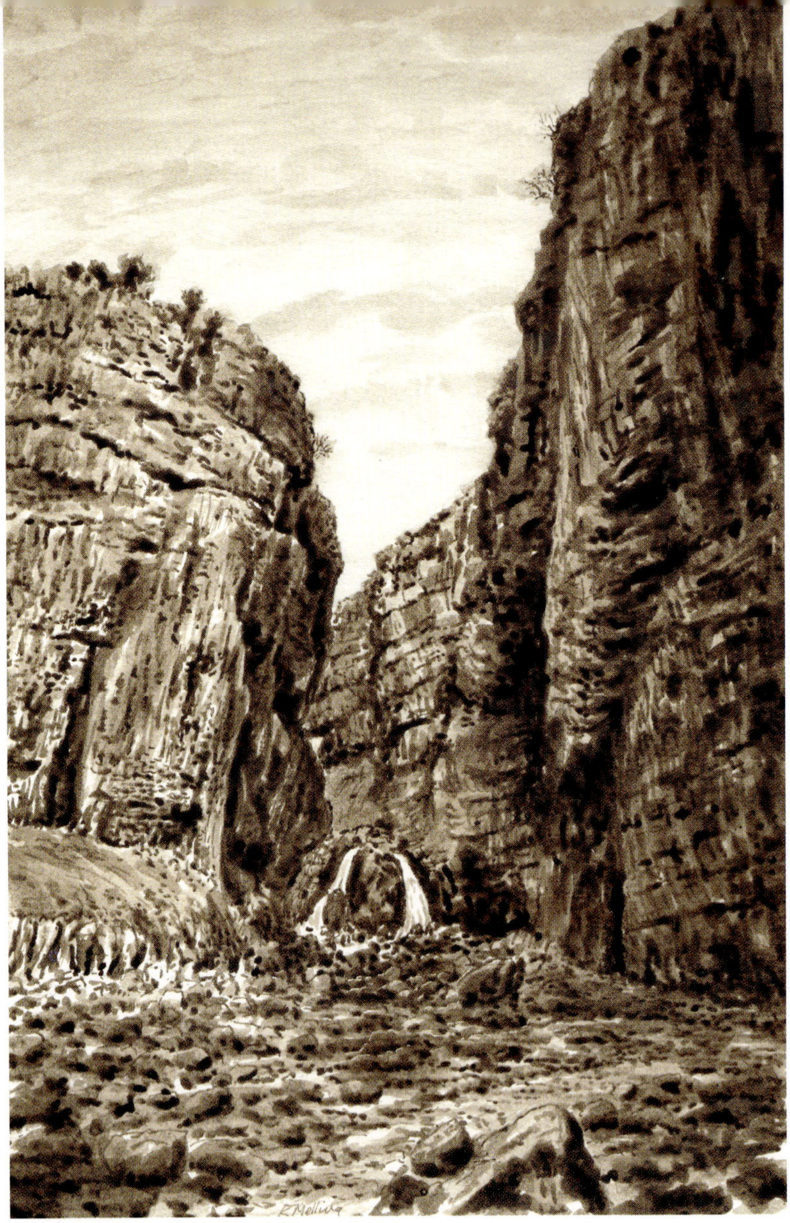

Gordale Scar

2007 French sepia ink 14.5 x 10in

Of the many impressive limestone gorges in the Yorkshire Dales, none can compare to Gordale for sheer scale and grandeur. Thought by some to be a collapsed cave, the huge cavity does have a certain cavernous feel, somewhat gloomy and oppressive yet always awesome. There is the roar of falling water, but this does not dominate and the faintest of sounds are amplified and hurled around the beetling walls in rapid returning echoes. When I was a child my parents used to tell me that this was cowboy country, it was never too difficult to imagine those ricocheting bullets of the 'Spaghetti Westerns' whistling over our heads.

Gordale, whilst being most attractive, has always posed problems for the painter, for it is virtually impossible to capture the scale and spirit of this place from a fixed viewpoint. Maybe a cubist approach would work better. My picture is a straightforward representation, executed fairly quickly with French sepia ink, the monochromatic qualities of which go some way towards portraying the pervading sombreness.

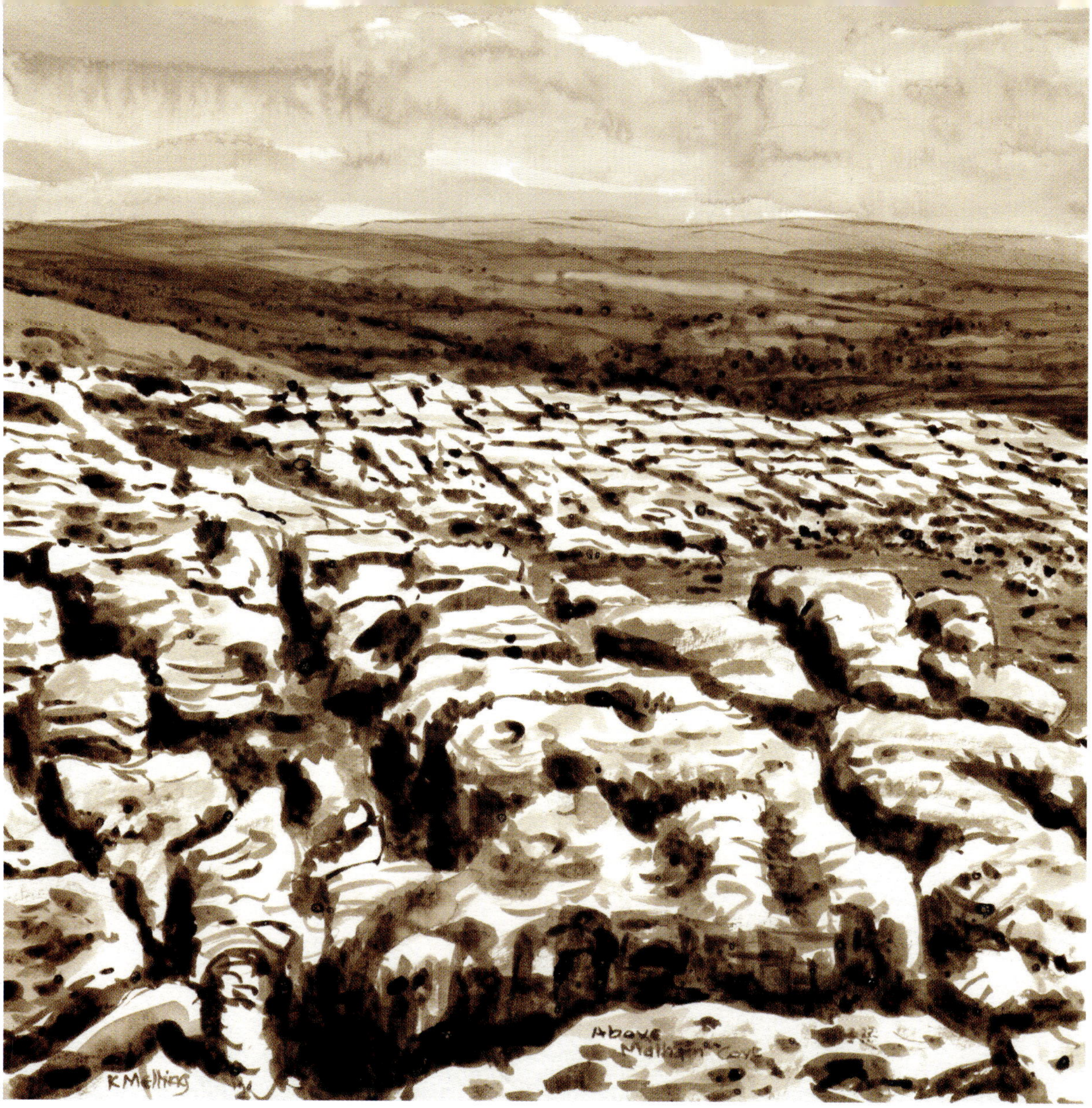

Above Malham Cove

2002 French sepia ink 11.8 x 11.8in

Malham's mighty crescent cliff is a magnificent sight from the valley floor and must have looked stupendous when the now extinct waterfall plunged in a thundering white plume over its broad dazzling face; the sheer drop apparently higher than Niagara. The fascinating limestone pavement directly behind the cove's lip is a wonderland of rounded clints and grykes, where, despite thousands of tramping feet, rare plants still grow.

We gaze out to the vapour laden hills of the southern horizon where the distant darkening Pennines crouch defiantly under threatening skies.

Deliberately emphasising the shadowy background to complement and contrast with the illuminated foreground, the drawing was freely and swiftly made with French sepia ink.

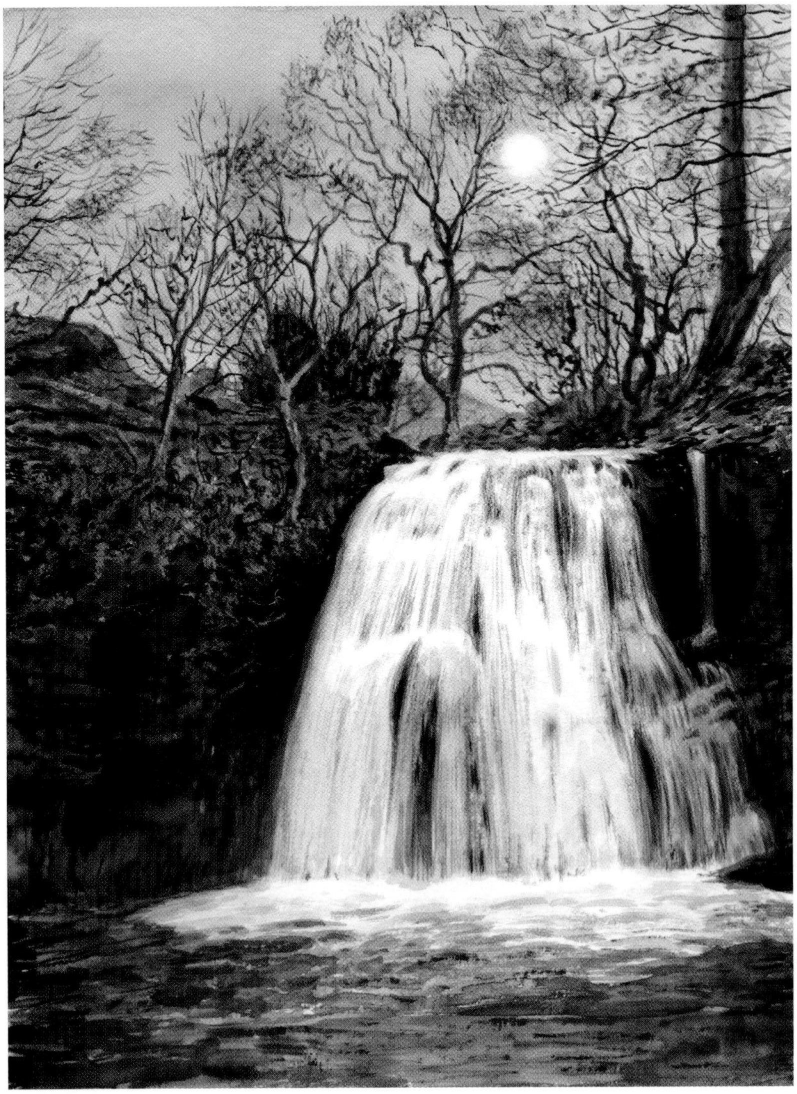

Full Moon Over Janet's Foss

2005 Ink 12 x 9in

This exquisite waterfall, adorning the entrance of an equally enchanting wooded clough on Gordale Beck, simply exudes mystery and romance. 'Foss' is a Nordic word for force and Janet or Jennet was queen of the fairies here. Legend has it that she lived (maybe still does) in a tiny cave on the far bank. When the moon rises and daylight dwindles, the imagination is prone to playing fanciful tricks; all manner of shadowy figures may be momentarily glimpsed. When here just after dusk I couldn't believe that the waterfall was still so bright, as if illuminated by its own inner light, perhaps it was Jennet's doing!

Although this drawing might have the look of an outdoor sketch, it actually isn't. I did a couple of sketches but not successfully and must confess to completing this picture entirely from photographs, which is another way of working. My natural inclination is to disapprove of artists who work wholly in this way, but there are no rules in art.

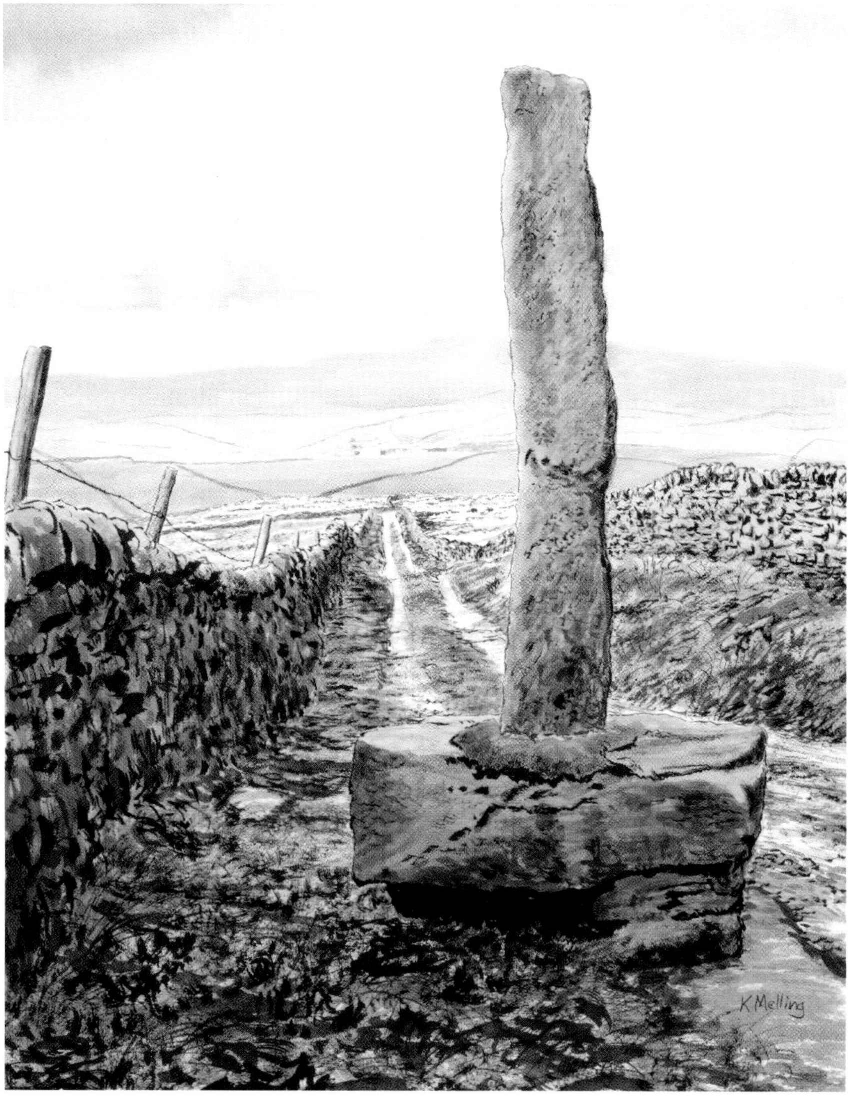

Weets Top Cross
2006 Ink 13 x 11in

This restored wayside cross has a sheltered hidden position, tucked behind the drystone walls near the summit of Weets Top, but it was here long before the walls were built and would have been much more conspicuous from afar.

The rough design is typical of these sturdy crosses, of which this is a fine example. Many were not really in the form of a cross at all, though some were incised with a small cross on the shaft. They were placed strategically beside the old monastic roads as way-markers; some could have been boundary stones. There are several other crosses in the area of Malham Moor, most consisting of only a base stone. Curiously, Nappa Cross above Pikedaw has been rebuilt on top of a wall.

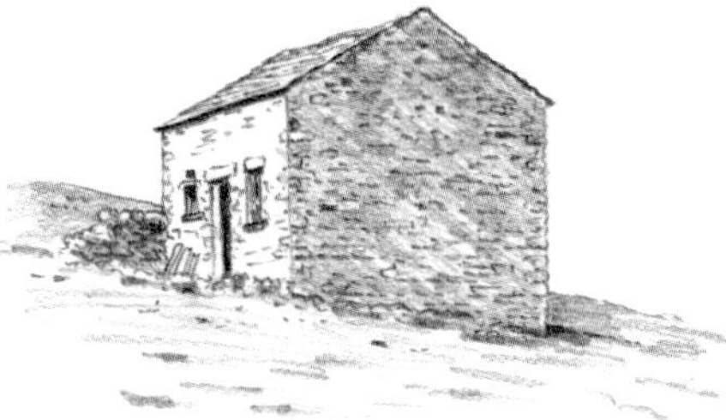

Nidderdale

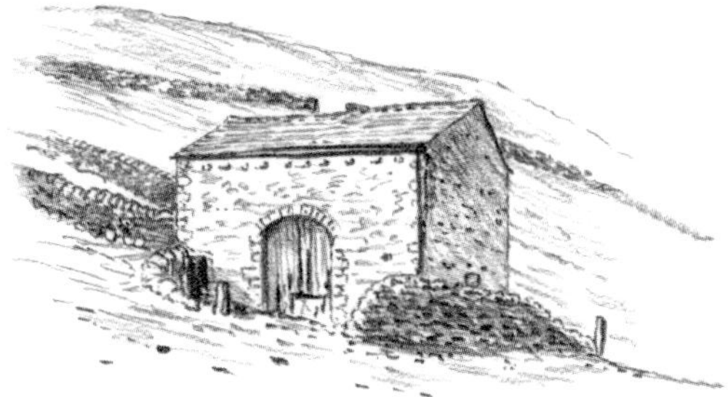

Wharfedale

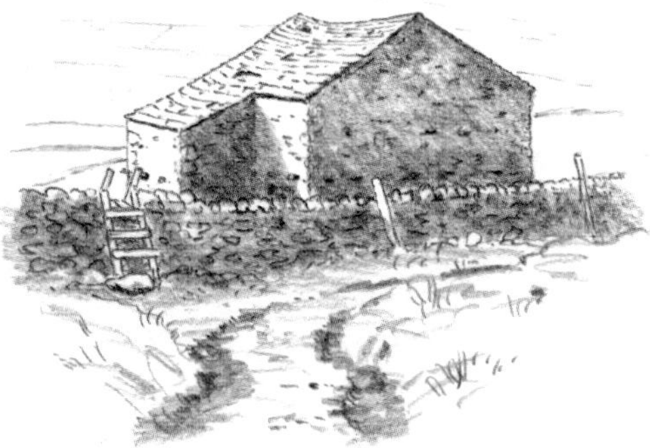

Ribblesdale

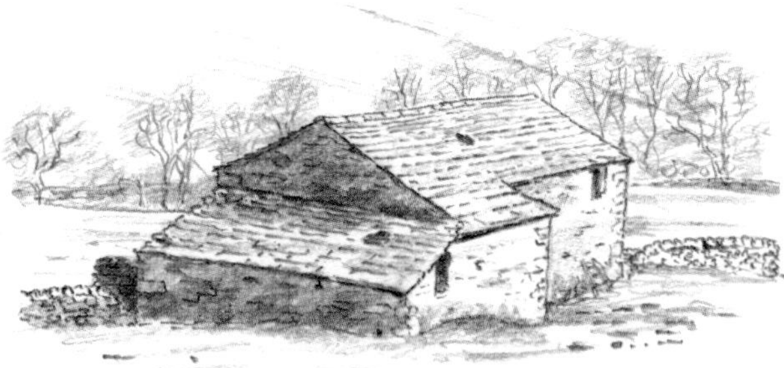

Littondale

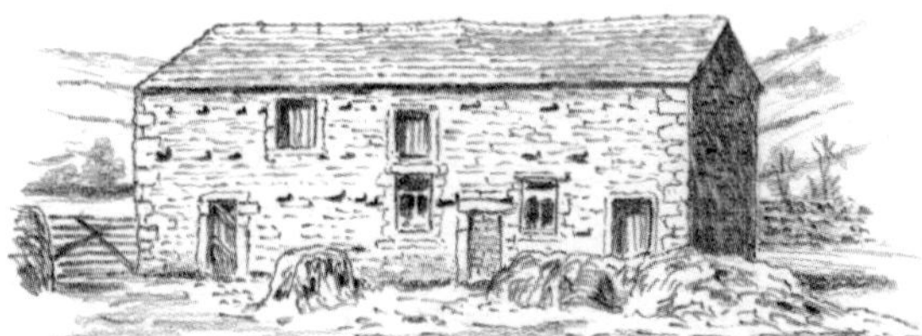

Swaledale

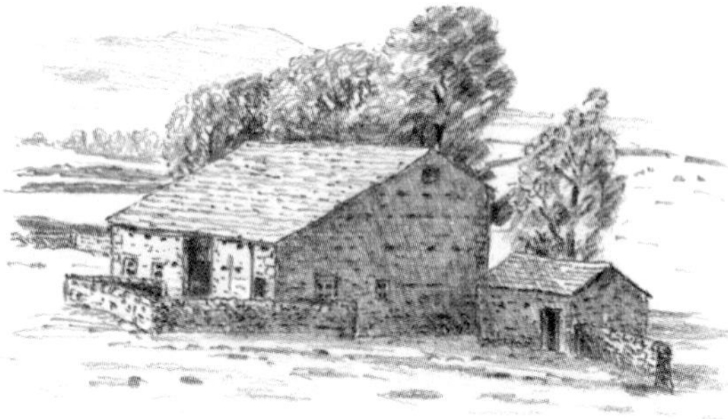

Wensleydale

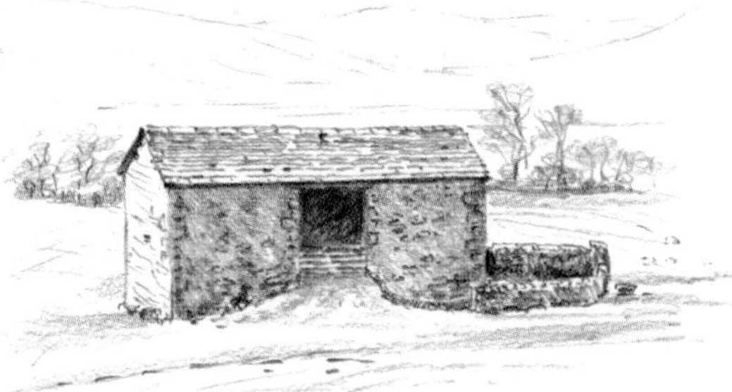

Dentdale

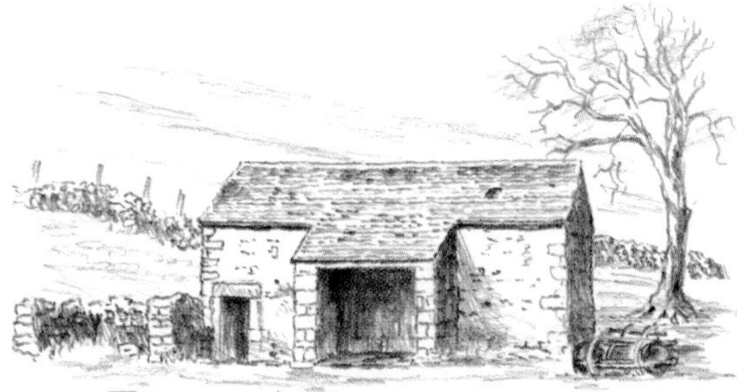

Malhamdale

Dales field barns

2007 Pencil 9 x 7in

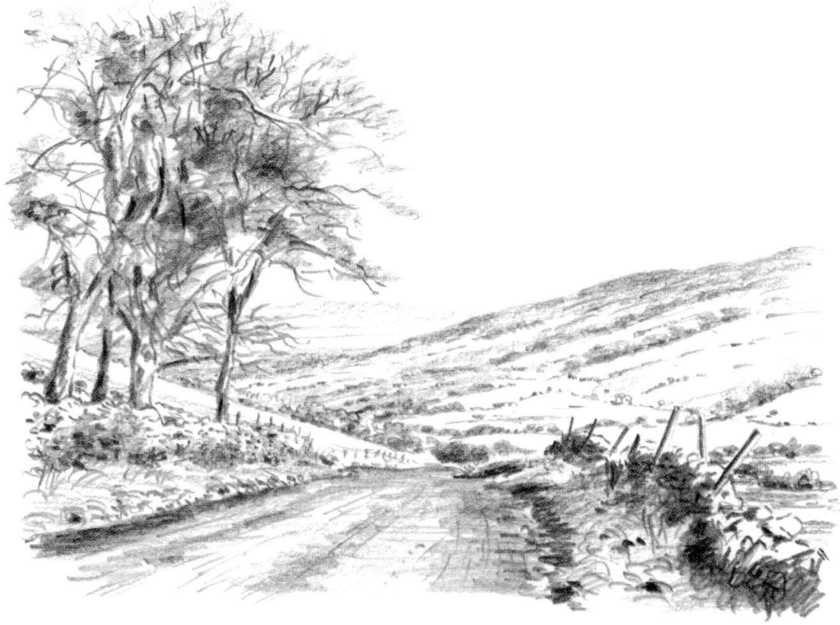

Bishopdale from Kidstones Pass

2007 Pencil 4.5 x 6in

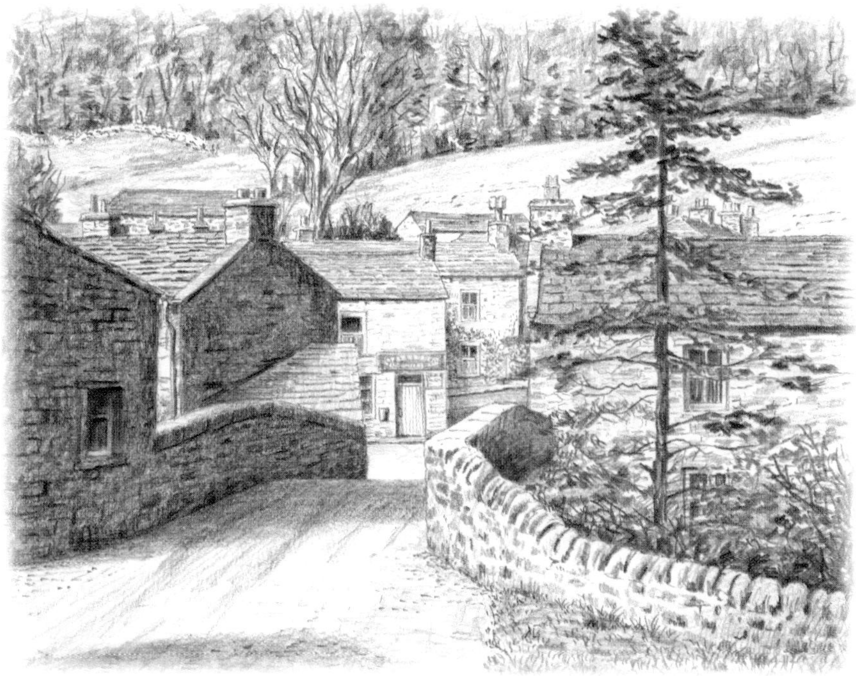

Langthwaite, Arkengarthdale

2007 Pencil 7 x 9in

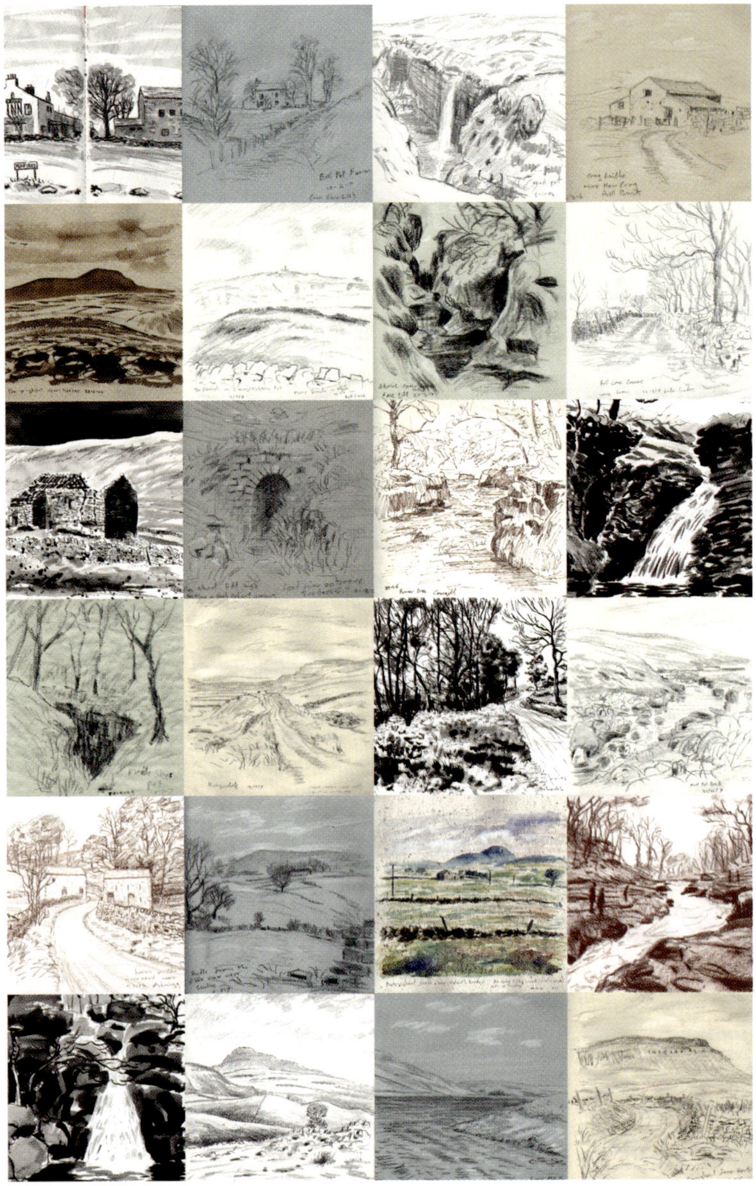

Sketchbook Pages

Various media, majority 9 x 9 in

When out walking and exploring possible subjects for painting, I often make 'lightning sketches', which are rapidly recorded in one of two sketchbooks always carried in my rucksack. Although I've not counted, I must have accumulated hundreds of these sketches. Of course, in practice, not many were made with painting in mind at all, but were done just for their own sake, as a personal reminder of things seen. Working directly from the subject is an enjoyable and valuable activity: the exercise in concentrated observation plus the correspondence between hand and eye, heightens visual awareness and is beneficial for the artist's general skills, not only in the great outdoors but also back in the confines of the studio.

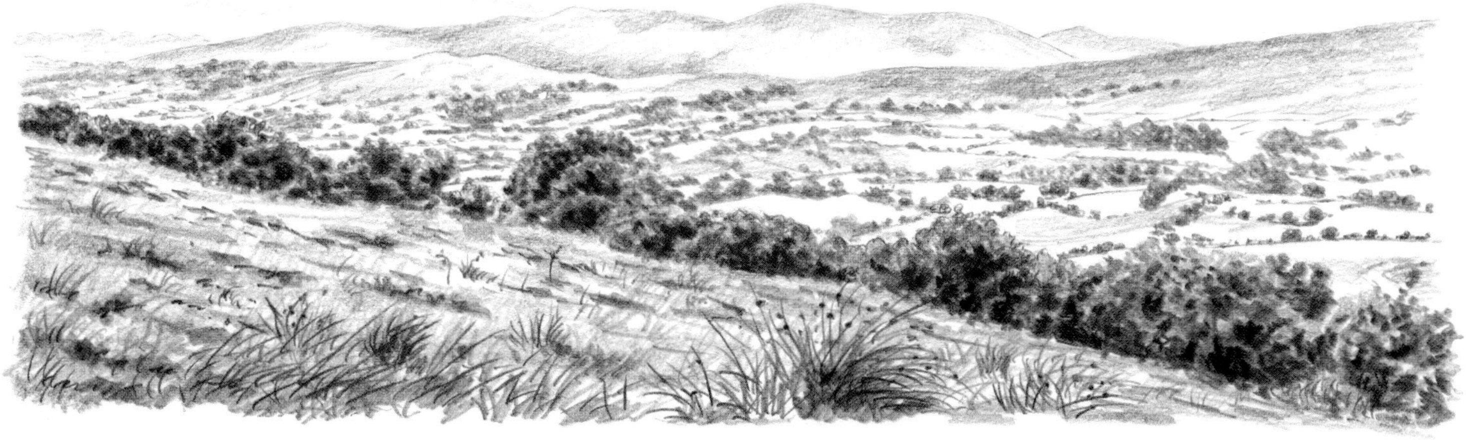

Across Dentdale to the Howgill Fells
2007 Pencil 4.5 x 11in

Although now in Cumbria, Dentdale is still part of the Yorkshire Dales National Park. A peculiarity of the area is that hedgerows rather than drystone walls divide the majority of fields.

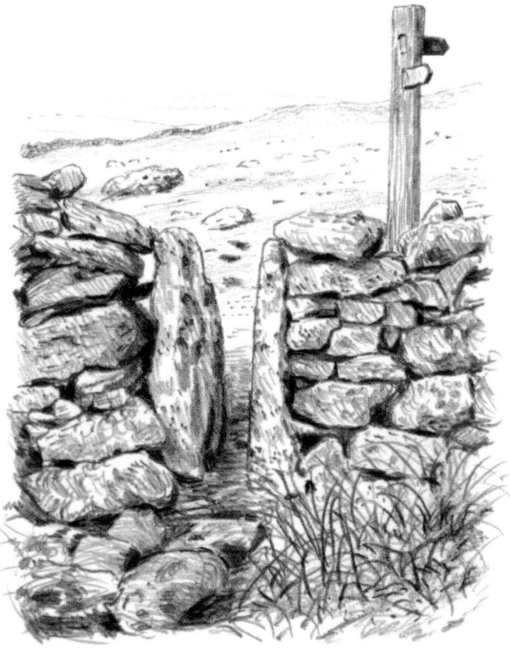

A Dales Stile
2007 Pencil 4 x 3in

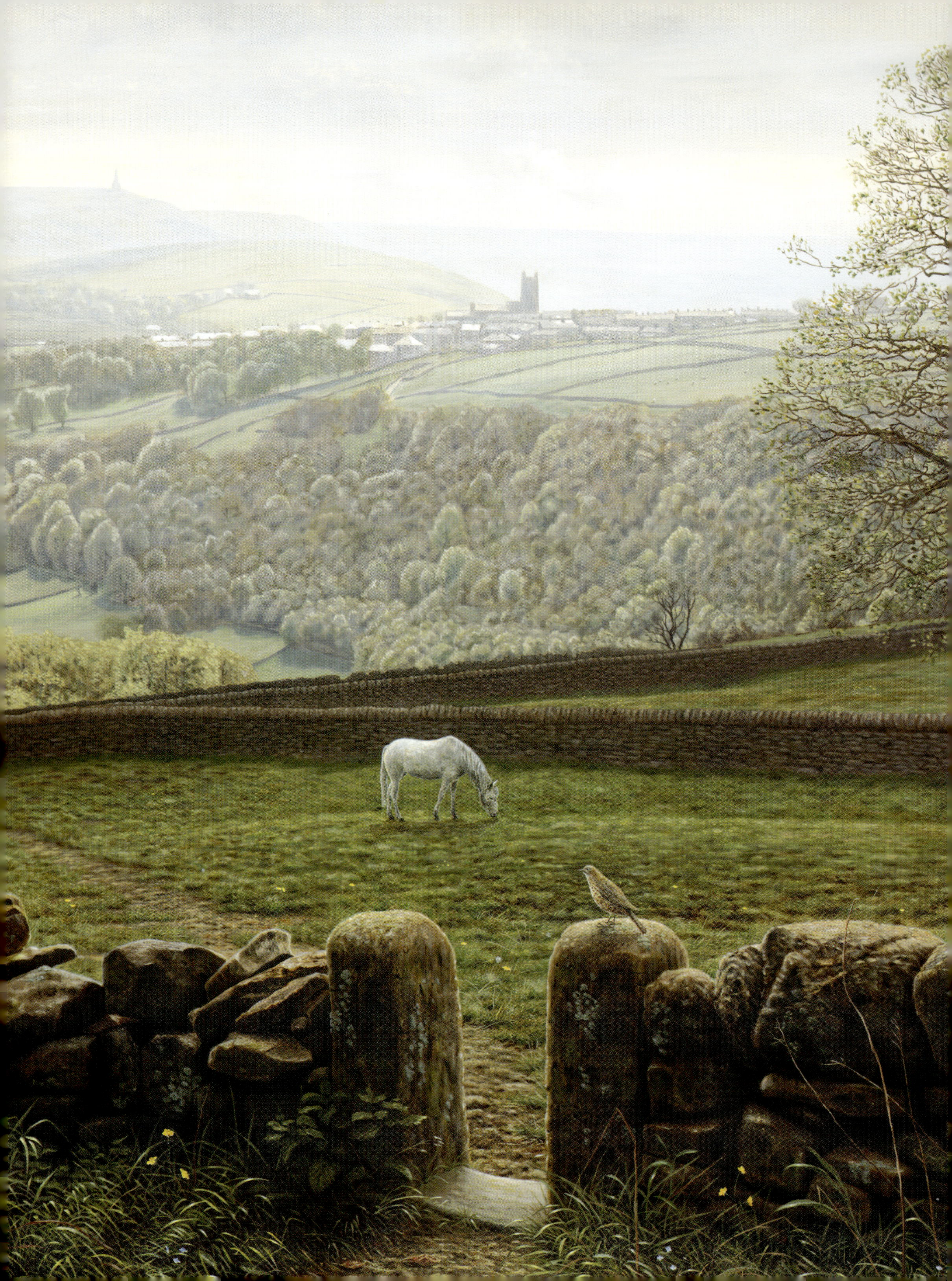

Not the Yorkshire Dales

I wrote in the introduction that the Yorkshire Dales was quite a well-defined area — and so it is. Or is it? Unlike the National Park, the exact whereabouts of its borders are more a matter for conjecture and open to debate. One 'truth' we would think, is that the Yorkshire Dales should be wholly within Yorkshire, but incredibly this isn't so. Since the county boundary changes of 1974, some sizeable chunks of the 'Dales' have been reallocated elsewhere. Dentdale and Garsdale are now in Cumbria and — Lancashire, which has lost its portion of the Lake District, has gained a little more of Ribblesdale and most of Bowland. Not that any of this would worry the lover of landscape, for it is the lie of the land, the natural geography that matters and not political divisions.

To confuse matters further, there are many other dales in Yorkshire not considered to be part of the Yorkshire Dales. The word 'dale', derived from the Old Teutonic 'dalum' is common in the north of England and means 'narrow valley'. There are literally hundreds of them. So the 'Yorkshire Dales' is a specific area on the map, albeit with loosely defined edges.

By including the following paintings, you might think I have strayed too far from the core topic of the book. But there is method in my madness. The inclusion serves to illustrate a point: that the Yorkshire Dales region doesn't exist in isolation like an island, but merges into and is surrounded by huge tracts of land which, though different in nature, can be equally dynamic and fascinating.

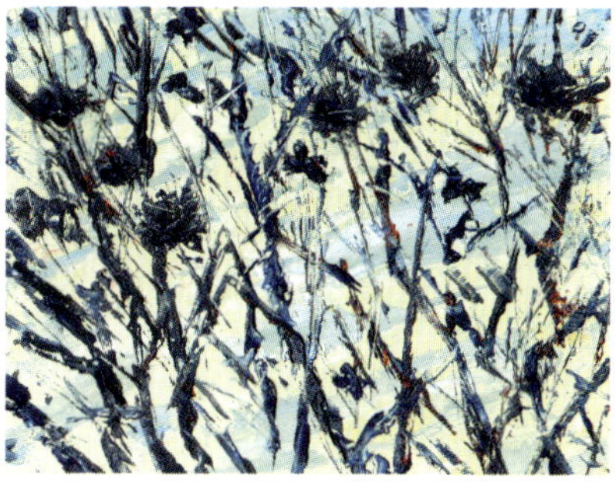

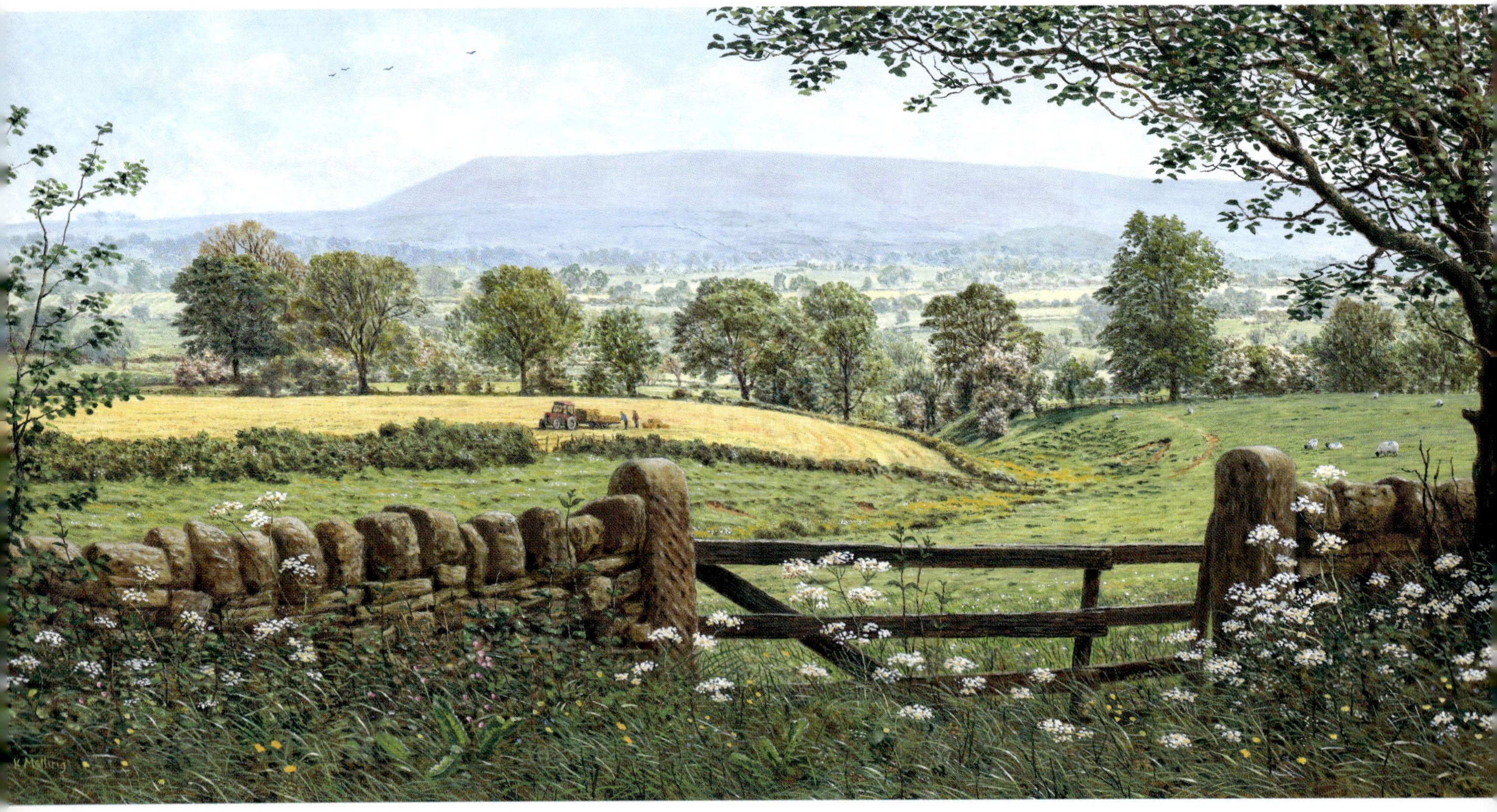

Ribble Valley and Pendle Hill

2000 Acrylic and gouache 8 x 16.5in

Painted from the tiny hamlet at Foxley Bank near Sawley, the River Ribble, hidden by the line of tall trees and banking, runs unseen through the picture from left to right. The scene, dominated by Lancashire's famous Pendle Hill is entirely in that county, though, prior to 1974 the river divided the 'red rose' from the 'white' for a good length of this stretch.

Heptonstall and Stoodley Pike

1986 Oil l 30 x 48in

In this painting we have moved south over the Aire Gap, well away from limestone country to Calderdale in the gritstone Pennines. The hilltop village of Heptonstall is seen from Pecket Well across the deep wooded valley of Hardcastle Crags. On the far horizon, perched high on the backbone of England, Stoodley Pike stands sentinel, keeping solemn watch over Calderdale. This 110 ft monument was built in 1856 to commemorate the end of the Crimean War. An earlier pike existed to mark the defeat of Napoleon and evidence suggests that an even older structure existed here. The rooftops of the old mill-town Hebden Bridge are glimpsed where the two valleys meet. The peculiar gritstone houses, built higgledy-piggledy into the steep hillsides, have to be seen to be believed. As in the Dales, drystone walls are a feature of the landscape, their regular patterns, especially on the distant hills — appearing as if a net has been cast over the land; their construction with 'millstone grit' renders them darker, sombre and more severe.

This was the earliest and largest of my Yorkshire pictures, painted with oil paint on a wooden panel 4 ft wide. It really felt like I was creating an epic and thought it never would be finished. The typical Pennine stile is a way into the scene, beyond which our eyes zigzag along the lines of walls and hill contours — resting at various focal points; the mistle thrush, grazing horses, shining roofs, church tower and the remote Stoodley Pike itself.

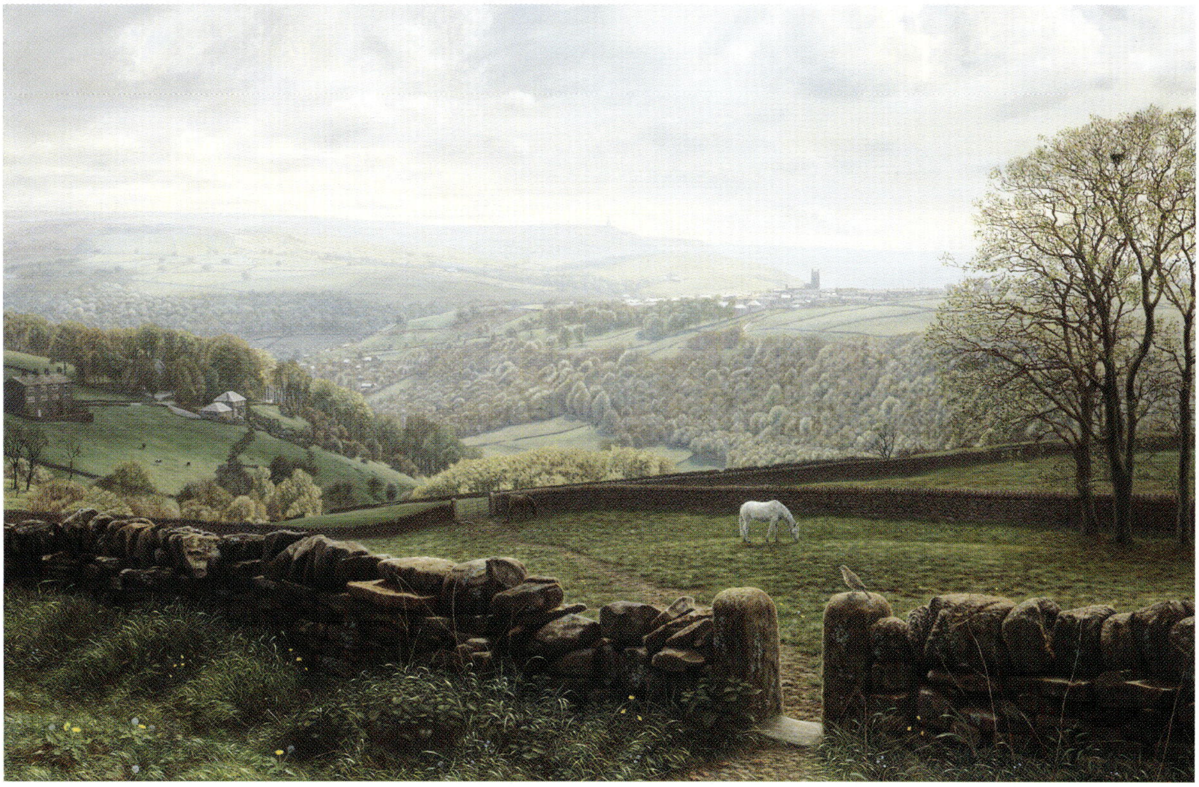

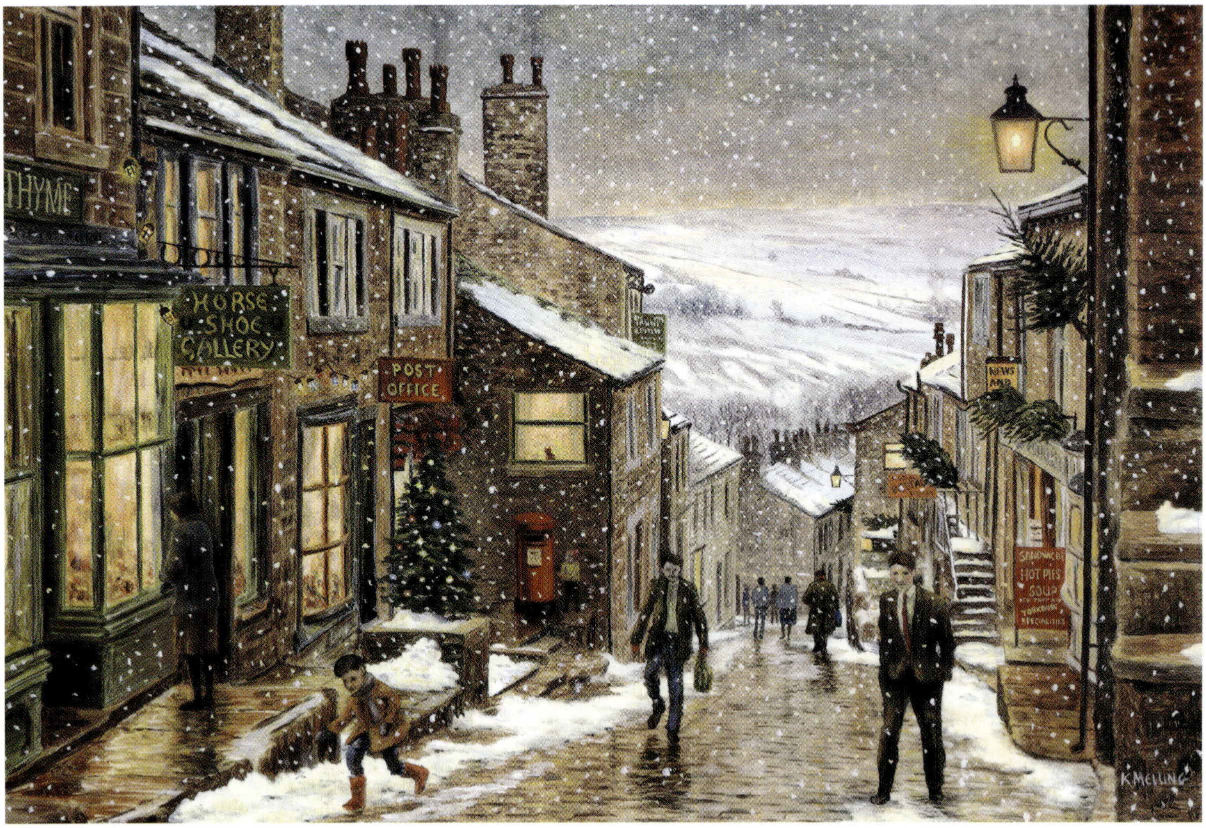

A Yorkshire Christmas

1993 Oil 9.5 x 12.8in

Again this is not the Yorkshire Dales although not too far away. The small town of Haworth is inextricably linked with the tragic story of the Brontë sisters who were so inspired by the surrounding wild moorland that they felt at a loss when separated from it. Their evergreen novels (works of genius) have been responsible for bringing thousands of visitors here. So much so that the footpath signs have been written in three languages, English, French and Japanese.

Like many other Yorkshire towns and villages, Haworth excels in this jolly festive season, tastefully balancing reverence with frivolity. Haworth also excels at attracting snow, thanks to its high location on the edge of the moors.

The subject matter for me is rather unusual — one of the few 'townscape' pictures I've painted. Of course it's the figures that animate the scene and I like to think that little stories can be woven around them.

Devil's Bridge, Kirkby Lonsdale

1990 Oil 9.5 x 12.8in

The fine old market town of Kirkby Lonsdale, formerly of Westmorland but now in Cumbria, remains within touching distance of both Lancashire and Yorkshire. As the name describes (church by Lune's dale), the town is beautifully located in the valley of the River Lune. The grand river has its beginnings way-up in the Howgill Fells and although its waters don't actually run through Yorkshire, sections of the eastern bank formed the western fringe of the old West Riding. The 19th century art critic Ruskin loved this area — writing 'I do not know in all my own country, still less in France or Italy, a place more naturally divine'. He described the view across the river from the church as 'one of the loveliest in England and therefore in the world'. The view is certainly lovely, but in my opinion there are dozens of views to equal or beat it in the north of England alone.

The origins of the medieval bridge are obscure, though it is believed that 14th century monks were responsible for its construction. There is an alternative theory however, a local legend much more imaginative and colourful....

An old woman was somewhat distressed because her cow had strayed to the opposite bank. The Devil appeared and offered to build a bridge in return for the soul of the first living thing to cross. The woman agreed but then played a trick. When the bridge was complete, she threw some food for her dog over to the other side. The dog ran across first and the Devil reluctantly had to accept its animal soul.

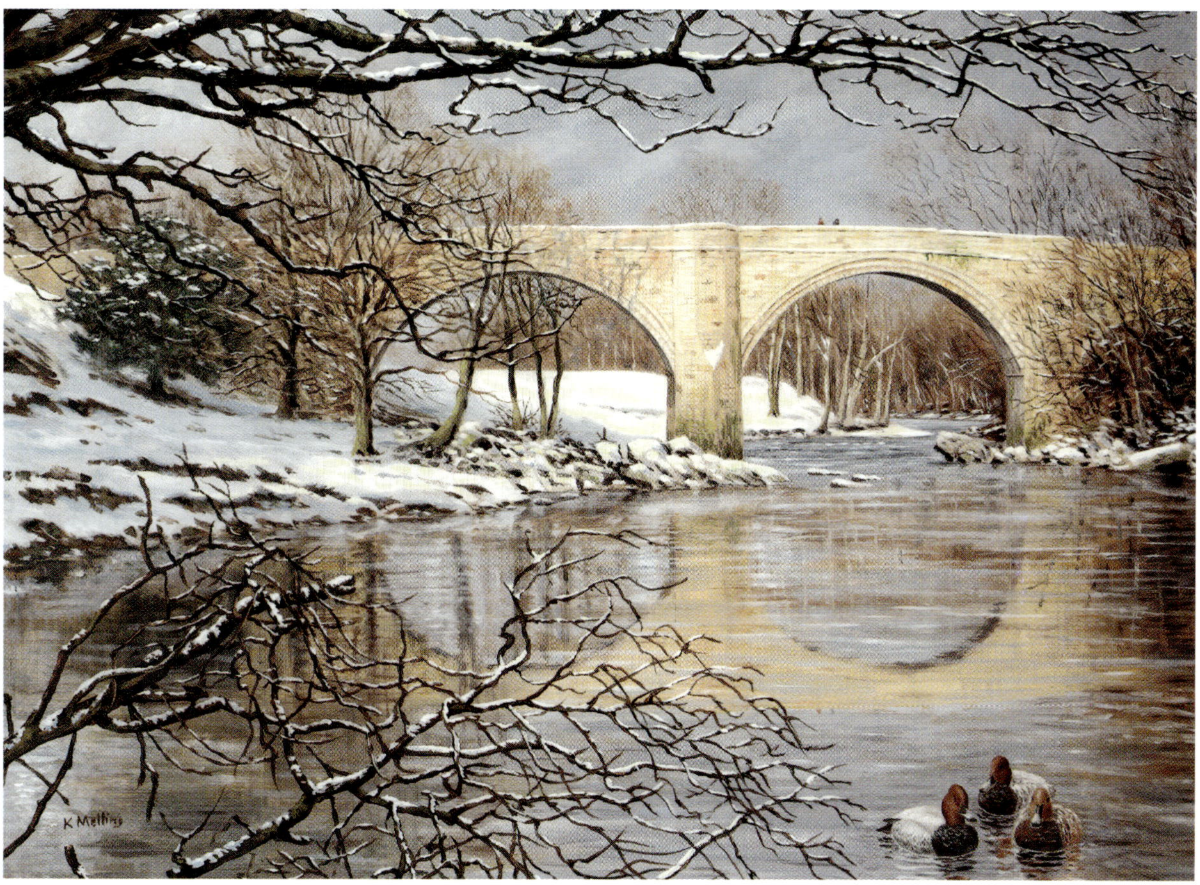

The River Aire at Kirkstall Abbey

1992 Oil 9.8 x 13.3in

Not in the Dales by a long chalk, Kirkstall Abbey is near Headingley, three miles from Leeds city centre: the River Aire though, does begin its varied life in Malhamdale at Aire Head Springs, which I hope is excuse enough for inclusion here in this book.

The abbey's history starts in 1147 with monks from 'Fountains' establishing a Cistercian community near Barnoldswick. They found the local people and weather so inhospitable that they relocated five years later to the Aire's banks at Kirkstall, a secluded spot with woodlands, water and grazing land close at hand. After the dissolution, the buildings miraculously avoided the great destruction suffered by many abbeys, and remains one of the most complete. Today, the well-preserved ruins and grounds are virtually surrounded by houses, making it a most precious oasis of peace in the spreading conurbation of Leeds.

When Turner's friend Thomas Girtin painted the Abbey in 1802, he faithfully portrayed the ruins as they were, within a broad sweeping pastoral landscape. I'm afraid I haven't been quite as objective; I looked for viewpoints that hid most of the houses and disguised the rest in a fuzzy background haze. Still, the subject is the abbey itself in its immediate setting, which I have concentrated on.

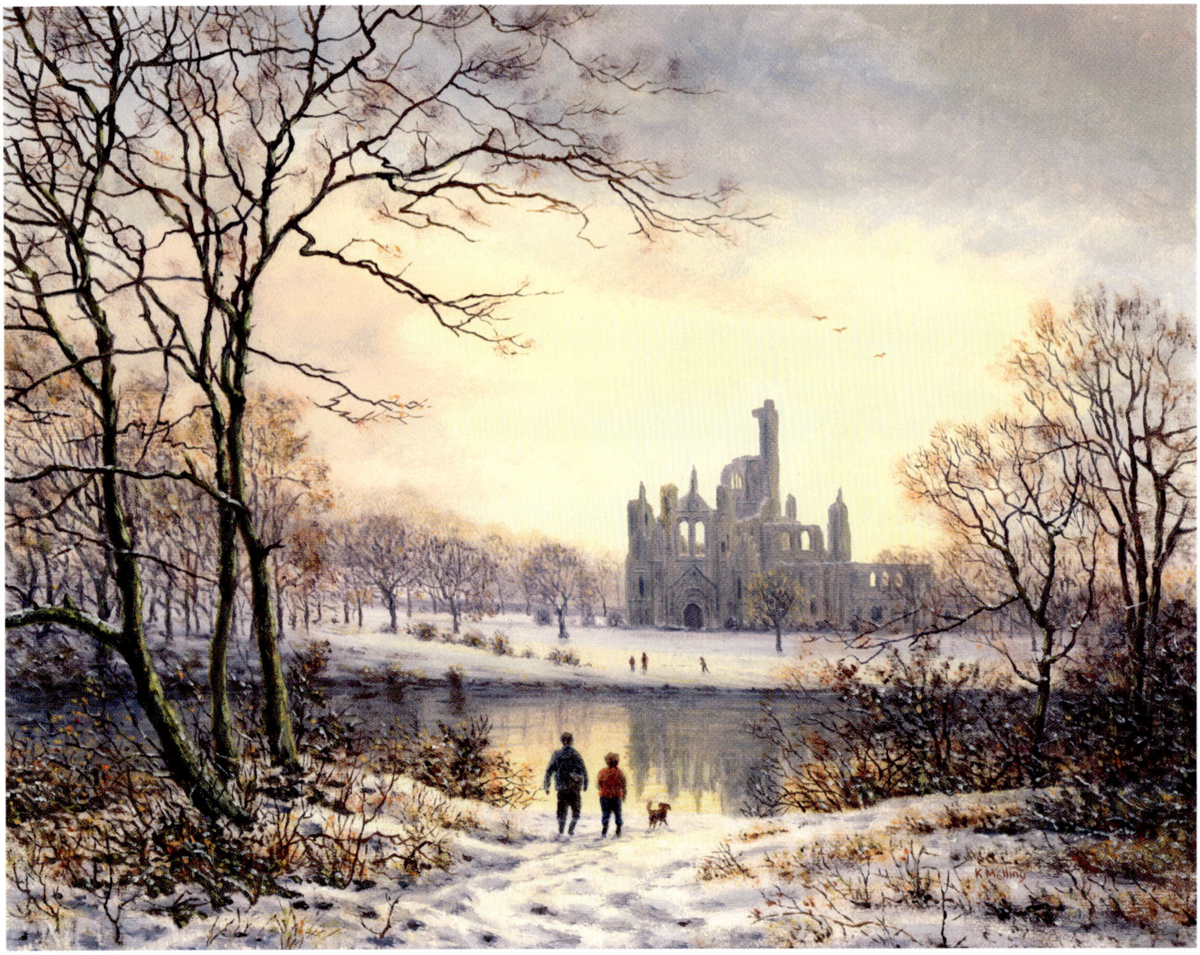

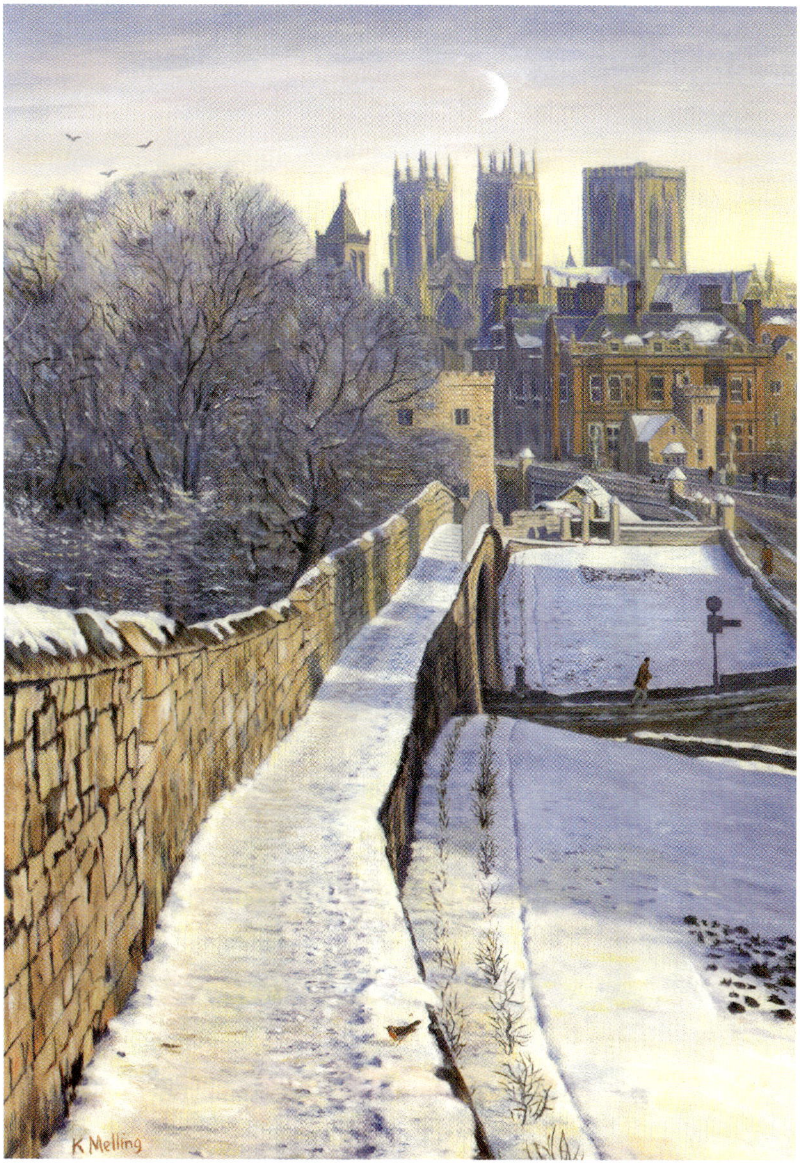

Towards York Minster

1991 Oil 12 x 8 in

The inclusion of York in this book is justified simply because traditionally it is the county town of Yorkshire, to which it lends its name.

The majestic River Ouse, which sedately flows through this fascinating walled city, is at times susceptible to severe flooding. Not surprising when we think of the five Dales rivers that join it; the Ure, Wharfe, Swale, Nidd and Aire. Not to worry though, York is also noted for its many pubs; reputedly, one for each day of the year. The saying goes that you can't stand anywhere in the city without a church and pub being visible.

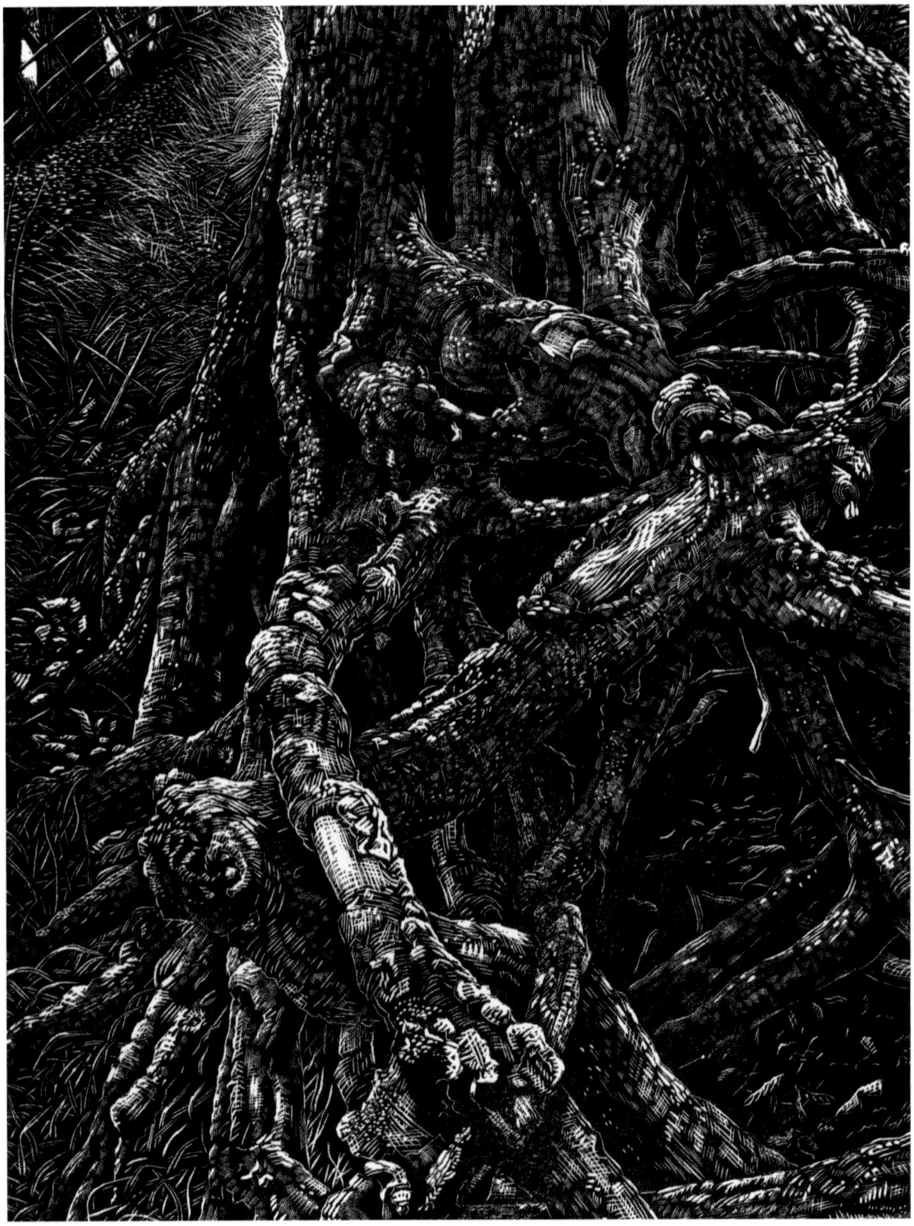

Roots

1995 Wood engraving 7.5 x 6in

I know that this could be anywhere — and I might have said it was near Dent or in Arkengarthdale (where I'm short of material) and nobody would be any the wiser. But in truth it's far from Yorkshire's borders, being in deepest Lancashire at Preston, where the local natives stroll by the dark waters of the River Ribble and claim it as their own.

Postscript

I've always believed that art should speak for itself and need no explanation beyond a title and, perhaps at most, a simple commentary. Of course we may (or may not) appreciate the most obscure avant-garde work without having the foggiest idea what it's about. That's the fascination of art, it's not a science, and it cannot be quantified. We can argue and debate till the cows come home but, when it comes to 'hey lads hey', it's simply a matter of taste and opinion. Matisse believed that 'art should be comfortable like a good armchair', while Picasso stated that 'art was a weapon of war'. Turner's view was that it 'was all a rum do'.

I sometimes wonder about my own motivation for painting certain places or even painting at all, and am forced to conclude that I don't really know. I've seen the Lascaux cave paintings and marvelled at the modernity and sophistication of the drawings there. These artists of 17,000 years ago tried to connect with the animals they were dependent on by incising and drawing their images onto the cave walls, perhaps in an attempt to invoke power over them. It may be a subconscious thing but I believe it still happens. George Harrison drew guitars in his schoolbooks and actors have been known to make doodles of the characters they are playing. So by painting and drawing places that mean so very much to me — who knows?

I must confess that painting comes to me more easily and naturally than writing. That's not to say I haven't enjoyed the writing, I have, but it's been more than a little trying at times. Thank goodness for the computer spell checker.

No doubt there will be places very dear to some folks' hearts that I haven't painted and I'm sorry about that. The book was never intended to be a complete systematic survey of the Yorkshire Dales (an impossibility anyway) but rather — as one artist's response to it — two artists actually; for my son Sam, who has accompanied me on many a walking and sketching expedition, has kindly allowed me to include two of his paintings.

I was first introduced to the Dales in the 1950's by my father (a Yorkshire man) and even as a child tried to draw my impressions of the landscape and wildlife. When I started painting seriously as a teenager in the mid 60's, my subjects varied immensely. Often I painted my memories of nights out in the local dance halls and discotheques; sometimes dingy and other times an array of throbbing colour. Pure abstracts were tackled on big 8 x 4 ft boards, mixing grit and sand into thick oil paint scooped from student quality tins. Yet it was the landscapes of northern England that returned with ever increasing frequency to my canvases that gave me the most pleasure and satisfaction. Indeed for the last 30 years or so, this has been almost my only subject.

Latterly I have concentrated all my efforts on the Dales and have really caught the bug. The startling richness and variety found there, not only in the grand panoramic vistas but also in the minutiae of the ordinary things, has cast an indelible magical spell. I hope that through my paintings and drawings I can convey some of that magic and encourage others to go forth and discover this wonderful region for themselves. I have been enthusiastic about this project and enjoyed it immensely; so much so that it has been difficult to know where to stop. Enthusiasm is infectious, and if I have done my job properly I sincerely hope that anyone looking at this book will catch a dose of what I have had.

Of course I will continue to venture into and paint the Yorkshire Dales, but in the meantime, I am turning my attention back to the landscape right outside my door — the Pendle area, which hopefully will be the subject of another book.

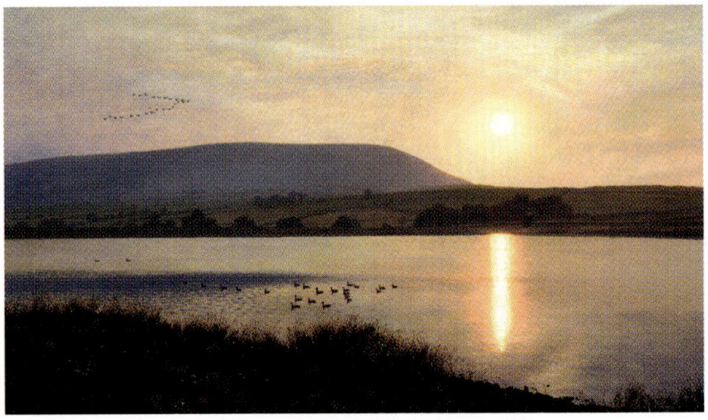

Black Moss and Pendle Hill

2005 Acrylic 17 x 29 in.

About the Artist

Keith Melling has gained a reputation as one of the finest painters of the northern landscape.

Born in Colne, Lancashire, in 1946, he showed from a very early age much enthusiasm and talent as an artist. Largely self-taught, his first exhibition of 40 paintings was held in 1966. At the time, Keith was serving a five-year apprenticeship in mechanical engineering — 'that really was the ultimate if you were from a working class area — art wasn't an option'. Later, after studying at Burnley School of Art and the Harris College Preston as a 'mature student', he worked in a number of occupations before turning fully professional in 1983.

Meticulous topographical accuracy has been his hallmark, combined with strong composition and 'feeling of place'. Keith uses a variety of painting mediums and techniques, although, oil paint made by him in the traditional way, is still a favourite. He enjoys the disciplines of wood engraving and etching and has also been a potter.

There is an ever-increasing demand for his fine quality prints, which have been published from paintings produced over the last 35 years. These have brought him considerable success and made his work available to a much wider audience. With the advancement of printing technology, recent giclée prints have given exposure to another side of his work not previously seen. His paintings have won many awards and he is represented in collections throughout the world.

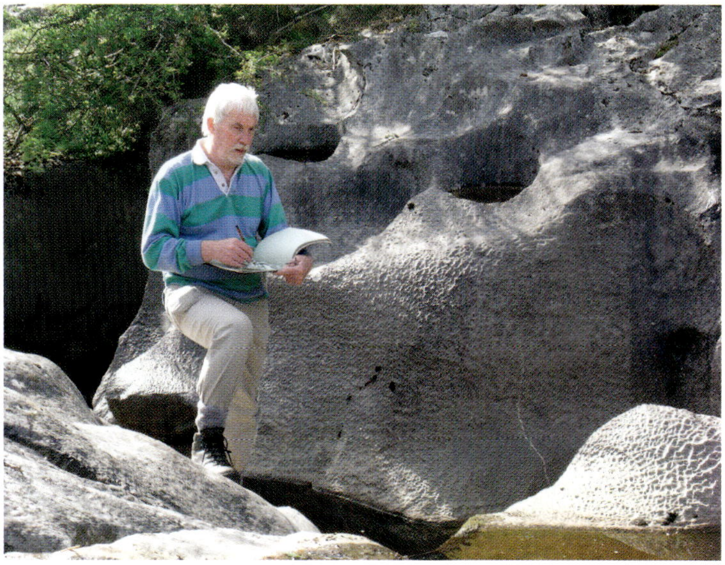

Keith has a keen interest in the natural world in general, wildlife, fell walking and exploring the countryside; all of which are inextricably linked to the activity of being a landscape painter. Outside of art, his other passions include: music (from Dylan to Delius), poetry (writing a little), football (supporting) and chess (playing for a team in the East Lancashire Chess League).

Over the last few years, calendars featuring Keith's paintings have been produced for the Pendleside Hospice; these have been a great fundraiser, accumulating an incredible £29,500 for Hospice funds from 2005 to 2008.

Keith lives with his wife June in the beautiful Pendle Forest area of Lancashire, they have two sons, a daughter and a granddaughter.

A comprehensive display of limited edition prints, cards and recent paintings may be seen at the family run, K Melling Studio-Gallery.

K Melling Studio-Gallery
486, Wheatley Lane Road,
Fence, Burnley,
Lancashire.
BB12 9EB

Telephone: 01282 696641
Email: kmelling@supanet.com
Website: www.kmelling.com